Here's the good news: If you're a woman facing down the daily demands of work and home, you don't have to wait for big fixes like national child care or female CEOs running the Fortune 500. Instead, if you shrug off a few limiting ideas about women, men, and work, you can make small changes that will transform your life.

GETTING TO 50/50

"Once in a rare while, a book comes along and changes the entire nature of the discussion. If *Getting to 50/50* doesn't spark a revolution in work/life balance, I don't know what will."
—Deborah Copaken Kogan, author of *Between Here and April* and *Hell Is Other Parents*

"*Getting to 50/50* solves one of the most important pieces of the work/life puzzle: the relationship between husbands and wives."
—Sylvia Ann Hewlett, president of the Center for Work-Life Policy and author of *Off-Ramps and On-Ramps: Keeping Talented Women on the Road to Success*

"A creative take on how to balance the demands of work and home. (Fathers may be surprised to find out how much they can benefit from these new arrangements.) Parents with children from 1 to 21 should rush right out and buy this book."
—Carolyn Pape Cowan and Philip A. Cowan, authors of *When Partners Become Parents: The Big Life Change for Couples*

"As an organizer for social and economic justice, a working mom, and a woman leader in a male-dominated sector, I found *Getting to 50/50* right on. It is full of great advice about how to negotiate for women and their families."
—Anna Burger, secretary-treasurer, Service Employees International Union (SEIU)

"Invaluable—should be required reading when any couple applies for a marriage license."
—Leslie Morgan Steiner, editor of *Mommy Wars*

GETTING TO

50 50

How Working Couples Can Have It All by Sharing It All

And Why It's Great for Your Marriage, Your Career, Your Kids, and *You*

SHARON MEERS and **JOANNA STROBER**

BANTAM BOOKS

GETTING TO 50/50

A Bantam Book/March 2009

Published by
Bantam Dell
A Division of Random House, Inc.
New York, New York

Book design by Glen M. Edelstein

Library of Congress Cataloging-in-Publication Data
Meers, Sharon.
Getting to 50/50 : how working couples can have it all by sharing it all :
and why it's great for your marriage, your career, your kids, and you /
Sharon Meers and Joanna Strober.
p. cm.
Includes bibliographical references and index.
ISBN 978-0-553-80655-7 (hardcover : alk. paper).
ISBN 978-0-553-90616-5 (e-book).
1. Work and family. 2. Dual-career families. I. Strober, Joanna. II. Title.

HD4904.25.M44 2009
650.1—dc22 2008045963

Printed in the United States of America
Published simultaneously in Canada

www.bantamdell.com

BVG 10 9 8 7 6 5 4 3 2

To our husbands

CONTENTS

INTRODUCTION

Imagine a Full Life— There's No Need to Choose

Do we know you?

You worked hard to get where you are. You pushed yourself in school, got a job, and gave it your all. You learned your trade and found your strength, spurred on by the challenge of doing things well. When you see the next mountain, you gear up to climb it.

Along the way, you think about meeting the right guy. Or maybe you've met him and he has joined your journey. Either way, you see how linking your life with a man's may change your course.

Setting out, it all seems simple. It's fun to be a twosome, and you help each other when the ground gets rocky. If he slips, you steady him; when you lag behind, he pulls you up. You map out your future together, and it's good. Two people joined by love and shared dreams. This is the marriage you hope for.

Then, one day, you take a grand new path: parenthood. No longer a couple, you're a family. While you pause to adjust to this miracle, your husband resumes his course. But with a baby in tow, you're carrying a bigger load and you wonder what pace you can keep. The mountain seems bigger than it did before—more forbidding, and a whole lot colder.

You look into your child's eyes and wonder, *How much will I miss you when I go back to work? Should I slow down to keep you safe—even stop altogether?*

Other voices echo yours. Those who once cheered you on now ask, "Do you have to work? Won't the baby need you? Do you really want to leave your child with strangers? Does your salary even cover child care?"

Back at work, some colleagues now see you differently.

"You seem less focused. We'll ask Jack to help you run that project."

"We restructured the group while you were out. Half your team now reports to Charlotte."

"Commitment is important. We'd like to see you here more hours." And you see things differently, too. *Do we need the third staff meeting? Is the trip to Tucson really necessary?* you start to ask—time is no longer something you give away freely.

You look to your partner for support, but he faces a steep grade himself. Convinced he must "provide for the family," he resolves to work even harder. You call to him for help—did he hear you? You ask him to take his share of the load, but he worries he'll stumble if he does.

"I know it's my turn to do day-care drop-off, but can you do it? I have an early meeting."

"The baby is calmer with you. He always fusses when I try to feed him."

"There are no other dads at the playground and the moms look at me funny. Can't you do the playdate?"

One day you wake up and wonder, *Why not just quit?* You see your paycheck depleted by child-care costs and your time vanish as each day repeats itself: dressing your child, feeding her, going to work, coming home, feeding her again, and putting her to bed (with hopes that she'll stay there). Weekends are cram sessions of diapers, groceries, laundry, errands, and the occasional night out that takes as much planning as a space shuttle launch. You begin to think of your spouse as a kindly roommate who usually remembers to put the seat down.

You're still giving it your best at work, but you're tired and scared about the not-so-subtle signs that no one thinks you'll stick it out. On bad days, you ask yourself, *Can't we make do without my income—just for a while?* You certainly wouldn't be the only working mother to "opt out." You can tick off a half dozen ex-colleagues, all mothers, all talented in different ways, who drove off into the sunset, children strapped safely in their car seats. You keep hearing that voice: *Is it really worth it?*

You bet your kid's college tuition it is.

We're going to show you precisely why working is worth it for you, your children, and your spouse, and how both your family and your career can flourish—when you tap into a powerful ally. It's not your babysitter, your BlackBerry, or your boss (though they come in handy). Here's a hint: You married him.

GETTING TO 50/50: THE LIFE-CHANGING JOURNEY

We are two working moms who believe that everyone wins when men are full parents and women have full careers. When both parents pay the bills and care for kids, this life is possible—we know from experience. In our homes, we don't assume that Mom is destined to be the "primary parent." Our kids see Dad as equal to Mom because we set it up that way. True, we did 100 percent of the breast-feeding and sometimes only we can make the monster under the bed disappear. But Dad loves parenting as much as we do—and he's good at it, too. There is also no "primary breadwinner" among us. Mom and Dad are both on the hook for the costs of raising kids, from groceries to braces, from housing to soccer cleats. The payoff? We enjoy rewarding careers and see that our families thrive—not despite our work but *because* of it.

"Don't you really need to choose? Won't I need to pick which comes first, my work or my family?" We hear this often from women in their twenties on campuses where we speak. (We rarely hear it from young men.) And even when young women are more hopeful, there's a big disconnect between what they hear (you're equal) and what they see. "These issues creep up on us without our being aware of them," one twentysomething told us. "I think women my age believe the world has changed so much that we don't need to worry. But then we look at the men in charge where we work and think, *That is not what I want my life to look like and it's clearly not feasible for me if I want to have kids.*"

We remember the angst we felt at their age, that somehow things would be tougher for us than they were for our guy friends. At times in each of our own careers, we shared the fear that we'd have to forfeit something big—a career or a husband.

"I'll never find the right guy if I can't ever leave the office," Joanna, then a lawyer in her first 24/7 job, complained to her mother. At her second corporate law firm, still unmarried but curious about the future, Joanna went to a meeting on work/life balance. The discussion leader, the only female partner with children, started to cry. Not inspirational. Joanna had grown up with a mother who mostly stayed home. So the discouraging signs around her at work did not give Joanna much conviction that she would want to keep working after she had kids.

Sharon, a child of divorced parents, assumed she'd always earn her own living. No man Sharon dated could miss the point. She grilled boyfriends for double standards and gave them books such as *The Women's Room* and *The Feminine Mystique*—which largely went unread. Working stock-market hours in San Francisco, Sharon was in the office close to 4 a.m.—and asleep by 9 p.m., making her an even more unusual date. As she was turning thirty-one, Sharon walked down the street after work one day with tears in her eyes. "No marriage is better than a bad one," she thought, "but how did I end up alone?"

Then we met our husbands and learned this: The most important career decision you make is whom you marry. (And the deals you make with him.)

When Joanna got engaged, her fiancé, Jason, told her he wanted to start companies. To take the risks that entrepreneurship requires, Jason knew that sometimes he would be putting more money into his business than he'd be taking out. When Joanna wanted to quit her job, Jason did his share of child care while Joanna transitioned to a career she found more satisfying than the law. Jason not only wanted to be a good father, he also knew Joanna's income bought him freedom to pursue his own career dreams.

"Women are more nurturing and should stay home with kids for a few years," Sharon's future husband, Steve, said on their first date. That evening did not end well. But Steve, an Iowan raised with the virtue of fairness, was curious (and a good sport). So he asked Sharon to put her thoughts on paper. "I want my husband to share every part of parenting with me 50/50. How do you feel about this?" Sharon wrote. Steve wasn't sure but kept an open mind until he and Sharon found a vision they could share.

We're not saying it's easy. Living this way takes lots of discussion and often debate. No matter how fair-minded your spouse, if you're anything like us, you'll still find plenty to argue about. But hundreds of men and women in this book tell you in their own words why they make the effort: The 50/50 mind-set can help you live the life you want.

THE MANY VOICES OF 50/50: KIDS, DADS, MOMS, AND BOSSES TELL IT LIKE IT IS

In *Getting to 50/50*, we'll lay out the challenges women and men face when they seek to combine work and family. We've talked to hundreds of two-career couples, from an array of professions and ethnicities, who live all over the country. Ranging in age from their twenties to their eighties, these men and women told us how they've forged marriages that support two good jobs and one strong family.

We've focused this book on men and women married to each other. We believe outdated views about husband-wife marriage cause problems for everyone (even people with other living arrangements). Most ideas that hold women back at work, that make it hard for fathers to spend time with their kids, that deprive children of the support they need, are rooted in these old beliefs. When more of us adopt a 50/50 mind-set, families of all configurations will gain. If you don't have kids yet, this book is for you, too. The odds are 80 percent you will be a parent some day. And if you'd like to see more female success where you work, you know that will only happen when more women stay in the game. All women win when mothers can pursue their careers—and so do men.

We spoke to men and women all over the country: nurses, engineers, teachers, lawyers, government workers, accountants, salespeople, doctors, CEOs, a rocket scientist, a football player, an ice-cream maker, and many more. We interviewed people who work for large institutions like Fortune 500 companies, hospitals, and law firms; we also talked to many people who work for small outfits or for themselves. What we learned is that 50/50 couples are everywhere. Using what researchers call the snowball method (where one contact leads you to many others), we were amazed by the groundswell of volunteers who emerged to share their stories. As one working mom told us, "Happy working couples are culturally invisible. That needs to change."

We told our interviewees we would describe their real jobs but give them fake names. We've found that this topic is such a hot one, few people will go on record telling you what they really think—they worry they'll rub coworkers and friends the wrong way. (And how many bosses will say this in public? "I discriminated," the ex-chief of a large company told us, explaining how he dealt with working moms.) So we gave anonymity to get you the real story.

We chose to focus most of our interviews on mid-career couples who talked about the rewards of staying the course. Though most are college graduates, these men and women are not "celebrity" working parents who can afford to outsource every domestic challenge. These couples devote themselves to their families and two careers because they believe it's a good thing—not because it's easy.

To get broader input, we also conducted an online survey called "The Real Lives of Working Mothers." Professional organizations, mothers' clubs, and school groups sent the survey to thousands of women across the country—who forwarded the survey to yet more women. The survey asked questions like these: Does your spouse prefer that you work or not work? Whose career is primary, yours or your spouse's, or are they equally important? When you returned from your maternity leave, what was your boss's attitude toward you? What do you tell your children about work and family? Over one thousand working moms wrote in to share their stories from a broad spectrum of careers.

Throughout this book, you will find quotes from the survey that we thought would be helpful to our readers and that represented the wide range of respondents' views and experience.

The respondents spoke frankly about hurdles they sometimes leapt, sometimes tripped, over. And they pointed out how much we'll all gain if women and men can talk about these issues earlier in life, more often, and with open minds.

"You need to consider the slippery slope of men's and women's job choices. We 'prioritized' my husband's job over mine because his income is higher and his job is less flexible, but he took that job and others thinking only about his professional and economic goals, not about how well they would work with being a father, and he has not pushed for flexibility within his jobs. [I chose my] path because I realized I would benefit as a mother from the flexibility it would confer. But I would have preferred a more balanced approach to co-parenting and working."

They also described the upside of continuing to work. One mother wrote, "I have wrestled with the decision to work since my older son was a year old. I have had to accept that I just can't be happy putting my career completely on hold while my kids are young. Work charges my batteries in a way that being at home doesn't—it helps me to be a complete person. I don't want my identity to be either just centered on motherhood or just centered on career—I want to be a mom, and a wife, and an individual."

Beyond stories, we went looking for facts. What does social science say about 50/50 life and how it all plays out? We'll share answers we've found in the vast pool of academic and government research to questions like these: How do children fare when both parents work? What happens to marriage? Does dual-career life make men and women more happy or less so? We not only combed the data, we talked to many of the leading academics who did the work. Experts on child development show how kids flourish with attention from engaged dads (and how working moms and child care can be helpful, too). Turns out that children don't need one parent home all of the time—but kids really benefit if they have *each* of their parents some of the time. Psychologists tell us marriages thrive and men and women find greater well-being when both spouses work. Look at the economics and you'll see the numbers add up in support of sharing the load—where men and women feel an equal duty to make money and care for kids.

WORKING: IT'S NOT ABOUT CHOOSING SIDES

This is not another polemic on stay-at-home mothers versus working mothers. Our goal is not to lecture, but to empower women who want to combine gratifying careers with a rich family life. We want to start a conversation, to get men and women talking—not just at home but in the workplace—about the limiting beliefs that knock too many moms out of full careers and keep dads apart from their children.

Some of our closest friends have left their jobs to focus full-time on their families, and we respect that choice; it's a deeply personal decision that some women never regret. But we are concerned when women lower their sights or "opt out" of hard-won jobs simply because they can imagine no other option. We see many of our peers pinned between two forces: a workplace oblivious to parenthood, valuing long hours as the *only* proof of productivity, and husbands who don't do their half at home. We hope this book will give people license to talk more freely—to ask "Why?" when mothers think they have to quit and fathers feel they can't get home for dinner.

The Fortune 500 spends $8 billion per year on workplace diversity, much of that aimed at supporting female careers. In accounting, law, medicine, and many other jobs, there is now more effort put into retaining talented women than ever before. But 85 percent of the leaders in most fields are men, still, and we haven't changed those numbers much in the last ten years.

In her sixteen years working at a large investment bank, Sharon logged many hours hoping to help more women succeed: speaking to new recruits, mentoring, hosting networking events, serving on retention committees. Sometimes these activities made a difference—and sometimes not. Then one day, Sharon got a cross-country call from, Emily, a young woman who wanted to see her for "career advice." Fifteen minutes into their meeting, the real topic emerged: "I need to work late in this phase of my career or I won't do well. I need my husband to step up with our kids. How do I tell him that?"

Venture into this terrain, the dangerous territory where personal and professional life meet, and you'll hear comments like these: "I'd love to take some pressure off my wife but if I leave early, my boss will think I'm a wimp." "My husband's so stressed out about his job, I can't ask him for help. I don't want a fight." The vise that squeezes women has two sides, family needs and work demands. In this book, we'll show you how successful working couples deal with both.

But when these issues aren't discussed constructively, out in the open, women continue to leave work—and the causes are misunderstood. "Few mothers drop out," concludes Joan Williams, an eminent expert on work and family who has studied the progress and perception of working mothers for decades. Instead, "they tend to drop from good jobs into bad ones." They accept inferior pay and prospects in return for a small amount of flexibility. In her report *"Opt Out" or Pushed Out?: How the Press Covers Work/Family Conflict,* Williams responds to the much-ballyhooed "opt-out revolution,"[1] a so-called trend whereby educated women are exiting the workforce *voluntarily* to stay at home with their children.

The stakes are high for getting this story right. "If women are happily choosing to stay home with their babies, that's a private decision," writes E. J. Graff, journalist and resident scholar at Brandeis University. "But it's a public policy issue if most women (and men) need to work to support their families, and if the economy needs women's skills to remain competitive. It's a public policy issue if schools, jobs, and other American institutions are structured in ways that make it frustratingly difficult, and sometimes impossible" to manage work and family obligations.[2]

When women quit their jobs, the repercussions go beyond the economics. Stephanie Coontz, author of *Marriage, a History,* notes that when women opt out, "Not only does it reinforce women's second-class position in the work force, but it reinforces Dad's second-class position in the family. She becomes the expert, and he never catches up."[3] Fixing this unfortunate dynamic—that skews outcomes for men and women at work and at home—is what *Getting to 50/50* is all about.

Myra Strober, a labor economist and Joanna's mother-in-law, is well known for a class she teaches at the Stanford Graduate School of Business called Work and Family. Professor Strober invites speakers to talk to her class about how they built their careers while raising a family. In 2004, we each spoke at this class and came away struck by one thing: Students, both men and women, were anxious. They worried that the jobs they wanted were incompatible with the family life they hoped for. As one student told us, "People say you can do it. But no one opens up and shows you how."

On another campus, a group of high-performing twentysome-things asked many questions about reentering the workforce after years away for raising kids. Sharon asked back: "How many of you are planning to take more than a year off?" Over 70 percent of these young women raised their hands. Are they aware that few jobs let you exit for years and return with ease, or with the confidence and skills you had before?

How many of these students would plan their lives differently if they had more facts? If they knew that research shows 50/50 couples enjoy much lower divorce risk?[4] Or that careers make moms happier, too? A major study published in 2007 found mothers "attain the greatest life satisfaction if they work." Based on surveys of ten thousand individuals, British researchers found that mothers with jobs are significantly happier than their nonworking counterparts. Interestingly, though most women expressed a desire to work part time, the study reported that "women with children are significantly happier if they have a job regardless of how many hours it entails."[5]

So let's tell young women this: Imagine a full life—there's no need to choose.

WHO WORKS?

One of the most interesting things we learned in writing this book is that the question of working impacts all women, regardless of income. While many of us feel we work because our families could not afford it any other way, it turns out what you can "afford" is a function of something other than dollars. At every income level, at least 30 percent of mothers don't work when their kids are under six—and moms work least at both the richest and poorest levels.[6] To work or not to work? Often culture trumps economics.

Poorest Quartile:	63 percent of mothers work
2nd Quartile:	70 percent of mothers work
3rd Quartile:	69 percent of mothers work
Richest Quartile:	58 percent of mothers work

SHARING THE JOURNEY, SOLVING THE PROBLEM—TOGETHER

When we started talking about this book, Sharon was a managing director at Goldman Sachs and Joanna was a general partner at Bessemer Venture Partners, a venture capital firm. We had small children and working husbands.

As moms with full-time jobs, we got our share of comments from the skeptics on the playground ("I can't imagine leaving my children every day") and at work ("Do you really want to do this? I love that my wife takes care of our kids"). But our spouses were strong allies and our kids were thriving.

In fact, our spouses have proven to be our best allies as we combine family and career, because we can rely on them to do their fair share. As we talked to hundreds of other working men and women, we saw a pattern: Couples win from standing in each others' shoes, day after day—committing themselves equally to raising their children and breadwinning for a family. Mothers work without guilt; fathers bond with their kids; children blossom with the attention of two equally involved parents.

As one 50/50 dad (a CEO) told us, "I love that my kids are excited to be with me and that they see both their mother and me as equals." "I did not expect to live like this," said another father, an entrepreneur. "I grew up in a very traditional household and my dad was the sole breadwinner. I married an amazing woman with a great career and I've reoriented my work so we can both raise the kids together. I'm very proud of the way we live, I feel on a daily basis we are contributing to the way that life should be."

We hear that men don't read books like this. But we've talked to hundreds of guys about what this book says and they love it—a lot of men really want a different deal, too. Pollsters say that working dads today express at least as much anxiety about work/family conflict as working moms do, and surveys now show more than 60 percent of fathers are willing to trade income and advancement for more time with kids.[7] Many couples have gotten to 50/50 in their own way and at different points in their relationships. For some, it started before marriage; for others, it took hold well into parenthood; for all, it's an ongoing quest, an ever-changing equation that lets both partners see that their duties and dreams rank the same.

"Fifty/fifty?" a male friend asked us with a worried look when we told him about our book. "Do you mean every day?"

No. Some days (or years) are 40/60 or even 90/10. That's why we talk about *getting* to 50/50—it's a process as much as a destination. A 50/50 marriage isn't purely based on how you divide the daily tasks of family life—50/50 is really about a core belief: that satisfying work lives and loving bonds with our children are equally important to men and women.

Right now, there's a talented young woman worrying she'll have to choose. All she sees is people around her working 24/7 and she can't imagine how she'll ever raise a family and succeed in her career. She's losing hope that what she wants is possible—and she's downsizing her dreams in ways her male peers don't have to. She thinks about gearing down her job to buy the flexibility that only women ever seem to ask for.

Right now there's a woman, a mother, at a computer solving a problem; in bed nursing a child; on her phone helping a customer; in her car driving to day care. Maybe she's preparing to teach her next class or see another patient; maybe she's helping with homework or volunteering at school. She's designing software or writing a press release or filing a brief—and planning the family dinner. She's working and being a mom. But she's losing hope and thinking of quitting.

We wish she would read this book first.

Part One

The Good News About Work:

Why Two Careers Are Better Than One

Chapter One	Mom *and* Dad: How Kids Can Get More from Two Working Parents

Why count sheep when you can count your worries? *Your child... your job... your spouse... his job... your marriage... your child... your job...*

Will getting to 50/50 let you sleep carefree? For us, that hasn't happened yet. But we toss and turn much less because we have good company, spouses who are equal players in the parent game. The many couples we've interviewed say the same: "It's worth it—especially for the kids."

The thoughts that keep you up at night start early. On a popular morning show, a parenting guru shakes his head. "You need to be there when your kids get home from school." (Does he mean you?) As you kiss your kids good-bye, you see a flier from the library: "Children's Story Hour: 11 a.m. on Mondays." You've never gone. "Would my daughter enjoy that? What is she missing?" you wonder as you shut the front door.

Midday, there's an e-mail from school. "Your son writes numbers backwards. Please practice at home." How, you wonder, will you wedge that in on weeknights? Your 3 p.m. meeting started forty minutes late and the Little League game is at 5. You said you'd be there and, as your son likes to say, "a promise is a promise." You arrive at 5:45

and the game is in progress. You sit down as your son goes to bat. The ball soars and he runs all the way to third base. He sees you and smiles—but you wonder why every day feels like such a fire drill. What about that guy on TV this morning: Are your kids getting short-changed? You start calculating how your family could get by on one income (not yours).

Then your husband grabs your hand and whispers: "Don't worry, I got here early. See what a little batting practice will do?" He smiles proudly as your son's foot hits home plate. Yes, your kids sometimes bring store-bought treats for the bake sale. But if you craft family life to give your children what they need... *does it matter?*

As working moms who care about our kids, we've taken a hard look at this question and learned many eye-opening things. We've read the research—and interviewed many experts who conduct it—to understand what the science really says. We've also gathered the stories of working parents (and their grown kids), who share their experiences complete with ups and downs. It turns out that children can gain a lot when both parents work: independence and self-confidence, cognitive and social skills, and strong connections with two parents—not just one. First, though, let's talk about an issue that can lead to more sleepless nights than a newborn: the question of child care.

THE TRUTH ABOUT CHILD CARE: THE KIDS ARE ALL RIGHT

If you played with dolls as a little girl, you'll recall the game had one rule: Babies need their mommies.

As you prepared to have your own child, you heard the same message, but the sentences got longer and the words got bigger. Experts talked about the human brain and the first few years of life, about how a child's emotional and intellectual development hinged on a mother's total involvement in these crucial early stages. The newspapers announced the landmark government study saying that children placed in day care are more likely to exhibit behavior problems than children reared at home. Friends at the playground traded tales about what a nanny cam caught on tape.

You enjoy your work—you need your work for many reasons—but all this "news" is making you wonder if your career shouldn't take a backseat. Isn't it better for the kids if Mom stays home? Isn't child care bad for children? Can anyone do as good a job as you? And don't forget what your sister said about that boy in your nephew's preschool class—the pint-sized bully who's getting kicked out—"His mom works full time, no wonder he's a problem."

Even when we feel good about the child care we've found for our kids, it's hard not to wonder about its long-term effects. You rarely hear the good news about child care, so wondering can quickly turn to worry.

The mother of all mothering studies

In 2006, the National Institute of Child Health and Human Development (known as NICHD—an arm of the National Institutes of Health) wrapped up fifteen years of research on 1,364 kids. The conclusions were unambiguous: Kids with 100 percent maternal care fare no better than kids who spend time in child care. And "child care" in this study included all types of nonmaternal care, from center-based and family day-care settings to babysitters or nannies. As one summary put it, "There is no reason for mothers to feel like they are harming their children if they decide to work."[1]

The study's key message: Child care is not the thing to worry about—how you parent is. In fact, kids in high-quality child care had higher cognitive and language skills than other kids—including those with at-home mothers. Children in high-quality child care also scored best on school readiness based on standardized tests of literacy and numbers skills (though, like *all* the effects of child care in the study, the effect was small relative to the effects of parents).

This is comforting to know if you're a working parent. But maybe you, like us, don't recall reading about this good news. That's because the media largely focused on one aspect of the study: For a small number of kids, long hours in child-care centers triggered "problem behavior," such as fighting or temper tantrums. Shouldn't parents worry about that? Not really, say the experts. The so-called "problems" weren't serious enough to warrant counseling. They were temporary, diminishing with age, usually between third and fifth grades, and could be reduced or avoided when these "problem" kids were placed in a different sort of child care, such as home-based care with fewer kids, and when their time in care was reduced. Don't fret like we did. When headline-seeking pundits claim child care will turn your kid into a bully, get the facts. You'll feel much better.

By 2006, the NICHD research network had collected millions of observations offering the richest data ever collected on any group of children. There has been a big time lag in getting these findings to parents—the NICHD published its first booklet for parents in 2005, covering only findings from the first four and a half years of the childrens' lives. To find out what happened to the kids after first grade, you have to dig into scientific journals—and talk to the researchers yourself—as we have done.

Here's the bottom line:

"Parents should focus on finding the best-quality child care they can and being the best parents they can," Kathleen McCartney, dean of Harvard's Graduate School of Education and NICHD investigator, told us. "There are some studies that show long hours in child care can pose a risk for behavior problems; it's a small effect, however, and children in child care do not show high levels of behavior problems that require professional intervention. If a child does show behavior problems, parents can do a lot on their own and in collaboration with teachers—for example, set appropriate limits, reward their children for good behavior, and correct bad behavior."

"The big news here is that the amount of time that mothers spent with their children does not seem to be that important; it is the quality of the interaction," said Aletha Huston, a University of Texas psychology professor, past president of the Society for Research in Child Development, and an NICHD investigator. "Many people don't have the luxury of deciding to stay home full time, but if you do, you should make the decision about using child care based on your own beliefs about the costs and benefits for you, your family, and your child as well as your judgment about the quality of the child care you can find. There is no credible evidence that being in child care as opposed to staying home full time with a parent is harmful to children. There is evidence that if you stay home full time when you'd rather be working or if you work full time when you believe it's harmful to your child, your unhappiness may affect how well you relate to your child. If you follow your own beliefs, you'll probably be a better parent."

THE NICHD STUDY OF EARLY CHILD CARE AND YOUTH DEVELOPMENT

In 1987, top child development experts launched what would become "the most ambitious (study) ever undertaken of early child care and its consequences."[2] Federal funding of about $126 million allowed the NICHD to design a study ten times larger and vastly more detailed than any prior research. According to Sarah Friedman, the study's scientific coordinator, child-care development experts spent two years agreeing on how to measure the effects of the many factors in children's lives.[3] The goal: to give parents scientifically based, authoritative answers (and end misleading headlines).

Researchers from leading universities competed to participate in the study and ten locations were chosen around the country. In 1991, researchers recruited 1,364 newborns and their parents—who had yet to make decisions about work and child care—from two dozen hospitals. These investigators studied the children in multiple environments including their homes, day care, and school. From birth to age fifteen, researchers tested these kids for cognitive skills, language, and behavior. Their parents, caregivers, and teachers were assessed for a variety of factors—most important, how they interacted with the children. Reflecting the ongoing challenges of child care in the United States, most kids in the study were in child care that did *not* meet the standards, such as minimum child/caregiver ratios, set by groups like the American Academy of Pediatrics or qualify as "high quality" according to the NICHD researchers.[4]

Despite the lack of high-quality care, the outcomes for children who had been in childcare were reassuring. Yet, polls continue to say most parents still believe that staying home with Mom is better than even top-notch day care. Alison Clarke-Stewart, University of California psychologist and NICHD investigator, observes that "researchers need to communicate better about the positive effects of care on children's development and family well-being."[5]

Until that happens, keep these FAQs handy.[6]

1. *Did kids in 100 percent maternal care score better on any measure than kids in child care?* No.
2. *Did child care harm child–mother attachment?* Not unless the mother was insensitive to her child and the quality of care was low.
3. *Did kids who started child care before twelve months have worse results?* No.
4. *Did kids have long-term behavior problems if they went to child care?* No. On average, children in child care showed a modest elevation in behavior problems that fell within the range of what is considered "normal." Problem behavior was concentrated in a small number of children, the level of misbehavior was pretty low, and the effect diminished over the course of grade school.

Why parenting will always trump child care

Your child's time in the care of another person is short-lived; your role as a parent lasts forever. One major finding of the NICHD study is that how you behave as a parent influences your child's emotional, behavioral, and cognitive development *at least two times* more than any form of child care. In other words, stop worrying about leaving your child with someone else and focus on what happens when you (and your husband) get home.

There are some things you may not know that can help you get a lot more comfortable with being a working parent—they've certainly helped us. For example, working mothers and at-home mothers don't spend drastically different amounts of time interacting with their kids. Nonemployed moms do spend far more hours in the house with their children. But it turns out that working moms spend only

20 percent less time than their at-home peers in "social interaction" with kids—playing games or reading books versus making dinner while the kids run around outside.

Looking at time diaries of over one thousand mothers from the NICHD pool, a University of Texas study found the following: On weekdays, nonemployed mothers spent two and a half hours per day interacting with their kids while working mothers spent one hour less. On the weekends employed mothers do some catch-up, spending three hours per day interacting with their kids (versus two hours for nonemployed moms, who are getting some well-deserved downtime). So, the working moms in the study had 80 percent as many hours of interaction with their kids as nonemployed mothers.[7]

How do kids see this? In a large study conducted in 1994, the Families and Work Institute surveyed children of both employed and nonemployed moms and found their responses remarkably similar. Whether mothers worked or not, children were equally likely to say they got enough time with Mom (about two-thirds said this). But while the majority of the kids felt they got enough time with Mom (whether or not she worked), 40 percent said they had too little time with their other parent: Dad.[8] More on *that* later.

Happy working mothers tell us that their jobs, in fact, help them to be better parents. In our "Real Lives of Working Mothers" survey, one woman offered this observation: "Before I had children, a coworker told me she was a better mother *because* she works. She said she appreciated her time with her daughter more because she didn't do it all the time. I was skeptical then, but now, with two sons of my own, I fervently agree with her assessment." Or as another working mom said: "I think there's a zone. There's a minimum amount of time your child needs with you but there's also an upper limit—where you stop being the parent you want to be, when you've had it with fussing and spilt milk. My mother said she loved staying home but I recall an awful lot of shouting. Knowing there's a clean office for me at work, I can laugh about the sticky handprints in our kitchen."

It turns out that parent education is another thing that raises a mother's sensitivity—and child care can give you a leg up. Research shows we can learn important skills—like setting boundaries and giving options—by watching and talking to well-trained child-care workers.[9]

TIME OUT!

If you sense that kids today get more time with their parents than you ever did—even if your mom never worked—you are probably right. At the University of Maryland, sociologist Suzanne Bianchi has tracked the changes in how married couples spend their time. This is what she found:

Percentage of children with breadwinner dad/homemaker mom:
  1965: 60 percent
  2000: 30 percent

Percentage of mothers who work:
  1965: 33 percent
  2000: 71 percent

Hours per week that moms spend on kids:
  1965: 10.6
  2000: 12.9

Hours per week that dads spend on kids:
  1965: 2.6
  2000: 6.5

What suffered? The number of hours spent on housework was down about one-third.[10] So, embrace your unmade bed as a sign you're prioritizing your kids.

But what about activities like those "mommy and me" classes that happen during the workday? Can you really tune in to your kids if you miss all that? When her son Jared was young, Joanna found herself rushing out of the office at lunch hour to join him at toddler classes like music, gymnastics, or story time at the library. Jared was always eager to go and enjoyed the other kids. Joanna found herself doing what the other moms did—talking with one another while the children played. *Am I here for Jared,* Joanna wondered, *or to talk with other mothers?* What Jared valued was his time alone with his mom at home, without the distraction of bouncing peers. And while Joanna liked the company of the other moms, she realized her son was happy whether or not she attended every class.

Don't hesitate to acknowledge how you really feel about *whatever* choice you choose, because if you're not honest with yourself, you aren't the only one who suffers. This leads us to another fundamental truth: *If you are happy with your decisions about work and family, your children (and your spouse) will be happy, too.* In other words, if you are confident in your choice to work, you will be a better parent.

Why children of working parents excel, even when the cupcakes aren't homemade

If you are like us, you have young kids and it's hard to see what's on the horizon—how your kids will fare as teenagers and adults. Talk to happy two-worker families farther down the path and you'll feel more secure about what lies ahead.

Alexandra, an executive at a multinational firm, has three children, the oldest a business school student. "It's harder when they are young," she acknowledges. "You get those notes from school, 'please send your child to school with a red ribbon tomorrow.' And by the time you get the note, you're just getting home from a business dinner, it's 10 p.m., and the stores are closed."

But now—with child care and permission slips mostly behind her—Alexandra runs a big business for her company and enjoys rich relationships with her children, one in grad school, one in college, and one in high school. "As our kids got older, other parents would complain their children didn't communicate. When I came home my kids *wanted* to be with me." Though she wasn't always able to oversee homework—a task her husband embraced—she now helps her daughter with her business school classes.

"Abby came home the other day during exams and said, 'You know, most moms teach their daughters to cook or sew. Here you are teaching me accounting.' I got to help her study, which was fun for me, and Abby did really well on her exam."

Like many working parents, Alexandra thinks that her children benefited from having a mother who didn't hover. "Working gave my kids more normal teenage years. I wasn't monitoring them one hundred percent of the time. They weren't feeling there was someone always watching, always eavesdropping. It gave them a chance to be themselves. It gave me a much better relationship with my kids than I had with my mother at that age."

There were certainly bumps in the road. Alexandra says she will never forget arriving midway through Abby's first-grade school play after getting waylaid in a snowy snarl of traffic. For years, Abby reminded her mother, "Remember when I was six and you were late to my play?"

"How do you do it all?" some of Abby's friends recently asked Alexandra. "You don't always," Alexandra told them, and she went on to recount the old story of the snowstorm and the missed opening number. "It wasn't *that* bad," Abby now says, though she admits that she sometimes wanted a June Cleaver kind of mom. Was it easy? No. But was it worth it? Just listen to Abby.

"Today, I'm doing what my mom did—going to graduate school, starting my career—and it's great to have her perspective. My mom knows me very well. She knows what I'm good at in a way no one else could. I realize now how amazing she was—raising three kids who did well in school and succeeding in a really demanding career. She was around for the important moments. She always went to my brothers' basketball games and to my track and swim meets. My mom really made an effort to be there for significant events. And if something went wrong that made it impossible for her to be there, she made it up to us in a way that made us feel special."

Abby's father's business allowed him to work from home. "I loved having my dad around," Abby says. "He was always there to help. I could always rely on him. Having a working mom really allowed me to have a good relationship with my dad and that was very valuable."

In this family, like many we've talked to, the children gained a lot from two working parents: an involved dad, an engaged mom, two role models. As Abby says, "What my parents have done has been a great example for me."

It's a bird, it's a plane, it's a helicopter . . . it's Mom

How do you help your child succeed? At the University of North Carolina, psychologist Martha Cox combed the NICHD data for answers, looking specifically at how kids performed as they started kindergarten. Having an at-home parent was not a factor, but Mom's and Dad's approach to parenting—what they believe and how they behave—was quite significant. It turns out that children with the greatest academic and social competence have mothers (and dads) who let go. That does not mean a parent should be detached, but letting a child do for himself builds self-confidence and problem-solving skills. The only factor with equal strength: having a good marriage (we'll come to that in the next chapter).

CONFIDENCE AND COMPETENCE:
Helping Kids by Not Over-Helping

As kids entered kindergarten, NICHD researchers asked teachers which kids were the most competent and least problematic. To focus in on what matters for children living in two-parent families, the study looked at only kids in two-parent homes. Three factors emerged as equally important:

1) Fathers who are sensitive and supportive of their child's autonomy: Dads were active with their kids, and in a positive way. "Fathers who don't want to be there don't help. But fathers who are glad to be with their kids are a very positive influence," Martha Cox told us.
2) Mothers with parenting beliefs that support self-directed child behavior: moms who said they favored "self-directed" child behavior, not

that "child behavior should be governed by adults." These mothers
scored as most sensitive and their children as more competent.
3) Parents who maintain an emotionally intimate relationship: When either fathers or mothers gave their marriage high points for "intimacy,"
children were more likely to do well. As other studies have also
shown, child competence is more likely to develop where there is a
"supportive marital relationship."[11]

Whether or not you work, it's tempting to pave the way and "fix"
things for your kids as much as you can—it just *feels* like what you're
supposed to do. But it's not. It may be easier to tamp down your zeal
to "help," and give your kids the kind of autonomy that will make
them stronger, when you and your spouse both work. Families with
two working parents have less time to micromanage, and they often
find that this lesson from the workplace applies on the home front:
Employees (and kids) learn faster when you let them do it themselves.

We risk undermining our children's faith in themselves, their ability
to make their own decisions and forge their own identities, when we
overdo it with our helping. In our quest to do everything we can to
support our children, we can deprive them of the chance to learn from
failure—to see if they can get up and try again. Laura Berk, a professor
of psychology and the author of *Awakening Children's Minds: How
Parents and Teachers Can Make a Difference,* cautions that parents who
constantly intervene on behalf of their kids stunt their children's self-
confidence and coping skills.[12]

Tony, a third-grader, is the son of working parents who have always
encouraged self-reliance. "When we ask him about his homework,"
his mom told us, "he says it's done. One day some other moms were
worrying about some huge project the teacher had assigned—I hadn't
even heard about it," she said. "I was so worried—had Tony just forgotten? Would he be in trouble? So I asked him about it and he said,
'Yeah, it's due tomorrow and I finished it yesterday.'" Adds his father,
"I look around and hear about all these 'helicopter parents' and I
know we don't have those problems. It's easier for us to separate—to

let our kids have their own space to achieve—because we both have our own careers." At eight years of age, Tony knows he's a competent person and can be independent.

In her book *Einstein Never Used Flash Cards,* child development professor Kathy Hirsch-Pasek points out that young Albert had "freedom to do as he pleased." Kids need to play—and to play with parents.[13] Her advice for us: "If you put the things in place so you have emotional time with the kids, there is no reason to believe there will be problems. Enjoy parenting. Put down the BlackBerry, look your child in the eye, and do what interests them."

LESS MOM, MORE DAD: HOW ENGAGED DADS MAKE A BIG DIFFERENCE

"We assume babies are these mysterious creatures," says Ross Parke, Distinguished Professor of psychology at the University of California–Riverside and director of the university's Center for Family Studies, who has spent decades researching and writing on fatherhood. "It turns out they aren't that mysterious. If you don't stick the bottle in their ear, babies are programmed to feed. And men can figure it out just like mothers do."

Men—the fathers of our children—can excel at parenting and provide unique benefits to our kids. That happens most readily when moms see dads as they are—people equally capable of parenting (even if they do it differently sometimes). When you have an ally in your spouse, you'll never face the challenges of working parenthood by yourself.

Let's go fly a kite: Involved dads as the swing factor

Did you see the movie version of *Mary Poppins?* Sure, by the end of the film, the kids had learned to follow some rules, but the big transformation wasn't in the Banks children—it was in Mr. Banks, their dad.

Mr. Banks starts out a workaholic, obsessed with time and order and oblivious to his children, a man who derives all his self-worth from being a successful banker and a model of male authority. But then

Mary pulls a fast one and forces Mr. Banks into a Victorian version of take-your-kids-to-work day. It's Dad's worst nightmare as the children fight his boss, cause a run on the bank, and get him fired. His world blown apart, Mr. Banks wanders the streets of London all night, stripped of his identity without his all-important job. At dawn, however, Mr. Banks emerges reborn, singing "Let's go fly a kite," eager to skip with his children. His bosses learn some lessons, too, and he gets his job back. As Mary Poppins floats away, we are satisfied that the kids will finally get what they need: an engaged father.

Ms. Poppins got it right. When it comes to raising happy, successful kids, Dad is the swing factor. Until twenty years ago, child development studies focused almost exclusively on the behavior of mothers. But now that the experts have their eyes on fathers, they're learning that active-duty dads make a huge difference. Kids who don't have fathers, or who don't live with them, can and do thrive, too. But we're zeroing in on the added value fathers can bring in two-parent homes. Fathers have a large impact on children, regardless of what mothers do.

One study that tracked the behavior of 1,250 fathers found that children had markedly better academic results if their dads ate and played with them and helped with reading and homework. Another large study found that better-behaved kids were the ones who had more involved fathers, after controlling for moms.[14] Psychologist Martha Cox analyzed the results from children in the NICHD study and found that sensitive support from fathers—more than mothers—significantly predicted children's social skills, the quality of their relationships with teachers, and the level of behavior problems.[15]

Not to give moms a complex, but some research implies dads can be *more* than just as good. In one study, kids with fathers as their primary caregivers had a greater belief in their ability to control events and had higher verbal scores than kids in traditional families. Why? Because these at-home dads set higher expectations for their kids than was the norm in traditional families.[16]

Abby, whose father worked from home, is now in her mid-twenties and preparing to start her own career. She remembers that her dad encouraged her achievement in especially memorable ways. "My dad really pushed us to do our best and it started early." In fourth grade, she entered a track meet and told her dad she thought she was a good runner, but she was worried.

"I really didn't want to do badly," says Abby. "My dad was great. For two weeks before the race he took me out and timed me so I could see myself getting better. We watched the movie *Chariots of Fire* to get me inspired. There's a scene where they're running barefoot on the beach and the coach tells them to pretend the sand is really hot so the runners pick up their feet. On the day of the race, Dad told me, 'Remember! Hot feet! Hot feet!' so I'd do the same. He was really competitive for a fourth-grade track meet, but it was fantastic because I won and my dad had shown me how to take control of a fear and go for it."

Abby's dad was on to something that would yield more than just blue ribbons for his daughter. Researchers say that grown women who report that their fathers spent adequate time with them during childhood have better mental health as adults.[17]

Forget the SAT tutors, just get Dad to the school play

It's not just child development experts who see the value of engaged dads. Educators do, too. In 1996, the U.S. Department of Education (DOE) interviewed parents of over twenty thousand children to see how much parental involvement matters. They asked moms and dads if they had been involved in any types of school activities during the past year: a general school meeting, a parent–teacher conference, a school event (like a play), or a volunteer activity. If parents said they had done zero or one of these activities, the parent's involvement was rated as "low." If they made it to three of any of these activities during the school year, they were deemed "highly involved."

The DOE found that "fathers' involvement in their children's school has a distinct and independent influence" even after controlling for parental education, income, and maternal involvement. "In two-parent families, involvement of both parents in school is significantly associated with a greater likelihood that their children in first through twelfth grade get mostly A's and that they enjoy school and a reduced likelihood that they have ever repeated a grade. Fathers' involvement has a stronger influence on the children getting mostly A's than does mothers' involvement."

Here's the bad news from the DOE survey. Of fathers in two-parent families, almost half (48 percent) scored low, meaning that they showed up at one event or none per year. Only 27 percent of married dads made it three times a year to earn a "high" score (married moms were the opposite, 21 percent rated low and 56 percent high).[18]

Strangely, schools may *benefit* in some ways from parental divorce. Single dads act like single moms when it comes to school involvement; nearly half of all single parents are "highly involved." Does this mean you should divorce your husband so he'll become more involved in your child's school? No, but you might consider the number one reason men cite for their absence: the need to make money. Your income can give Dad the courage to leave the office and get to school. When a wife can pay the bills, a dad can more easily be there for his kids. NICHD researchers found that when moms worked more hours, dads were more involved—even if the fathers held "traditional" views about how families should run.[19]

THE DAD DIFFERENCE:
Self-Esteem, Smiles, and Salaries

Kyle Pruett is a child psychiatrist who drew on two decades of research at the Yale Child Study Center to write *Fatherneed: Why Father Care Is as Essential as Mother Care for Your Child.* His findings reinforce the correlation between paternal involvement and cognitive skills (such as higher IQs and better verbal and math scores, particularly among girls). In addition, he shows the correlation between what he terms the "moral behavior" of children and paternal engagement. Researchers found fewer negative behaviors among boys and girls with involved dads, including lower incidences of acting out, lying, depression, and sadness.[20]

The positive impact of paternal involvement is especially impressive when you look at what happens over a lifetime. Getting enough paternal love predicts higher self-esteem and life satisfaction in both men and women. Some researchers found "the most powerful predictor of empathy in adulthood for both men and women was the paternal child-rearing involvement when they were five years of age." Others discovered that adults who enjoyed higher-quality marriages and friendships were most likely to have experienced paternal warmth as children.[21]

If emotional benefits aren't enough to convince you that engaged dads make a difference, how about degrees and dollars? University of North Carolina demographer Kathy Harris used the results of the National Survey of Children, an eleven-year study sponsored by the Foundation for Child Development, to find links between parental involvement and adult success. Based on data for 584 children who lived in two-parent families throughout the study, Harris found that "paternal involvement in childhood was associated with adult children's higher economic-educational achievement and lower delinquency, whereas maternal involvement was not."[22]

Who says Mother knows best? Let Dad give it a shot

If you embrace 50/50, your kids will get the benefits of two parenting styles. Even if you and your spouse are in agreement on the big stuff, rarely will you approach your children in exactly the same way, and that's good (and often more fun) for your whole family.

"I think it's really wonderful for Ben to have two really different points of view about life," says Maggie, his mom, an intensive care nurse. Maggie's husband, Marc, is a writer. "Marc won't realize we're missing food in the house," says the practical-minded Maggie. But she values his freewheeling approach to problem solving with their son. "I'll ask Ben, 'Why would you do *that*?' Marc asks the opposite question: 'Why *wouldn't* you do that?'"

When dads get involved, kids get twice the range of interests. For example, one 50/50 dad we talked to said, "I know reading to the kids is important, but it's not my thing. If I do story time at night, I fall asleep. But my wife loves to do it. On the other hand, I love playing chess and math games with the boys. And my sons and I go skateboarding (while my wife worries too much that we'll all end up in the ER!)."

"In general," Maggie says, "I think men are more spontaneous with children." Playful, inventive, comic—that's how many 50/50 wives describe the fathers of their children. In fact, we're often envious of our husbands, because they don't seem burdened with the sense that there is a "right" way to parent. This means they can have more fun with the job.

Christina found a note in her kindergartner's backpack. "Please help Joel memorize his letters. He's not quite where he needs to be." Christina's first instinct was to head for the store and buy books, puzzles, and flash cards about letters—all things that her son had no interest in. Christina's husband, George, had other ideas. Why not make letters out of pretzels or trace them in the air with their son's prize possession—his light saber? Guess whose method worked? Joel and George combined learning with laughter, not drudgery.

Sharon's son insisted on doing a particularly time-consuming puzzle right before bedtime. When she told him it was too late, his face fell and his shoulders sank as he told his mother, "If we can't do it tonight, I . . . Well, I will NEVER do it!" Sharon tried to reason with Max but he just dug in.

Then Max's dad walked in with a different approach. Steve glowered and began stomping his feet on the ground, chanting, "If I can't do it now, I'LL NEVER DO IT!" Max tried to keep frowning. "Or," Steve went on, "you could do it like this." Steve started jumping up and down, saying, "If I can't have my way right this very second, I'll NEVER, EVER, EVER DO IT!" Max lost his composure and laughed, bouncing up and down with his dad—puzzle forgotten and meltdown averted, thanks to his funny father.

In *When Mothers Work,* author Joan Peters relates the story of her young daughter who came home sad after fighting with a friend. Peters wasn't home and her husband consoled their daughter. Unable to get her out of her funk, the girl's father switched on *Winnie the Pooh.* When Peters got home, she was not pleased—did they want to teach their child to drown her sorrows in TV? "What's wrong with escape when you feel bad? You and all your women friends never miss one emotion. The worse you feel, the more you have to dwell on it," her husband said, defending his methods. "I don't want her to be a girl in that way. I'd rather she had more of a buffer." Peters later admitted he had a point—and that his way had worked.[23]

It's hard for us to face, but sometimes dads see things clearly that we moms just miss. The good news is that our kids benefit from two different mind-sets.

"I WANT TO BE LIKE YOU"—WORKING PARENTS AS ROLE MODELS

"Our daughter Melissa uses a backpack I got at a conference," says Kathy, a physicist and mother of two, whose husband is also a physicist. "It says something about particle physics on it. When Melissa started wearing it to school, the kids started asking her, 'What are you, some sort of rocket scientist?' Melissa would tell them, 'No, but *both* my mom and dad are!'"

Even if we're not rocket scientists, our children can sense why work is good and how it serves as a source of pride—how it serves as a parallel to what they do during the day. We both tell our grade-schoolers that we work to make money and do our part in the world, and that when they grow up they will do the same. For now, our kids know that their "job" is to go to school and have fun as they learn new things.

Discussing work seems to open up channels of communication between parent and child. Our struggles with the office jerk generate a dividend—parables to share with our kids and a chance to show how we mess up, too. "I tell my daughter about my day, the people I like, the ones I don't like, the battles. I bring my work into our relationship," says Maya, a mother of two. "She sees that I have ups and downs in my life. That I have struggles a lot like hers. And that opens the door for her to tell me how she's really feeling at school." (Interestingly, both of Maya's children attend an all-girls school that has more working mothers than any other private school in her community. "The principal told me they actively work to attract the children of working moms—the school wants their girls to have working mom role models.")

Kathleen Gerson is a professor of sociology at New York University and the author of the forthcoming book *Children of the Gender*

Revolution. In the early 1990s, Gerson randomly selected a pool of young adults and asked how they saw their parents' choices about work and home life. One notable finding: Children of dual-career homes were more likely to embrace their parents' choices than those who had grown up in more traditional homes. Four out of five told her they preferred having a working mom (approval was even higher among girls who valued their working mother role models). Their parents may have missed ball games and worked late some evenings, but these children grew up viewing dual-career life as the "best option." Gerson also spoke to adult children who grew up in homes where only the father worked. These children of more traditional homes were almost evenly divided, with 48 percent concluding that "it would have been better if their mothers had gone to or stayed at work."

These adults in the survey had the benefit of hindsight. Had Gerson interviewed her subjects at age nine, perhaps some of them would have longed for Mom to pick them up from school every day. But as it turns out, a full 90 percent of the young women Gerson interviewed say they want to follow their mother's example and combine work and family, while two-thirds of the men intend to "share parenting and work."[24]

By showing that it's possible to combine work and family in a positive way, you're shining a bright and hopeful light on a path your kids can happily follow.

"Ladies' lunches," family dinners, and reflections on a full life

Linda is now in her sixties, a tenured professor at a leading medical school. She and her doctor husband raised two children while working full time in very demanding careers. Her mother, a college-educated woman with four children, did not work. "She really fell apart from frustration and boredom. The lesson was, you have to have something in your life that's not your kids. I feel so lucky—I had my life and my work. My kids have their life and their work. I didn't live vicariously through them."

But Linda worked hard to stay connected with her kids. And there were challenges. When her daughter Ellen was six, "she told me I wasn't as good as her best friend's mom because I was working," said Linda. "So I started doing special things with her, like a 'ladies' lunch'— I would take her out, just the two of us or sometimes with her friends." Making these kinds of efforts "helped a lot. By college Ellen e-mailed me all the time and we grew very close."

Even when two jobs made it hard, Linda insisted on getting everyone together for dinner. "Our kids now tell us we were the butt of jokes at school because we seemed to be the only family still having family dinners. Sometimes I had to return to the hospital after dinner or I went to the study to finish up the day's work. But ninety-five percent of the time, our family ate together," says Linda. "I expected my husband to be there and, generally, he was."

Experts say this kind of effort pays off. According to psychologist Kathy Hirsh-Pasek, a two-parent family dinner helps kids see how to ask for and receive advice: "It is wonderful for children to see parents asking each other for feedback. Establishing that we can count on each other and call on each other for support gets conveyed indirectly but clearly that way. A shared dinner hour (even a truncated, twenty-minute dinner hour!) gives the message that each of us, and what we do, is important in our own unique way." Research has also shown that kids who regularly share sit-down dinners with family perform better in school.[25]

Linda's children are now in their twenties. On a recent visit home, the kids decided on a twist for family dinner: They gave Mom and Dad a "report card."

"They told us they always feel loved and love us, they respect and admire us for what we do in our work, that we always made them feel important. They think both parents should work as we did."

Linda's son and daughter also believe parents should share responsibility for child care. For instance, "they have this idea that one parent should be home when the kids get home—like every other day Mom and Dad switch off getting home early, even if the kids are on the phone or doing homework."

Two devoted parents who value their work, who are equally engaged in family life, who nurture and inspire their children to do the same is what getting to 50/50 is all about.

Chapter Two

What Your Husband Wins from a Working Wife

You may be thinking, "My children will have plenty of time with their father and he'll be an equal parent, whether I'm at home or in a job." In many families today, both dads and moms want to be involved with their kids whether or not both parents have careers.

But consider this: If you stay home, you're likely to take on more family work—and your husband is less likely to make it home for dinner. Being the *sole* breadwinner for a family is stressful (and sometimes scary). Contact one last client or race home for bedtime? Facing this choice, the sole earner may tell himself, "the kids don't really need me" and make the call. Asked to fly cross-country to meet a customer, the sole breadwinner may feel it's too risky to suggest a conference call and skip his son's school play instead.

As children grow and become more expensive to raise, the pressures on a sole provider increase. At the same time, that breadwinner becomes more competent at work and less competent at home. The 50/50 couples we've talked to tell us it doesn't have to be that way. You can choose to be competent both at work and home, no matter if you're called Mom or Dad. For this to happen, women need to work more so men can work less.

THE HIGH PRICE OF THAT PICKET FENCE: HOW SOLE BREADWINNERS GET HEMMED IN

"How am I going to tell my wife?" Zach wondered, after a bad review with his boss. Zach has a great education and makes a decent salary, but he hasn't enjoyed his work for a long time—he'd really like to change jobs.

When his wife was working, Zach could have called it quits and made a new start. However, his wife, a Harvard-trained physician, left her job six years ago to stay home with their two kids. So the family now relies on Zach's income for 100 percent of its needs. *She wants a new house. She wants more children. She is going to be so disappointed in me.* All these thoughts keep Zach in his current job even though he is so anxious he is unlikely to perform well. So he is stuck—unless his boss makes the decision for him.

Remember Darrin in the sixties sitcom *Bewitched*? Whether you watched the series growing up or on Nick at Nite reruns, you may have felt frustration on his behalf. As he scrambled to please his intrusive boss, Mr. Tate, and his nutty advertising clients, Darrin's angst was the grist for the show. When Darrin got into a jam, Samantha wiggled her nose and got him out of it. What Darrin could *not* escape was his joyless work life. What if Samantha had gotten a job?

One income, no options

Becca runs human resources for a semiconductor firm, where most employees are male. Men tell her personal stories about what they like and don't like about work. But it's *Becca's* personal setup that most interests her male colleagues with at-home wives. "I'm jealous of your husband. He doesn't have to take as much crap at work as I do," one man told Becca. Another told her how boxed in he feels. "My last boss was a jerk; now I've been transferred to a bad division. But I can't afford to protest or change jobs." He's obliged to grin and bear it since his income alone supports his family. "If I were married to someone with a real career like yours, I wouldn't have to suck it up twenty-four-seven," he says. "I feel trapped, like my only option is to stay here."

Two incomes are a safety net. If a husband's work is jeopardized or vanishes because of "right-sizing," a working wife keeps the lights on and provides security until the next job comes along. If your husband leaves his job (or his job leaves him), your income gives him choices—more good ones. He won't have to panic. He'll be free to take his time and decline what one man called the "soul-killing" jobs because you've got things covered.

In the wake of the tech bubble, 9/11, and Enron, many people got pink slips they weren't expecting. Ethan was one of them. He worked for an Internet company that went bankrupt. His wife, a pediatrician, had been working three days a week and staying home the other two to be with their children. When Ethan's job vanished, their solution was simple: His wife returned to seeing patients full time so she could support the family. That gave Ethan a lot of breathing room and he used it well. It took six months, but Ethan found a good new position where he has done well. "Many of my friends had to take jobs they weren't excited about," he says. "Sometimes they had to move across the country. Their spouses didn't work and they were stressed about paying the bills. I was lucky that I could be more discerning because my wife was our safety net."

When wives don't pay their way, men often pay a price—they have to compromise themselves, sticking it out in work environments that don't reflect their values. "Your business is filled with people who don't put family first," Sharon's husband, Steve, said to her when they first met. Steve had interned on Wall Street one summer. One of his strongest memories was of Nick, a respected banker, who was forced to choose between attending a "mandatory" recruiting event or his son's birthday party. Nick felt the culture wouldn't accept how he felt: that his son was more important than summer interns. So what did he do? Nick stealthily tiptoed out of his office at 6 p.m., ducking down between the cubicles as he went for the elevator. Steve's takeaway: "It wasn't a life I was willing to lead." Steve hasn't had to—and Sharon's job meant Steve hasn't had to worry that his family would go wanting if his career had a hiccup. But he did make a compromise. He supported Sharon's career in a business he'd intentionally avoided.

"Be your own man." That's what we teach our sons and, after a fashion, our daughters. Yet a dad can't *do* that when he's the sole provider. Freedom to walk out on a bad deal at work, to tell the truth—that's a big part of what husbands win with a working wife. But it's more than just avoiding the negatives. Men also gain an advantage in their careers (and lives) that often goes unnoticed.

Should his heart race for his boss—or for you?

Let's say your spouse supports your family while you stay home, but dreams of bigger things or wants to change tracks. If he's a responsible guy but hasn't yet won the lottery, what's the chance he'll get to act on his desires? It's hard to be a frontiersman without a grubstake or a second income that acts as one. When men yearn for open territory, wives can block the way or pave it.

Pablo came to the United States when he married Celia, a public school teacher. He left behind a job as an accountant to start over in his adopted country. To work in health care, he needs credentials and Celia's full-time teaching salary pays for the classes that will certify him in his new specialty. Alex was a successful sales executive at a large company but wanted something more in life. His wife, Deb, ran a public relations business and together they had three small children. Deb's job meant that Alex could go to graduate school and launch a career he found more rewarding. Maggie's husband, Marc, is a writer; they knew when they first married that her nurse's salary would probably provide the steadier income stream and that it would allow him to write. He makes money when he sells his work and her income pays the bills in between.

If your husband is burning to move into a new field or start that business he's been talking about since college, he has a fighting chance, if you have a job. In fact, he's more likely to spread his wings. The research group Catalyst reports that when both spouses work, one or both are more likely to take career risks. Says one man in a survey Catalyst conducted, "[my wife] made enough that I was able to go off and do something far more entrepreneurial than I would have if we were relying on one income."[1]

Craig took three years off to redirect his career and is now CEO of a software company. "I'm paying myself a lower salary and giving myself more upside in the company because [my wife's] income makes that possible. I'm putting in a lot of sweat equity and I couldn't do that if I needed the money to pay our bills. I have friends who would kill to do what I'm doing. But they can't take the chance because they're the only income in the family."

That's been the story in our lives, too. Both of us married men who enjoy taking risks. Because their wives work, they've been free to forge their own paths.

Joanna's spouse is a "serial entrepreneur" who thrives on creating new ventures. Before they married, Jason sat her down and said, "I don't want to be a corporate drone. I don't want to work for anyone else." He was prepared to live simply, he told her, if he could enjoy his work. But to support a family they'd need a steady income, and early on Joanna made the decision that consistency would come from her work. Jason was able to pursue his entrepreneurial career, starting successful (and some not-so-successful) companies.

When they married, Sharon's husband, Steve, worked for an established real estate developer. But the year they bought their first house, Steve made a big move: starting his own company. Since Sharon could make the whole payment if Steve's firm folded, the bank granted their mortgage. Steve was able to go with his gut and pursue his dream without fear that he would lose the family home.

Your work, his wages—how does it all pan out?

Your work adds a layer of security and freedom that your spouse will appreciate, but how does it affect his income? Historically, experts believed that men with nonemployed wives made more money (around 15 to 20 percent more) than men with working wives. They concluded that a working wife must create disadvantages for her husband that lower his wages.

Economists have now shown that this view confuses cause and effect: The wife's job does not determine the husband's wage—it's the other way around. After men have achieved high earnings, some percentage of wives cut back their employment. The increase in the man's wage creates a disincentive for women to work more hours. In the *American Economic Review,* one study controlled for variables like number and age of children and wife's age and education. The result? The wage "premium" from having a nonworking wife shrank to 5 percent or disappeared entirely. Bottom line: Don't quit your job because you think it will help your husband. There's likely no benefit at all, and there may be a big cost.[2]

When we stop believing that a woman's job will hurt her husband—and realize that it might help him instead—we free women to see the importance of their jobs as clearly as men do. Until we do this, women will not approach making money in the straightforward way men tend to. "I want to be able to support myself" is what we heard when we asked young women why they work. Do they ever think about supporting dependents? "It's a good idea in case my husband dies or we get divorced" is another frequent comment, as if it's optional, like flood insurance you might let lapse if the river dries up.

But when men talk about their incomes, they see the need to earn a living as clear, present, and perpetual—to look after their spouses, kids, grandkids, friends. Making money is not a contingency for most men. It's required. If we want men to treat us equally in the world, we have to take our paychecks as seriously as they do theirs. We owe it to the men we love to take half the burden (and joy) of making money. (How many people know that 30 percent of wives make more than their husbands?)[3] Whether we earn a lot or a little, men can worry less and enjoy life more when wives are committed to their careers.

"For a single-earner man, there's a lot of pressure to continue doing things he may not want to do. They can't take risks, they can't explore other things they might like better or be better at," says Laura, who shared breadwinning with her husband while raising two now-grown kids. "But if you have two careers, you have a lot more financial resilience as a couple. That is a big, big deal for women to understand."

MARRIED, FILING JOINTLY: WHY YOUR JOB MATTERS TO YOUR MATE AND YOUR MARRIAGE

Flying cross-country, Joanna found her seatmate eager to talk about his life. He asked Joanna what she'd been doing in New York and told her about his job. They compared notes on the elections and local schools. Then, this man blurted out a confession of sorts.

"I miss the days when my wife came home with stories about her work. Now, every night, she tells me what's going on in preschool. I know what she's doing is important and I like hearing about our son's day. But I miss the camaraderie we once had, when she was working, too.

"I never envisioned myself in this sort of marriage," he went on, saying he'd be willing to do more child care if his wife returned to work—"but she doesn't seem interested."

This wife may have many reasons for quitting: wanting to spend more time with the kids, perhaps believing that her children will suffer without a mom at home; disliking a job where she felt less appreciated or could not get control of her schedule, and was uncertain that she could steer her career to a better place; needing more help at home from her husband than she was getting (*before* he realized how much he wanted her to keep her job). We don't know how this couple fell into their rut, but we do know you and your husband can avoid it.

Life on the same page—fewer secrets, more sex

Many people ask us, "Isn't it easier to run a household if one spouse focuses on home and the other concentrates on making money?" True, logistics may be simpler if one parent mostly covers the home front while the other mostly pays the bills: There will probably always be milk in the refrigerator and clean underwear for everyone. When only one career is at stake and the possibility of relocating for a better job arises, the decision making will be easier. There will certainly be fewer day-to-day questions about who does drop-off and what's for dinner.

But is this necessarily good for a marriage? No. In fact, a lot of research shows that marriage can be a lot more rewarding (and fun) if both parents jump into family life full force. And in our interviews, many couples said that sharing their career lives gave them more mutual respect and excitement in marriage.

Studies show that once a child enters the scene, spouses begin to gradually disengage from one another if one parent leaves the house for work each day while the other stays behind.

"My male colleagues with wives at home have a hard time. They have a constant battle because their wives really don't understand why they have to work and travel so much," says Maya, who works at an investment firm and has two children in grade school.

When we started our careers, we saw the same thing Maya did— that trust and respect often suffer when husbands lead lives that become too different from their wives'.

At her first office holiday party, Joanna recalls talking to the non-working wives of some more senior associates. "How do you like the firm?" one wife asked Joanna. "Most of the time it's great," said Joanna. "But there are some things that are a little awkward. Like when we finish working late and the whole team goes out with the clients to a strip club." The next day, the woman's husband came to Joanna's office and closed the door. "What do you think you're doing telling my wife about strip clubs?" It hadn't occurred to Joanna that her peers would hide these things from their wives.

Sharon's firm lost a lot of money one year. For months, everyone knew their pay would be down. On the day compensation was announced, Sharon walked by a man she liked on the trading floor. He was on the phone with his wife trying to break the bad news. His face was strained. His nonworking wife wasn't taking it well. Sharon and her colleagues felt bad enough. They'd all sacrificed, put in round-the-clock hours, only to make less money this year. But for this man's spouse to berate him about something beyond his control—that seemed too much. Sharon called her then boyfriend, a journalist, and told him her own pay had been cut. "Gee," he joked, "can we still afford to eat?"

When you both have jobs outside the home, your daily experience remains more similar, even if you work in entirely different fields. If either of you has had a rotten day or a stunning success, it's nice to have someone who still knows what it's like to work with colleagues *and* with kids.

Jeff's wife, Tracy, returned to a demanding full-time job after five years at home. "Our experience with the kids is now more similar and that's good. When Tracy went back to work, it caused me to rethink getting up and running out the door to work at seven a.m. I had to be aware of where our three kids were. With both of us at work all day, it helps the dynamic in our family. It focuses our time together and simplifies our priorities. When we get home, we both agree that it's time to be with the kids."

WHEN HE DOES WINDOWS...

More career options, more companionship—your job gives your husband a lot of benefits he can discuss with his parents when they wonder if your career is good for him. But men smile most broadly when we get to the private reason couples enjoy life when they share roles: more sex. (Probably best to let your husband decide if he wants to tell that to his mom.)

In 2006, a survey of 360 married men found that men who did more chores at home fared much better in the bedroom. "The more satisfied a wife is with the division of household duties, the more satisfied a man is with his marital sex life," according to the survey. These married men reported that when wives were happier with their husband's household work, the *frequency* of sex was also higher. And, confounding many skeptics, the survey found that "the more hours a woman works at the job, the more sex she has at home."[4]

Why would this be? Aren't dual-career couples more harried and tired? Maybe, but fatigue may be a smaller factor in who gets sex than how couples interact.

If you look at the wealth of research, couples who share work and family life more evenly have three factors on their side. First, wives are less likely to see their husbands as slackers at home (less "you jerk" effect); instead, wives may find husbands more appealing *because* they snuggle their kids (more "BabyBjörn" effect); third, employed wives are statistically more likely to be happy with themselves (more "self-confidence" effect).

For years, noted marriage expert John Gottman has told husbands that dumping family chores on wives is an anti-aphrodisiac. Gottman and other couples therapists have identified household conflict as the toxin most likely to stunt married sex life.[5] In a ten-year study of young parents, Berkeley psychologists Philip and Carolyn Cowan found "the greatest interference with what happens in the bedroom comes from what happens between partners outside the bedroom." When parents get siloed—dads at work, moms at home—there's a lot of room for misunderstanding and anger. So, in early parenthood, with so little time to sort things out, disagreements fester. And then, as the Cowans point out, partners "feel 'not in the mood.' "[6]

The NICHD study on child development also looked at the behavior of parents and found this pattern: When wives work longer hours, husbands do more child care. And when husbands do more child care, wives report greater "marital intimacy." (Men reporting the highest intimacy were also the guys rated "most sensitive" with their kids.)[7]

More sex may also be a function of more contented wives. Author Stephanie Coontz points to the many studies showing that "working wives report fewer feelings of distress than wives who stay home and they are more likely to believe that their marriages are egalitarian."[8] Joshua Coleman, psychologist and marriage counselor, told us "the biggest predictor of marital satisfaction for women is how much 'emotional work' the husband does. While this is typically defined by his capacity for empathy, expressiveness, and sensitivity, it's clear that doing his fair share of housework and parenting communicates that he cares about her feelings and doesn't want her to feel overly burdened or unduly stressed. This kind of participation makes for a happier wife, and, in general, happier wives make for happier husbands."[9]

Want to halve divorce risk? Then halve the load

Today, more men than women see marriage as the "ideal" lifestyle, points out Stephanie Coontz in her book *Marriage, a History*. Studies consistently show that men enjoy more psychological benefit from marriage and suffer more depression from divorce than women. Why? One theory is that men may concentrate more of their emotional energy on marriage since men on average don't have as many intimate friends as women do.[10]

So, if men need stable marriages at least as much as their wives, what kind of marriage is most likely to succeed? In 2006, the *American Journal of Sociology* published a groundbreaking study by sociologist Lynn Prince Cooke. Historically, experts believed that working women were more likely to divorce, if only because they could survive without a man's income. But prior to Cooke's research, no one had really focused on the effect of *male behavior*—how much household work husbands do or don't do—on divorce.

It turns out that among American couples, whether wives work or not, if husbands do more housework, the odds of getting divorced are lower. Couples where the husbands did 50 percent of the housework and wives did 50 percent of the earning reduce their odds of divorce by more than 50 percent as compared with couples where the wife did all the housework and the husband earned all the money. That's dramatic. Two interesting notes: Couples where husbands did around 40 percent of the housework and wives earned around 40 percent of the family income had the rock-bottom odds of divorce, because we are apparently still more comfortable "doing gender" the old-fashioned way. Cooke believes gender norms will probably continue to change over time, shifting even more toward a 50/50 solution.[11]

When a dad has to go it alone making money, it can be a long, lonely haul until the kids graduate from college and he gets his gold watch. Relationship experts agree that two of the biggest stressors on a marriage are often lack of money and concern over kids. When both spouses work, there are two backs to carry the financial load—and less

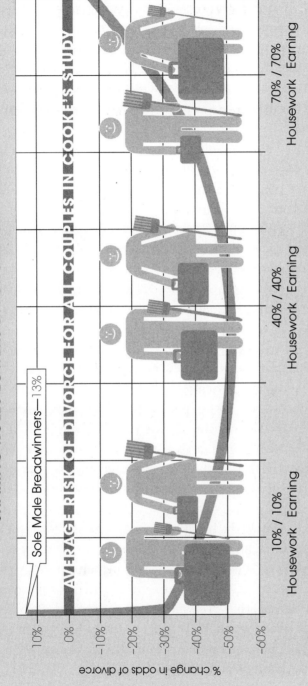

SHARING ROLES LOWERS DIVORCE RISK—A LOT!

AVERAGE RISK OF DIVORCE FOR ALL COUPLES IN COOKE'S STUDY

Sole Male Breadwinners—13%

% change in odds of divorce

10%
0%
-10%
-20%
-30%
-40%
-50%
-60%

10% / 10%
Housework Earning

40% / 40%
Housework Earning

70% / 70%
Housework Earning

- For sole-male-breadwinner couples where the husband did no housework, the odds of divorce were 13% higher than the average.
- Divorce risk drops sharply when a wife has a job, even if she earns little money and the husband does little housework.
- At 50/50, the odds of divorce were 48% lower than the average.
- Couples who split roles approximately 40/40 had the lowest divorce risk, 51% below the average.

stress on both of you. If you parent equally, you have the best salve we know of for the agitation of child rearing—companionship. Sociologist Scott Coltrane, author of *Family Man,* points out that joint parenting supports marriage in another way, too. In his study of dual-career couples, Coltrane found that when men were more engaged and sensitive parents, their marriages often improved and they "paid more attention to emotional cues from their wives."[12]

"I really stayed a workaholic when our first two kids were small," says Peter, an executive at a Fortune 500 company. But when his wife, Jen, a writer, got pregnant with their third child, Peter offered to take a month's paternity leave so Jen could finish a manuscript. "It did really good things for our relationship. It shifted how Jen thought about me. There were traces of anger from how she felt when our first two kids were young and she really bore the brunt of the work," says Peter. "So when I offered to take this leave, Jen began to see me in a different light—like a great guy. She was not alone but truly had a partner to stand by her and empathize."

Most couples we talked to see having two careers as a source of strength in their marriages. Says Rachel, a stockbroker whose three children are now in their twenties, "Our relationship is much closer because I work. You see a lot of people who raised kids together and then they split up. Sharing the experience when you both have careers is more protective of marriage than you would think. You are closer to each other's world. You understand the rhythm of each other's lives. You don't have the buildup of resentment on one side or the other."

Psychologists Rosalind Chait Barnett and Jane Shibley Hyde studied divorced parents and found they chose something different when they later remarried. "They engaged heavily in joint parenting so as to avoid the rift that traditional parenting had caused in their previous marriages. As a group, they overwhelmingly endorsed their 'peer marriages' and felt that the quality of these relationships was markedly better as a result of their extensive community of interest."[13]

Translation? Common ground.

Isn't that why you married each other in the first place?

Trade in the old saws for things men can love

"A brilliant wife is a plague to her husband, her children, her friends...everyone," wrote French philosopher Jean-Jacques Rousseau in 1762. Rousseau was not the only smart guy to say dumb things about women (he also abandoned five of his children, giving him a low 50/50 aptitude score).[14] But his notion—that women are less appealing, loving, or devoted to their families if they demonstrate their talents in the world—still haunts us. Centuries later, we can laugh at Rousseau's brazen words, but our behavior says we, as a group, still think he's on to something.

Successful 50/50 couples show us that the best way to give men (and women) the lives they want is to reject the received "wisdom" that leads a lot of couples off track.

Consider what happens when women gravitate to lower-paying careers or to men who make more money than they do: When a child arrives, "of course" it's the wife who cuts her hours—her work is deemed less valuable to the family. Trade "man" for "woman" and you quickly see how this logic falls apart.

Betsy runs a department within a large company and her husband, Paul, teaches school. Another woman told Betsy about her daughter. "She's a teacher," she told Betsy. "She doesn't make enough money to pay for child care, so she had to quit." Later, Betsy laughed. "Imagine if I said that to Paul! 'Honey, your salary doesn't cover our child care. Why don't you leave teaching?'" Income isn't everything. When *men* choose jobs—musician, soldier, clergyman—where success is not measured in dollars, no one demands they put their calling aside to look after the children. Wives like Betsy appreciate the nonmonetary contribution their husbands make, to the world and to their families. Likewise, there are lots of men who see the value in their wives' work apart from the paycheck.

"It is slightly stressful that we both work," admits Josh, a software executive married to a professor of French history. "But the fact that Sasha wants to work reflects that she is a passionate, engaged person and I love that I married her. I appreciate her contribution to our economic well-being, but the money is not the point. The important thing is that she is engaged with the outside world, not the money."

Sam runs a jobs program for inner-city children and his wife, Jody, is a public defender. "I like the fact that Jody defines herself in part by her work. We define ourselves by our family and our work, both are important," Sam says. "We feel we are contributing to the world, trying to make a difference in people's lives. Our evenings are always rich and interesting because we have things to connect on beyond the kids."

"What I fell in love with was a talented, ambitious person. I knew I was never going to be bored," says Bob, Maya's husband. "It benefits our entire family. There are obviously challenges with two careers but the benefits outweigh the challenges, hands down. It creates more harmony than conflict because we don't take each other for granted. We are both doing things that fulfill us and I think that lets us have a healthier, happier family."

FAMILY MAN: HEALTHIER, HAPPIER, SUCCESSFUL AT WORK—AND WITH THE KIDS

Remember Zach, the latter-day Darrin of *Bewitched,* stuck in a job he hates? He's stressed out all day. His evenings probably aren't much better. He stays at work late because maybe, just maybe, that will impress his boss and salvage his job. And if Zach does go home, how good is an angst-ridden dad to his kids—did Darrin ever *play* with Tabitha, or just quash her magic tricks?

It's not clear that Darrin's bossman Mr. Tate—always at the office or client dinners—did much better in his fathering role. In the cover story "Why Grade 'A' Executives Get an 'F' as Parents," *Fortune* magazine explained that "successful executives and professionals often have more trouble raising kids than all but the very poor." Looking at the children of executives, most of whom were male, *Fortune* found these kids were more than two times as likely to seek drug abuse or psychiatric treatment than kids of nonexecutives covered by the same health plan.[15]

In our first chapter, we talked about what kids win from active dads. But it turns out that fathers need their kids—for health and long-term success—as much as children need their dads. A study conducted by the National Institute of Mental Health confirms that a man's experience as a parent, not as an employee, is "the strongest predictor of whether he would have stress-related physical problems."[16]

Psychologists Barnett and Hyde add, "Multiple roles are, in general, beneficial for both women and men, as reflected in their mental health, physical health, and relationship health. Adding the worker role is beneficial to women and adding or participating in family roles is beneficial to men." In fact the men who have the strongest relationships with their children score the highest in mental health.[17]

So, in four decades of work life, what kind of a man would you bet on to win the marathon of long-term work success? The guy who overworked in his thirties and forties—and spends his fifties trying to connect with his estranged children? (In the end, even Rousseau went looking for the kids he'd abandoned.) Or the father who prudently kept both parts of his life healthy and afloat?

"When I got home each night my daughter would come running," says Doug, a professor of psychiatry who now has grown children and runs a large institute. "And I'd have to put aside my work miseries, my worries about getting tenure. My kids kept me from losing perspective. I think if you are overfocused on your work, you lose perspective and make mistakes." Would he have been any more successful without the burden of kids? "No," he says.

As University of California psychologist Ross Parke told us, "Fathering is good for men. It makes them more likely to contribute to the world. It improves their self-esteem, their sense of efficacy, and their emotional range because with children you can be more emotionally vulnerable. We raise men to be tough and closed and many active fathers report discovering emotions they didn't know they had."[18]

"Becoming a father made me better at work," said one 50/50 dad we interviewed. "You learn not to take yourself so seriously, to be more patient, and boy, do you develop stamina."

Many men fear that spending more time with kids will hurt their earning power. But the numbers don't support that either. Economist

Robert Drago at Pennsylvania State University looked at data from the 2002 National Study of the Changing Workforce. Drago wanted to see what happened to the wages of married men who said they did most of the child care or "shared about equally." Not much. The hourly pay of men who did half or more of the child care was not statistically different from men who said they did less.[19] In fact, tracking 240 men over forty years, one study found that "involved fathers are more likely to have career success." They are less likely to make bad career moves due to the excess stress of being the sole provider.[20]

To look inside the statistics, we interviewed a variety of men who took parental leaves, cut work hours, or just made time to do their part at home (we'll share their stories in Chapter 5). How do they feel? If there is a price, it's small, it's temporary, and it's worth it.

Hidden guilt: How dads suffer from the fathering deficit

In Chapter 1, we saw that the average dad today spends three times as many hours with his kids as his own father did. But also recall that that's only 6.5 hours a week—half what today's moms spend. Hidden in these statistics is a surprising fact: Working dads feel just as guilty as working moms and maybe more.

For the last three decades, polls have shown that working fathers are as anxious as working mothers about how their work hours impact family life. In a large survey of boomer men, 78 percent said they felt guilty about their lack of time with their children (as compared to 76 percent of wives).[21] Polls also show that male anxiety over finding time for family ranks as high as fears about breadwinning. In 2005, *USA Today* reported a survey in which 62 percent of fathers said they would sacrifice job opportunities and higher pay for more family time.[22]

Ellen Galinsky, co-founder of the Families and Work Institute, notes that employed dads and mothers used to sound different when she interviewed them. In the 1970s, Galinsky told us, "men and women used to talk about work and family life and sound very different. Now, if the timbre of the voices was disguised, I couldn't tell which was which. The men are saying, 'I don't want to live this way. I want to be with my kids.'" Galinsky says that men used to trail women in their surveys on work/family conflict, but today 53 percent of employed dads say they experience conflict versus 52 percent for their female peers. Interestingly, men with nonemployed wives reported the same level of work/life conflict. "So it doesn't matter whether men are married to stay-at-home moms or employed moms—they want to be more involved in their children's lives and they are feeling the pull between these responsibilities even more than women."[23]

Just ask men and they'll tell you. One dad, a corporate CFO, blogged on a parenting website: "My wife takes the brunt of the day-to-day responsibility for our kids. But I am certainly not immune to the guilt triangle of three competing forces: 1) if I spend too much time with work, I am failing at home, 2) if I spend too much time with family, I am failing at work, 3) if I spend too much time with family and work, I am failing myself."

Remember the classic Harry Chapin song, "Cat's in the Cradle"? A father and son just can't seem to get in sync. The boy asks, "When you coming home, Dad?" and the father never has an answer, but only a promise, an empty one, that they'll be together "then." By the end of the song, the boy is a man, the father is old. Now it's Dad asking to see his son, who—like his father—can't seem to find the time. Fatherhood deferred became fatherhood denied.

Since 1990, college-educated men (the ones who set most work hours) have given themselves a dubious raise—today they work ten hours a week more than twenty years ago.[24] In aggregate, and as much as they'd like to do things differently, our male peers are consigning themselves to sing Chapin's song, unless we, their wives, do more to help dads get home.

Carl's wife is an academic who works full time and Carl has been able to pursue his goals—as a screenwriter, businessman, and father. "I was a corporate securities attorney and I hated it," Carl told us. He worked long hours before he quit to write for the movies. He now runs a family business, too, but has constructed a life that lets him have time with his kids. "I'm one of the more involved dads at the school. I know as much as my wife about our kids," says Carl.

Carl sometimes sees what other men miss when they keep their killer hours. "There are a lot of dads who spend a lot of time working. Some men come home and their kids are a bit foreign to them. When they get a little block of time with their kids, they don't want to set boundaries. They want it to all be fun and games," says Carl, reflecting on a Cub Scout outing with his son. "I'm glad I never find my time with my kids to be so limited that I can't be a parent. But that's not true for a lot of dads."

While saying "Not now," "That's enough," and "No, you can't have that" may not be the elixir of parenting, drawing the line gives you kids you can be proud of (a result that *is* fun to see). Pressed for time, some dads feel they can only provide the parenting equivalent of junk food, so when their kids get out of control, these men start to believe that dads are inherently worse parents.

"My dad was a traveling salesman, he was on the road a lot. He really seemed scared of his kids," said David, one 50/50 dad who has built his life differently. "I love coming home every day to hear my kids say 'I want Daddy!' when they jump in my arms. We play family tag, we duel, we wrestle—even my three-foot-tall girl." David, an active volunteer at his daughter's preschool, despite a busy career in real estate, told us, "I don't know why more men don't make room for their kids. Dads are such a novelty in the classroom that I feel like a superhero every time I go in."

Teachers are fans, too. One grade-school instructor told us she loves having more dads in the class. "Fathers come in energetic and excited to lend a helping hand with the children." Volunteering at school means something special to dads, she says. "These men have rearranged their work schedule to come in. For these fathers, this time seems to be golden."

Jon's wife, Beth, was a medical student when they had their first child. She took two months off. Then Jon, who was already a practicing doctor, followed with a two-month paternity leave. "I spent eighty hours a week with our baby daughter. It is one of the best memories of my life," Jon said. Over the next six years, as their family grew, Jon rose to lead his medical practice while Beth worked part time at a large hospital. But Jon felt he was becoming distant from his kids. He also wanted to write a book. So Jon and Beth swapped.

Jon is now home one day a week to be with the kids and write. "For me, my time with my kids has been like a spring of water—fresh, new, exciting. At the end of the day with them, I'm always beaming," says Jon. "I could have kept going along just being a successful doctor at a big hospital. But that way seemed limited. My kids, they're what gives me oxygen," said Jon, who continues to lead his practice while getting more time with his kids.

Dads often feel as isolated on weekday playgrounds as women feel in mostly male boardrooms. "I used to take our son to Gymboree. It was a little awkward to sit there with twelve mothers who were breast-feeding in a circle," said Matthew, a corporate executive. "At first it was intimidating for me. But there was always one mother who was more friendly and I would say 'hello' and see if we had anything in common. I just pretended I had no fear."

The 50/50 dads who've found the courage to dive in told us how much they feel they've gained. "I go through the day feeling very lucky," says Mark, who works as a headhunter and is married to Rose, a TV executive. "Yes it's stressful. But it's also cool I'm doing this. I love it that my kids are excited to see me and that they both see Rose and me as equal."

"The big driver for me is that I want to have the quality time with my kids that I think both parents should have," says Gus, the CEO of a consumer products company, about role sharing with his wife, an engineer. "Yes, my dad was around on weekends but even that was not so consistent. When our kids need something, it's not just 'Mom!' they shout. They kind of go back and forth 'Mom!' 'Dad!' 'Mom!' 'Dad!' until they get a response. They go to either of us. My kids are getting the best of two people instead of the best of one."

William Pollack, Harvard clinical psychologist and co-director of the Center for Men at McLean Hospital, has done research for over two decades on parenting boys (and wrote a bestselling book on the topic, *Real Boys: Rescuing Our Sons from the Myths of Boyhood*). He found that when active fathers take their sons' emotional development seriously, these involved dads satisfy their longing to do a better job parenting than their own fathers did, making themselves more available, both physically and emotionally, to their sons.

These men also bond with their wives in a new and different way, because as a couple they are now sharing a task long considered the sole domain of mothers. Their wives tend to see them as more relaxed and loving. And in families where Dad is both present and participative, there are generally more hugs and play. Importantly, these fathers feel enhanced self-esteem and receive the bonus of increased marital satisfaction and of greater personal and professional success.[25]

Your husband gains more from your work than the peace of mind bestowed by a second income. He gains a better shot at a satisfying career, a true partner in marriage, and a chance at being the dad he wants to be. As one 50/50 mom told us: "I appreciate that my husband makes a good living but I can make money, too. No amount of my mothering can replace our kids' relationship with their dad. The time my husband gives our kids is invaluable and unique."

Chapter Three | What Women Gain from Working Motherhood

Why do you work?

"To make money."

That's an honest response you'll get when you ask workers—both male and female, parents or not—why they get out of bed each morning and go to their jobs, and perhaps it's the first thing that pops into your head, too. But let's reframe the question.

Why do you *want* to work?

We're making some assumptions here—that you have a job you like or can see a path to getting one. We're not saying it's easy, or that you have the perfect job. In fact, a lot of days are pretty banal and some just stink. But when well-intentioned people ask: "Do you *love* your job?" you know that men seldom get the same question.

Why? Because people assume men need to support themselves and their families. Let's assume the same for women. You don't have to adore your job to realize its value. Work is called work for a reason—it's not always fun.

You work to support your family (and yourself). You're also working because—bad days and bad bosses aside—you like having a career. Spending time with your child may feel more compelling than your job sometimes and you may worry about the beautiful moments at home you will miss. But you know that having a career, a purpose in addition to your family, is good for you and everyone you love.

BREADWINNING: TO BAKE YOUR OWN LOAF, YOU NEED SOME DOUGH

Here's one great reason to work: You get to be a breadwinner. You often hear women say their salary doesn't cover child care—but they're not doing the long-term numbers. In fact, no matter how little you make, your family will be more secure with two careers. Every year you work you acquire skills and contacts and build your market value. That gives you options.

Sharon recalls the day she earned enough money to pay off her (large) student debt. Euphoric. That's how she felt. For the first time in her life, she knew she had the power to look after herself.

Many working moms express similar feelings—pride, gratification, relief—about knowing they can pay their own bills and build a future they want. Look at children and you know that drive for independence is pretty primal (Sharon's daughter Samantha said it with her first sentence: "I Sammy. I do it myself"). And when you grow up, for better or worse, to do it yourself you need some dough. So why do many women seem to forget this joy, to forget why having your own job and your own paycheck is a pleasure?

Of love and (your) money

"I'm so sorry you have to do that," a woman in her thirties with many hard-won degrees said when she heard Joanna worked full time. "I'm so glad my husband makes enough money so I can stay home."

We are all free to prefer different things. But we're concerned about preferences driven by fear. We've been surprised by the number of our ambitious female peers who've felt a demanding job would limit their marriage choices or damage their husband's career. What surprised us more (and worries us for our daughters) is how many women in their twenties seem to feel the same way.

"My mom told me I should change jobs," a young woman told us. "She thought it would freak men out that I make good money."

"I have dated a lot of wonderful men but I still think that there are so many barriers for all of us successful women to find men who want to be with us," another twentysomething wrote in an e-mail about our book.

The facts say otherwise. According to Stephanie Coontz in *Marriage, a History,* "college graduates and women with higher earnings are now *more* likely to marry than women with less education and lower wages, although they generally marry at older ages." High-achieving women, we now know, are also as likely as their peers to have kids.[1] But we still haven't banished the worry: Does the handsome prince gallop off if your paycheck rivals his?

An unspoken reason women don't gun for better jobs—and have a harder time being breadwinners—is they fear it will cost them love. Fifty years ago, magazines advised women to lose at card games with their husbands. Now it's just our careers we're advised to mismanage. Writing about today's young women, psychologist Peggy Orenstein notes that they "reflexively factored inequality into their futures: They assumed they would move in and out of the workforce and that family responsibilities would limit both their advancement and earning potential—but not their husbands'."[2]

We've all been raised in a world where men learn that to be manly they must be "strong"—but somehow it's not enough to cede men dominance in actual brawn. When wives show strength in other ways, things can get uncomfortable. Our husbands, like many, have never loved our business dinners when they are cast as "The Spouse," unrecognized for their own careers.

"The power thing is really important. I think a lot of women worry what their own success might mean for their marriage—it seems like an unknown cost because you don't know what could happen if you end up being more successful than your husband. Few women would sacrifice the marriage for career success," says Rachel, the stockbroker.

Yet, she and her doctor husband have raised three children over twenty years, all the while enjoying good careers. When men are satisfied with themselves, they don't need to win by squelching the success of the women they love.

Frank, an entrepreneur (married to Vera, a lawyer), says this: "It's wonderful to be proud of your wife, proud of what she does, the way she thinks." Frank is happy to invest in Vera's success. "I want her to do well. I'm always thinking about what she can do to advance her career and encouraging her to move forward. If there's a goal my wife wants, I'm going to bust my ass to help her get it."

"Why is this hard for other men to do? I think it's lack of confidence," says Jamie, a former NFL football player with a second career in business and a wife who became a CEO. "Some guys lack the confidence that you can be successful on your own, that you don't need to drag someone else down."

Women need to know that there are plenty of men who find female strength appealing. A recent piece in *Men's Health* magazine asked, "Are women too aggressive?" The guys say absolutely not. It won't shock us women to learn that men most want our aggressiveness in the bedroom. But they'd also like it in most other realms, too. They want us to say what we want—not expect them to know.[3]

A life built for two: How your job helps your marriage

There are many reasons to protect your income stream—college savings, a trip to Grandma's, that daily latte. An added bonus: more marital bliss (and less bickering). When a women sees her job as important, her marriage will likely be more equal, and when marriage is more equal, couples—and particularly women—fare better.

Janice Steil, professor of psychology at Adelphi University, has spent her career researching the links between marital health and how women see themselves. Husbands and wives are more satisfied with their relationships when "women and men regard themselves as equally responsible for providing financially for the family, as compared to those who see the husband as responsible for providing," according to Steil. These couples had a "greater likelihood of confiding and showing affection, and the wives were less likely to be depressed."

Steil notes that couples reporting "that household work was equally shared scored lower on measures of dysphoria than those who said the wife was primarily responsible. Men and women who said that child care was equally shared reported a greater sense of fairness, less stress at home, and more benefits from having responsibilities both in and out of the home, including feelings of competence and feeling like a well-rounded person who is able to use one's talents." What kinds of families are more likely to have more equal sharing? Those with a working wife.[4]

"I've been married thirty years and my husband is a wonderful man," said Leslie, a woman in her sixties with two grown daughters. "It's not like he ever said, 'I make the money so I'm in charge,' but even when I was working he made five times what I did. I never felt I could ask him to watch the kids on the weekend. He would say, 'I worked late every night this week, I need time to myself.' He made the money so he had the final say," Leslie told us. "While he never used his power directly, it was tacitly accepted between us that my husband's 'say' was worth more than mine because he was the primary earner."

Leslie has encouraged her daughters to work because she feels it's good for marriage. And she's not alone among women who come to learn that variant of the Golden Rule: He who has the gold rules.

As Steil says, when men and women see themselves as true equals, they can enjoy "more intimate relationships based on a mutual reliance and respect."[5]

It's the money, honey

We need only look to our parents' generation, when far fewer women had incomes of their own, to see how money can shift the balance of power in a relationship. As one woman said to us, "My mother enjoyed her life and didn't work. But in our house my dad was kind of a prince. My mom has always encouraged me to work because she wanted her kids to have more equality in their marriages."

Sharon recalls her parents arguing a lot about money. Her mom didn't work, her dad did, and power and money were intertwined. The price tags stayed on every new dress, coat, or sweater until the purchase received her father's approval. When Sharon made her own money, clothes were no longer a source of conflict; they became a pleasure. Once married, Sharon found that she and Steve agreed on most things, but if Steve thought something was a "waste of money," Sharon bought it on her own dime.

Reflecting on how money shapes marriage, one woman in her sixties said, "It surprises me that this still goes on, but some of my wealthiest female friends are put on budgets by their husbands. And it's not just an upper limit on what they can spend, their husbands actually review their credit card receipts as if their wives were subordinates. It's quite belittling."

Shopping with a friend for work clothes, Joanna realized that even thirtysomething peers could see money as their husbands' domain. "Won't Jason be angry when he sees that bill?" her friend asked. Joanna explained that she and her husband have equal say on money—that they both contribute and trust each others' spending decisions.

Maria, now in her eighties, spent her life raising six children with a military spouse who was frequently stationed out of the country. Like Sharon's mom, she depended on her husband's income, but Maria also had a secret weapon of sorts: a monthly check from a small rental property she successfully managed for decades. Whenever Maria wanted to buy something that was not in the budget, like a plane ticket for herself or a piece of sports gear for her kids, she used the rental income. Maria and her husband argued over finances, too, but she often cut those conversations short by telling her spouse, "I paid for it with *my* money."

Money can't buy you love but it can get you the freedom that makes it easier to love everyone in your life. Being a breadwinner lets you provide for your family—and take care of yourself, too.

The Four Horsemen of the Apocalypse: death, divorce, disability, downsizing

Worst-case scenarios—they're why the insurance business stays afloat, and why we can't sleep some nights. Marriage is no fun when we dwell on the dark side of *What if I'm in this alone . . .* , but it's a powerful feeling knowing that you can fend for your family if you ever wind up in that position. And it's a helpless feeling if you rely entirely on your spouse's income and something goes awry.

He can get sick, fired, or worse ("worse" being the euphemism for "die" or "divorce you"). Maybe he just wakes up one morning and decides he's in the wrong profession. If you're in a good relationship, you'll want to hold hands with your husband long after the birds leave the nest—we certainly do. But sometimes the rug gets pulled out right from under you. Or sometimes you make a wrong choice and you need to replace the carpeting. Either way, we get no pleasure from the following facts, but when we ignore them, women (and kids) get hurt.

Rose, a media executive, told us how her own mother became the family breadwinner. "The environment changed in my dad's business and he didn't do well for a lot of years. I saw how that can put a lot of stress on your marriage and that it's a big mistake to stop working and rely on someone else's income. Women have to work for the same reasons men do—to build a financial base for their children and to feel the pride that comes with working."

Statistics show most women still behave as if they don't need to rely on their own funds. Fifty-eight percent of all boomer women have less than $10,000 socked away in a pension fund or 401(k), which means that many of these women will have to keep working for many years after their male peers are retired.[6] Forty-one percent of private pension funds leave nothing to a widow, and the Social Security Administration is not particularly kind to wives who leave the workforce; they face a 50 percent decline in living standards when their husbands die.[7]

Today, 87 percent of the impoverished elderly are women, and not enough boomer females earn enough to reverse the trend.[8] If we, their younger sisters and daughters, don't seize our chance to support ourselves, how will we do better?

Divorce is hard on a family and hell on a checkbook. Though the courts have made child support more available than in the past, women who rely on it and on alimony as a major source of income suffer. *While 80 percent of married women think that they would get alimony in a divorce, only 8 percent actually do.*[9] About 27 percent of custodial parents (mostly divorced moms) get timely payment of what the court orders dads to pay; the other whopping 73 percent get nothing or a fraction of what they are owed, or must wait more than a year for the money they need to pay living expenses, to hold on to a car or house, to clothe and feed a family.[10]

In 1979, Terry Martin Hekker wrote a book called *Ever Since Adam & Eve,* recommending that women stay home and take care of their husbands and children. Then on her fortieth anniversary, when she was in her early sixties, she was served with divorce papers. She now writes, "For a divorced mother, the harsh reality is that the work for which you do get paid is the only work that will keep you afloat... modern marriage demands greater self-sufficiency."[11] Even if calamity never strikes, the day-to-day payoff is large: Your income gives you liberty to worry less.

THE BEST HEALTH PROGRAM AROUND: YOUR JOB

"My job is driving me nuts!" Who hasn't said that? Yet, next time you think work is stressing you out and making you crazy, consider this: Numerous studies have found that women who work enjoy better physical and mental health than their nonworking peers.

Mining fifty years of public health data, UK researchers found that women who had been wives, mothers, and workers were significantly less likely to suffer poor health than women who did not play all three roles. Women who had been homemakers for most of their lives and who had not held outside jobs were most likely to report that they were in poor health (followed by mothers without partners and childless women).

And you can stop worrying about the pizza at the airport or the three cookies at the afternoon meeting: Your job may make you thinner. In this same study, women who worked were less likely to be overweight than women who rarely held jobs.[12] You may burn calories pushing your child's swing, but it could be that commuting, negotiating, managing, and drumming your fingers on your desk are as good as doing crunches (and no one pays you for doing crunches).

Hey, I'm home (and I'm happy to be here after a day at work)

"I truly believe I'm a better mom because I work at a job I love," says Celia, a public high school teacher in Los Angeles. "I feel stimulated and fulfilled."

"The deeper I got into working," says Tracy, who works for an energy firm and recently returned to work after five years at home, "the more I saw it was great for our family, both financially and emotionally. It even made me more appreciative of family time."

Research says that employed women (whether or not they are wives or mothers) have greater well-being than their nonemployed peers.[13] It also pays for women to keep their aspirations high—women who reach bigger jobs report the highest well-being of all. But we all reap rewards from our work no matter where we are on the company ladder. Studies of women in blue-collar jobs say that in addition to the money, they enjoy working as a way to meet other people and lead "a less restricted life."[14]

A happy mother is a good mother, and if work makes you hum, your whole family sings along. By contrast, if staying home makes you miserable—well, fill in the blanks. For decades, Brandeis University psychology professor Rosalind Barnett and her colleagues have studied the relationship between employment and depression in women across many kinds of work and social circumstances. Like many other researchers, Barnett and Hyde found that employed women have a lower risk of depression than nonemployed women.

How *much* does it matter? A 1989 study of 749 blue-collar and professional midwestern women found this: 30 percent more psychological distress among women who quit work after having a child compared to peers who returned to their jobs (women who cut back to part time show 10 percent more symptoms of distress).[15]

It turns out that spending too much time caring for family members may not be good for you. How can people you love harm your health? University of California at San Francisco psychologist Elizabeth Ozer points out that in our society, families are expected to come up with individual solutions, and those solutions fall disproportionately on women—who are still raised to believe that the well-being of the family, particularly kids, is all on them. Yet no one truly has the ability to control the happiness of another person, so "mothers often experience self-blame whenever their children have any problems," says Ozer.

Ozer concludes that work/family stress has less to do with work and more to do with excess responsibility for home life. The least happy mothers are those in her study who see running the family as their task *alone*. Solo parenting has the same occupational hazards as a bad factory job: "a low degree of decision latitude…time pressures and conflicting or heavy emotional demands." In roles like these, workers tend to feel stressed out and inadequate and their health suffers. The same often happens from excess time on the parenting job.[16]

This effect is not exclusive to mothers. Dads who leave jobs to focus exclusively on kids suffer the same heightened risk of depression.

Sometimes, just a taste of staying home will set off your inner alarm and help you see work in a better light. Maya stayed home for six months between jobs, caring for her two daughters. "It taught me a lot," she says. "At first, it was great. I saw friends for lunch, went to the girls' soccer practice, did the family photo albums. But then I started getting obsessed with stupid things like thinking I had to make gourmet dinners and that I had to drive the girls to all their activities myself. I thought this was what I was 'supposed' to do if I wasn't working. It made me irritable. I had less quality time with my daughters. I found myself snapping at them. I didn't enjoy it because it wasn't me."

When we interviewed Ann, a political science professor, she had just devoted large chunks of time to finishing a book. "I had all this pent-up mommy guilt. I had a light teaching schedule after I finished my book so I thought, *Great, I can spend lots of time with the kids.*" But after just four days, she realized something—and so did her kids. "It was more about me and I was being led by guilt. I had this sense of 'I must enrich my children.'" In a fit of quality-time-gone-wrong, she found the names of the world's largest fish and created "the research project from hell," thinking her kids would enjoy factoids about massive fins and gills. "The kids were like, 'Who cares? Let's go outside and play soccer.' And I really didn't want to play soccer myself."

Wisely, Ann's grade-school children and spouse did what amounted to an intervention. "The kids got together with their dad and said, 'Mommy has to go back to the office.' They took me for a walk around the block to break the news. 'Come home at 5:30—that would be great. But you are not a happy parent spending this much time in the house.'"

Tracy stayed home much longer than Maya and Ann—she took a break from corporate life for five years while she raised her two children. "I was the 1950s mom extraordinaire," she recalls. "My husband, Jeff, was working so hard—I did everything for our family so he wouldn't have to. Buying and selling houses when we moved, meals, schools, playdates. I did all of it out of guilt. I just had this idea that I'd be betraying my children if I went back to work. But not working made me feel taken for granted and financially dependent. I felt bad that only Jeff was working. And I just knew: This isn't thirty years ago, jobs aren't stable, and it felt really risky to rely on one income."

Sharing the load, it's much easier to clear hurdles. Men who do more relative to their spouses have wives who experience greater well-being—even if they don't reach 50/50. One surprising discovery in Ozer's research: Even if their husbands did not share in child care equally, women who *believed* they could count on their spouses enjoyed the best psychological health. A dad who is willing to help when called gives his wife a safety valve—and greater well-being.[17]

Psychologists Vanessa McGann and Janice Steil make a related point: When women see that they *matter* as much as men do (and feel men are no more deserving of respect or resources), many good things happen: They achieve better jobs and pay compared with women who compare themselves only with other females. Steil has measured female attitudes on a scale of self-reliance and self-assurance (SRSA) and found that high levels of these qualities predict less depression for women and more say in their relationships. And among married women, higher SRSA is "associated with higher levels of sexual assertiveness and sexual satisfaction."[18]

Lest we pretend that only Prince Charming will be pleased with this by-product of wives' self-assurance, guess what *women* rate as their leading source of happiness? Nobel laureate Daniel Kahneman and his colleagues asked 909 Texas women to record their daily activities and score how they felt during each of them. Sex was the standout favorite, scoring 5.10 on a 6-point scale. Interacting with spouses outside the bedroom rated 4.11, beating out time with the kids at 4.04. Unsurprisingly, moms enjoyed their time with children more when they didn't feel rushed.[19] Put it all together and 50/50 is a formula for giving women a lot more of what we really want—sex, time with our husbands, and help with our kids.

As we discussed in Chapter 2, when women (and men) play multiple roles—worker, spouse, parent—they enjoy higher self-esteem, too. "My mother's always told me you can't be the best career woman and the best mother at the same time," a female college student told the *New York Times* in 2005, explaining why she intended to be a stay-at-home mom by the time she was thirty.[20] Comments like these reflect a sad misperception. And as we'll show you, rewards are big when you escape this either/or mentality. "When people are psychologically at the top of their game, feeling good about themselves, they perform better," says Laura, who has spent her career in technology. Recalling the year when she both got promoted and had a baby, she adds, "When you're really feeling confident, you can perform really well and do lots of different things."

Having more roles is good for you. If it's making you sweat, don't worry. Working motherhood is a workout that makes you stronger.

A TASTE FOR GRIT AND GLORY

In our survey, we asked women to tell us what advice they plan to give their daughters about work. We think this mom said it best: "I will tell her that having a career that allows her to use her mind in a productive, ethical way is a gift to be savored every day."

But many girls don't get the message that work is a good match for motherhood. "I'd like my daughter to meet you," a venture capitalist told Joanna. "Her mom doesn't work and neither do any of her friends' mothers. The stay-at-home-mom life looks pretty good to her and I am worried that's a dangerous message."

When we don't tell our children clearly how much women get out of working and how successful they can be, we perpetuate a view that women really are the Second Sex. In a survey of one thousand Michigan elementary school students in 1995, girls and boys were asked if they saw any advantages for the other gender. Forty percent of girls saw real advantages to being male: better jobs, more money, and more respect. Ninety-five percent of boys saw no advantage to being female.[21] Perhaps reflecting this sense of the limits ahead, female risk of depression rises fourfold in adolescence (though it is similar to the male rate in childhood).[22]

There's no need for advantage to be so unevenly split and in Part II we'll talk about how to change that for yourself. Here, let's focus on what *you* win from working, the unique things you get from a job: the highs and the lows, the thrill of achievement in the outside world.

Let's acknowledge to ourselves and to others that success at work can give you one thing your children shouldn't: glory. The sense that you, and you alone, really aced it, solved the problem, made a difference. Kids need their own victories (and they don't like it when parents horn in). Women have egos just like men do and glory is not just a male pleasure—we need it, too.

"Without a career, my mom had an almost palpable need to suck the glory out of her kids. Anytime somebody gave me a compliment, my mother would say, 'Aw, it was nothing!' both co-opting and belittling whatever accomplishment I'd had," said one woman. "If my mom had had a career, we would have had a different dynamic."

"I'm a pretty ambitious person and my job is a really good way to channel that ambition," says Ann, the political science professor. "While I was trying to be home, I'd say 'let me see that homework'—

I was putting too much stress on my kids. I really didn't want to live through my kids—which is what my mom did with me. I think you are born with a certain amount of drive and you can't turn that switch off. So you have to channel it in ways that are productive."

Today, we see the face of female glory in sports—the Williams sisters lofting trophies in the air, Mia Hamm and her team leaping in joy, Paula Radcliffe breaking the tape at the New York City Marathon ten months into motherhood—and again a year later. But these images are hard to find in most jobs. A female colleague of Sharon's used to complain about the "testosterzone" at work, a spot on the trading floor where men would high-five each other with zeal when they won a big piece of business. Was she complaining because these guys expressed their unfettered glee—or because she had no place to express hers?

Eyes on the prize

In her *Harvard Business Review* article "Do Women Lack Ambition?" Cornell University psychiatrist Anna Fels explores what it takes for women to go for their goals—whatever they may be. She finds that female ambition is often drained by the fact that female victory is often ignored. When studies show men to be more confident than women (regardless of their skill), this is an "accurate reflection of the praise and recognition" gap and little else. Men get roaring cheers. Women get quiet nods. And over time, women (regardless of their skill) start to believe the audience, that their accomplishments just aren't that exciting.[23]

So how do successful women stay psyched up instead of getting psyched out? They recognize what they, themselves, win from working. They find an extra clapping section to fill the void. And they enjoy the sound.

"The only person who takes more pride in my career than me is my husband," says Grace, an advertising executive.

"I can just see it in my husband's face. Every time I get a bonus or promotion, he's so thrilled for me," said another working mom. "He knows how hard I work and my success seems to give him a lot of joy."

"An idea and a little money in the bank, that's how we started," says Ruth, a human rights advocate who founded a nonprofit five years ago.

"Now we are a multimillion-dollar operation with an international reputation—freeing kids forced to become soldiers, protecting refugees from violence, getting journalists out of jail. I love knowing our efforts are making that kind of difference, in the face of incredible odds. One of my best days came when my ten-year-old son looked at me and said, 'You are about making a difference in the world, Mama.'"

"My mom worked for the phone company," says Steve, Sharon's husband. "Her goal was to make enough money to send each of her kids to junior college—when she exceeded that goal, it gave her a lot of satisfaction to know that her work had done that. After a lot of years, she was senior in the union and got invited to the White House. All of us kids were thrilled for her."

Psychologists say there are lots of reasons women have a hard time envisioning their own success—few role models, discomfort with power, overcoming bad assumptions. The Implicit Association Test (or IAT) is a test that helps each of us see just how biased our assumptions are, how easy it is for us to associate stereotypically paired words (like "Jane–nice" and "Dan–strong") and how hard it is for us to break out of that thinking. The test times how quickly you make the easy associations—and how much slower you are to connect words like "woman" and "powerful."

While IAT research has exposed how subtly biased we all are, it has also revealed a possible cure—surrounding ourselves with examples that counter our bias. In a 2003 article titled "Seeing Is Believing," researchers at the University of Massachusetts at Amherst shared an exciting finding: Female college students who were exposed to a high number of female professors saw their implicit bias drop. (In contrast, the majority of college women—with mostly male professors—experienced a rise in their implicit bias.)[24]

Mahzarin Banaji is a professor of psychology at Harvard and a leading researcher on implicit attitudes. Banaji has devised a clever fix for her own environment that we can all emulate. "Knowing what I know about how the brain works, I reprogrammed the screen savers on my computer. One of them is now a slide show of women scientists, famous and ordinary. Whenever I'm at my computer, I'm informing my mind that women are just as plausible as scientists as men are."[25]

Happy working mothers know their wins *are* exciting. "I love the fact I've become an expert, that people seek me out in a room for my opinion," says Christina, a mother of three who advises start-up companies.

Tara has been a producer for decades and is the mother of a grown child. "'Why don't you want to retire?' a male friend asked me. 'I like being able to okay big projects. I like having an impact and influence,' that's what I told him. 'Oh, you like the *power*,' he said. He's right. I do like the power."

"Having an impact on multiple people, maybe thousands of people. There is something fun about that," says Liza, who built a division of a large technology firm and has two small children. "Expanding your business, learning new things, it pushes you to grow and achieve. It's pretty fulfilling."

Voicing for yourself what you get from your job is important. And in line with Banaji's work on shaping your environment, we find it's important to put ourselves in the company of other women who are excited about their work, too. Seeing how few women have continued to pursue the leadership track, Liza also spends time bringing together working women outside her firm. She hosts periodic speakers and casual dinners at her house just to get working women together. "I'm trying to create a community of support. It keeps us all thinking bigger picture. It lets us inspire each other."

More pride (less prejudice)

Holding on to your ambition is key, but many working moms say finding satisfaction in the day-to-day is what keeps them going. When her son was a baby, Dana would lift him out of his bed each morning before the babysitter arrived and she left for work, for breakfast and a cuddle. Once he could talk, he would tug at her sleeve and ask, "Mommy, are these your work clothes?" On weekend mornings, he'd pat her arm and ask, "Mommy, are these your relaxing clothes?"

"At first I was a little sad that he'd already figured out the adult world of 'workday' versus 'weekend,'" she says, "but frankly, I was also proud—of him for learning to discern the two worlds, and of myself for getting up, getting dressed, and heading out the door to a publishing job I enjoyed that allowed me to support him. I had a sense of purpose and was proud of what I did at the office each day. Our son knew that I'd come home at night and change into my 'relaxing clothes' and that I couldn't wait to see him."

"My kids are so proud of what I do," says Darcie, who has the kind of job that's every kid's dream: She develops new products for an ice-cream manufacturer. Her kids say to friends, "My mommy *invented* that ice cream!" When they drive past her office, they clamor to stop in. "Let's go see all the new flavors they are making."

"I love marketing," says Darcie, who worked for a wine company before she switched to ice cream. "I get to create things. I have an idea and after some time it shows up in the grocery aisle. It's a great challenge to figure out what customers want, how to manufacture it, how to make it profitable."

Though we can't all be ice-cream makers, we can each find the personal reasons work gives us satisfaction, even when our work involves dry spreadsheets, dusty chalkboards, or late nights in the ER. "It's great when I feel like I've developed real wisdom about something in my job. I look at the exceptional guys in my field—they are masterful, they seem to get results effortlessly," says Kara. "I love it when I see glimmers of that in myself."

Seeing our own growth and the difference we make, having a sense of purpose—these are things that give us pleasure at work. And even more, work lets us define ourselves more broadly and expand our sense of who we are and what we can do.

Diane has grown children, but when they were born, she put aside her fledgling career as an editor and stayed home for five years. But then, she says with a laugh, "I found I wanted to talk to someone taller than three feet high and to discuss something other than the price of lettuce.

"So there are lighthearted reasons I wanted to go back to work, but serious ones, too. For many women, even today, their identity is defined by others. They are 'Bob's mother' or 'Sally's mother.' Their status in life is directly linked to their husband's status or their child's success. Their lives are validated by the actions of others. Yes, I am a wife and mother—and these are very important parts of my life—but I am also a separate person. Validation as a valued and important person in my own right is a key part of why many women seek independent careers."

There are noble and necessary reasons for working, but sometimes there are not-so-lofty reasons, too. When you've worked hard in school and paid your dues starting out, you can feel possessive of what you've achieved—not only are you proud of it, you like how you feel about yourself at work. Maybe it's the office with a closing door that you finally earned, a pristine (spit-up free) outfit, or a computer without mysterious bits of Play-Doh lodged in the keyboard; maybe it's having your own network of friends and colleagues, your own daily rhythms, even some "alone time" as you commute to and from work.

There's nothing selfish about holding on to these aspects of work life, particularly if you put in years of effort to earn them. When men talk about the traditional "perks" of their jobs, they may mention expense accounts, golf outings, and company cars. Women, particularly mothers, talk about different fringe benefits of working.

It's the satisfaction that you get from holding an uninterrupted, interesting conversation with another adult, the fact that you can dash out at lunch and get a haircut, away from the chaos—and strange competition—of child rearing. It's London for a sales conference, or maybe it's Lubbock, but no matter the time zone, you don't have to make the bed or pick up the towels. It's just a job that you like, and that likes you back, and sometimes that's a good enough reason to keep at it.

Curing the disease to please: Grit as the antidote to "perfect"

Many working mothers say they've gotten better at their jobs after having kids. Why? They freed themselves of Polly Perfect. Too many women believe that striving for excellence means striving for perfection—an attitude few men share. Sure, men may say they want to put up the "top" sales numbers or be the "go-to guy" for their boss. What guy says he wants to be the "best dad" or the "best career man" (remember what our college student said in the *New York Times* about the impossibility of being "the best career woman and the best mother")? Women who keep working eventually learn that "best" is bad and focus on just being very *good*. Often that's better than "best."

"Before I had my family, I could never quite understand why my editors kept complaining about my constant fussing with my stories... I self-righteously felt they resented my perfectionism," says Kathy Ellison, Pulitzer Prize–winning journalist and author of *The Mommy Brain*. "If you have limited other outlets in your life, you may tend to grasp your work too closely, making small things into big things, and end up being a pain in the neck to your coworkers."[26]

Sharon once told her sister that some colleagues seemed light on the details. "The bigger problem," her sister said, "is that you seem to know too many!" Even the services of an executive coach barely made a dent—Sharon still felt compelled to probe the depth of every issue and cross the last thing off her daily to-do list (she'd do e-mail in bed, a favorite with her spouse). One thing changed all that: Sharon had a son. Time finally had a price. So she tried deferring those last little items (or ignoring them entirely) and saw that no one cared. In fact, when Sharon forced herself to triage, her team became more productive—and so did she. Surprised, she mentioned her "less-is-more" discovery to another working mom. "The same thing happened to me," said Sharon's friend. "After I had kids, I dropped the marginal stuff and did better at work."

"I am less of a perfectionist, I use student TA's to take care of any possible detail they can manage on their own," says Celia, a public school teacher in L.A. "But my classes have never run smoother and I still seem to have time to invent new lessons."

Apart from skipping the quest for "best," working moms get in on another secret: Defeat is the start of victory. Working moms learn to stop worrying about their bruises, get back on their bikes, and keep pedaling.

"I was twenty-two, I went to work for IBM right out of college and you have this sense you're on a clock—'by the time I'm thirty, I have to be a sales manager.' You get brainwashed into thinking that if you're not following this perfect plan, you're not doing well. I was lucky enough to get over this but some people don't," says Laura, who's spent her career at big technology firms and rose to become a company CEO. "It's just not true that you have to follow a linear path. I mean, Bill Clinton ran for Congress, and he lost. I wasn't always totally successful with everything, so I had to deal with my failures. It takes a long time to learn. It takes the school of hard knocks."

My mother, myself, my 401(k)

Women are quick to mention their own mothers when they tell us about how they became working parents. Women who'd grown up with at-home moms were very aware they were following a path their mothers had *not* and talked about how their mothers' experience had influenced them.

For most of Sharon's childhood, her mother did not work. Her mom, Jacqueline, poured her many talents and vast energy into the lives of her three children. Energetic, innovative, tenacious, resourceful, Jacqueline was a formidable advocate for her kids. Sharon often wondered what work-world feats her mom could *also* have accomplished if she'd had access to a bigger stage (or boardroom).

When Sharon had her first child, Jacqueline expressed concern about Sharon's travel. "You do plan to cut back, don't you?" she asked. In fact, Sharon's job required more travel and Jacqueline jumped in to help—flying to meet Sharon and her grandson to babysit when she could. Years later, Jacqueline said something that meant the world to Sharon: "I wasn't sure it was possible. But I can see now how well your kids are doing and how much you get out of your job. I'm so proud of what you are doing."

Joanna's mom, Judy, worked part time and enjoyed it. But Judy knew she was lucky her life worked out well and didn't encourage her daughters to depend on chance. She taught Joanna that if she wanted to live in the adult world with the same comforts she'd enjoyed growing up, then she had to develop the skills to make a good living of her own. Joanna and her sisters all have careers with incomes that can support their families.

Maya's mother was a nurse who quit when her children were born.

"She didn't leave my side my whole childhood. When I was getting ready to go to college, she went back to work part time. All of a sudden she had friends, she had office gossip—I had never seen her that happy in my life. I couldn't believe she'd given up that happiness for me. I felt guilty. I had not even appreciated what she had done until I could see the contrast. I knew I would do something different," says Maya, who has two daughters and works full time.

"My parents had a real partnership," says Jody, the public defender. "They set the bar high—working in jobs they loved and loving each other, too. Making a contribution to the world was a very important value in our household. My sisters and I all internalized that and that's what we try to do through our own careers.

"Yes, when I was young, I wished my mom helped at school more and went on more field trips. By around sixth grade, I noticed something: The moms who were around all the time weren't wanted by their kids—those kids wanted their own space. But *I* still really valued having my mom come in when she did. My mom has been a great role model."

Daughters, destiny, and demographics

When we started writing this book, we convened a group of successful women from a variety of fields and asked them what they would like to have known earlier in life. "I wish you could show younger women just how good things look once you make it up the steep incline," a female entrepreneur told us. "When they're halfway up the hill, all they see is a tough slog and they don't realize how much easier it gets once you gain some altitude. The hill flattens out and you've got a great view."

Stephanie has three kids, the oldest in high school. Now a partner at a consulting firm, she feels good about herself and her accomplishments. "It feels really great. I wish I could show young mothers that the hard stuff goes away pretty fast," Stephanie says. Thinking back to the stress she felt when her kids were younger, Stephanie recalls that "it felt so scary in those early years trying to manage the chaos at home and climb the ranks at work. I am really glad that I didn't stop and kept going. Now I have a career that is better than I ever dreamed I could obtain and really wonderful kids. I've accomplished something. I'm really proud of myself."

If we stick with it, we can also be proud of how we change the workplace we leave our daughters. Surveying a thousand executives, the research firm Catalyst found that women who reached higher levels in their companies report having a woman as the most helpful person in their careers. Women, Catalyst concludes, need other women as both role models and sponsors.[27]

In 2007, sociologists Philip Cohen and Matt Huffman published the conclusion of a massive study drawn from U.S. Census data on 1.3 million workers in 155 industries. They found that when more women are senior managers, women in lower positions are better paid. This is the first time experts have quantified how female bosses affect the wages of other women.[28]

But researchers have long known that women draw strength from greater numbers. For decades, studies have shown that when women are a small minority of an applicant pool they are judged more harshly than when they are more than one-third of a group.[29] In a study of women in math, science, and engineering, psychologists Mary Murphy and Claude Steele asked how men and women feel (and perform) when there are dramatically more men than women involved. When outnumbered (three to one), women had higher heart rates, sweated more, and had a lower sense of well-being and desire to participate. When part of a balanced group, women were more at ease — and likely to perform better. Men functioned the same in both scenarios but said that they preferred the environment with more female peers. So let's stay at work for the good of our sons, too.[30]

Getting to 50/50—clearing the path so more families have the lives they want

Picture a world where the odds are even, where the rewards of career and family life are shared equally by men and women. That's the place we'd like to work and it's what we want to leave our kids.

We have worked as managers with organizations of all sizes and

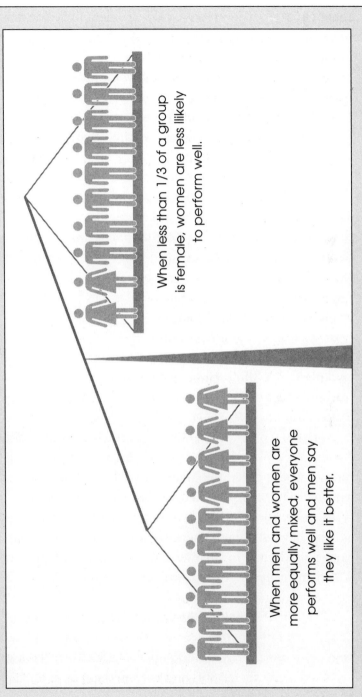

spent hundreds of hours trying to help talented people make the most of their careers. We've logged years on committees charged with retaining women and setting compensation. What we see is a circular problem. This is a numbers game—when women don't make up half the long-term workers, we don't have the votes to change the workplace. When the workplace remains unpleasant for women, they lose faith they can win there, they lower their sights, accept lesser jobs—and many leave.

In 1996, Sharon asked a senior male colleague his view about paternity leave. "Nice idea but not in our lifetime," he said with a smile. Three years later, Sharon's firm launched a leave policy for new fathers. What changed? A cohort of senior women emerged in that period and, along with many men who supported the idea, made paternity leave a priority. It was not merely that there were more senior women to cast votes for pro-family ideas. The presence of more senior women changed the way many *men* saw things, too.

According to the numbers, progress has stalled in the last decade—not enough women get enough power to accelerate change in the workplace. We think there is a way out of this rut—voicing three truths about women, men, and work that will empower many more people to get to 50/50:

Truth #1: Women Don't Quit Because They *Want* To. When women downshift or leave their careers, it is most often due to the many features of what's called the Maternal Wall. We'll discuss both that wall and how many moms find a door through it in Chapter 4.

Truth #2: Success Does Not Require 24/7. Many active parents told us how they built highly successful careers while avoiding round-the-clock work hours. In Chapter 5, we'll share their stories and the wisdom of management experts who know why fewer hours can be better for the bottom line.

Truth #3: It's Not a Fair Game—but You Can Even the Odds. Despite a lot of progress, women still face a cluster of "taxes" that eat away at the rewards from working. In Chapter 6, we'll show how working women give themselves breaks from these taxes and make getting to 50/50 more feasible for everyone.

Part Two

**Three Truths to
Bust the Myths
About Work,
Women, and Men**

Chapter Four

Women Don't Quit Because They *Want* To

Here's the good news: Women are breaking new ground every day in the work world, filling jobs and gaining status once reserved for men. They're fighting fires, running hospitals and corporations, they're serving in the military and as leaders in academia and the arts. At home, fathers are more engaged than in any prior generation, doing more housework, spending more time with the kids, taking charge of carpools and school committees.

Young women want to believe that the battles are mostly won. We know; we wanted to believe it, too. As one lawyer told us, when someone inferred she might have trouble as a working mom at their big firm, "That's so forty years ago!"

The reality is this: Women have come a long way but we've got much further to go—leadership in most fields remains more than 80 percent male. The majority of college students are now female and women get good starter jobs. Women earn 40 percent of MBAs and 50 percent of JD and MD degrees—and it's been this way for a decade.[1] But further up the career ladder, numbers dive. Today, fewer than 16 percent of law partners or Fortune 500 corporate officers are female and women have even fewer leadership roles in medicine.[2]

You often hear that women, particularly working mothers, "choose" to quit their jobs. They just don't *like* work as much as men do (we'll discuss that it Chapter 6) and prefer to focus on home.

However, if you probe just a little, that's not what women tell you— even those who "opted out."

When we became mothers, we started paying close attention to the frequent press about women dropping their careers. As we watched our female peers leave the workforce, it rarely looked to us like they were choosing to quit. Yes, some were drawn by a desire to focus full time on kids, but more often, the women weren't leaving because of a deep desire to spend all day, every day with their children. Instead, these new moms were caught in a vise—between husbands who weren't doing their share at home and bosses who wouldn't give an inch at work. These women couldn't get their spouses to assume more family tasks. And they couldn't get bosses to accept the often minor changes that would have allowed them to stay. Overwhelmed and disillusioned, these women made the seemingly rational decision to stop working until the storm had passed.

A 2004 study of professional women who left their jobs to stay home confirms what we saw among our peers. Only 16 percent of the women who stopped working felt the decision was a "relatively unconstrained choice or preference to become full-time, stay-at-home mothers." Most women said their husband was a primary reason for their decision—that his work hours, lack of participation in child care, or desire for an at-home wife drove the decision to quit. And this was true even though fully one-third of these women earned as much as or more than their husbands.[3]

The other key issue was the "amount, pace, and inflexibility of work" in today's 24/7 world. Even when women wanted to continue in their careers, employers acted on what they "knew" (that these women couldn't possibly handle their old jobs with babies), or demoted them to lesser work, or refused to acknowledge that a piece of work e-mailed from home is as valuable as one completed in the office while you miss family dinner. "The truth is women leave reluctantly, after long, drawn-out efforts to find a way to stay, begging for small amounts of flexibility—which they are often refused," Joan Williams, director of work/life law at UC Hastings law school, told us.[4]

YOUR OWN SHRINKING ICEBERG:
HOW CLIMATE CHANGE MELTS CAREERS

Sometimes it's sunny and pleasant when you announce your pregnancy and sometimes it stays that way for a while. But women often feel an environmental change when they become mothers. It's often hard to pinpoint when the clouds started to roll in—when you came back to work, when you got a new boss, when your job changed? In some cases it's intentional; in many others, it's just an employer's reflex, an ingrained attitude that may not be seen as harmful or off base. Whether you're a newly minted parent or you're already a master at checking homework, you may have asked yourself this question: "I get good reviews, so why do I feel I've been written off?"

You're not hallucinating. Studies show that people do see mothers differently: as nice but less competent. Even young people raised in a more recent era when mothers worked (very ably) in a variety of jobs have this attitude. In 2004, Princeton researchers gave a group of students a survey that asked the following question: "We'd like you to read the profiles of three consultants at McKinsey & Company's Manhattan office and give us your first impressions . . . Imagine you're a client, trying to choose a consultant from very little information." They asked these students to rate fictional consultants on a variety of traits (like capable, efficient, organized, sincere, warm, trustworthy).

Among the characters were Kate and Dan, professionals described identically except for their gender. The description went on to say that Kate/Dan was a new parent and telecommuted to work three days a week. The results? Kate was rated least competent of all workers, although she scored highest for warmth. Curiously, Dan, a father who worked at home most days, received the second-highest rating for competence (the only person rated more competent than Dan was the female professional without kids).[5] The only conclusion we can draw: Flexible work arrangements don't ruin your image at work—but motherhood might.

Why do people think this? "You have too much to do at home— you have two jobs now. Aren't you going to cut back at work?" asks your neighbor, watching you take out the trash. "You're still taking business trips? The kids must miss you a lot," your in-laws say. Their assumption: that you're working under duress—that you've become a harried, hare-brained (but "warm") victim of working motherhood.

Even when they come from people you like, these lines can rankle. The bigger problem? The classic lines at work, the ones rarely uttered aloud by your boss and colleagues, but floating overhead in a giant thought bubble (almost visible when you return from the pediatrician at noon): "Are you still committed?"

The road gets very rough when the people who hold these views, even if they have the sense to hold their tongues, are the ones in charge, the ones who make decisions that affect the day-to-day scope of your job, and your future.

We've heard a great deal about the "glass ceiling," but in her copious research Joan Williams shows that most women never knock into it because they never get near enough. Instead, they run up against what Williams has named the "Maternal Wall," the assumption that any woman who is a mother is the primary parent—and unable to commit to her job in the way a father could.[6]

When women take pregnancy-related leaves, they generate real costs that their employers may not like, but those costs are finite. What can seem like a bad deal to bosses is the ongoing volume and un-certainty of child-related downtime that takes workers out of com-mission (child-care snafus, sick kids, school-related obligations). Too many people assume women will do all these things without the help of their husbands. So working moms can begin to look like pretty un-desirable employees and these unchecked assumptions erect a wall that too few women get over.

It's time for employers to face the facts and ditch the assumptions about the effect of motherhood on work. "On average, the depletion that is so feared by organizations...does not exist," organizational be-havior expert Nancy Rothbard told us. Rothbard, who teaches at

Wharton, studied a sample of 790 employees at a large public university to explore how engagement in family impacts engagement at work. Her study found that when women had stress at home they were *more* engaged at work and (consistent with the research that multiple roles are good for people) that a good family life gives women more energy to be good workers. Rothbard concluded: "I suggest to organizations that their beliefs about women may be wrong. As a manager, don't make the automatic assumption that a woman with a rich family life is not going to be engaged in her work. She could be very engaged. Her time may be limited, but her focus may be very much all there."[7]

Hitting the (maternal) wall

In our survey of more than 1,100 women, we heard story after story of how women lost jobs they loved or saw them radically altered when they became mothers. For some, the shift happened immediately, for others after many productive years as a working mom. As one woman noted, "Many of the changes were not 'formal' but informal. For instance, because I took maternity leave, it was more difficult for my office to provide a rating. As a result, I ended up with a lower rating, which resulted in a lower performance bonus. Similarly, I also found a lot of subconscious expectations that I would want to go part time or be less aggressive in my career trajectory because most people expected me to leave (my staying on in my job was considered unusual)."

And sometimes the maternal wall feels more like a door being slammed in your face. "I was pregnant with my first child," Eve told us, "and I landed the biggest client of my career, an account worth millions to my firm." A week after her baby was born, Eve's doorbell rang. There stood her boss, Al, along with Joe, a new salesperson who'd joined their company. The office had already sent a gift. Eve knew something was up.

"Eve . . . your new account is very important to our office. You won't be back at work for a while so we're going to ask Joe to take it over. What do you think?"

Eve was shocked. Her boss had come to take away her most valuable professional asset—under the pretext of visiting an infant?

"Well," she said, stunned, "I guess you've made up your mind, but you know the client only signed with our firm because of me. No offense to Joe."

"Yeah, I know, but we'll see how it goes," Al replied.

Eve spent her leave infuriated. Her client threatened to pull his business in protest and Joe kept calling Eve asking for tips on how to manage the situation.

When she returned, Eve petitioned Al's superiors to get her client back but got nowhere. Within months, a competing firm made Eve an attractive offer and she left—taking her client and millions of dollars of revenue with her. This mother's story has a happy ending, but it illustrates how destructive bad assumptions about mothers can be when we allow them to go unchecked.

BAD NEWS/GOOD NEWS

In our "Real Lives of Working Mothers" survey we heard an outpouring of frustration from many moms when we asked them what happened when they returned from maternity leave. "I was no longer viewed as a rising professional." "I was seen as the mother of that child." "I was moved from one group to a less respected group without being consulted about the move." "I did not receive a promotion that I was entitled to, it was given to someone else." "Cases were reassigned and not transferred back to me on my return and it was a long time before my workload was full again, while my billable hour requirement remained the same."

But here's the good news. In our survey, we received a spectrum of stories—from the terrible to the terrific. In Chapters 8 and 9, we'll share what we've learned to help you navigate a successful leave, like these women: "I was promoted in title and did not miss a beat." "I actually received the top ranking after returning from maternity leave and received a promotion within a few months of returning. I was really lucky." "They appreciated me more when I returned because no one was able to cover for me while I was away."

Molly was a tenured professor of art history at a large university where she worked happily for many years as a mother. Then her department hired a new chair, Jack. " 'How are the kids?' was Jack's special question just for me," Molly told us. "Never, 'How is your work going?' He'd ask other colleagues about their work, even when they hadn't published in years." If Jack had been sincere, if he had been genuinely fond of children and supportive of working parents, Molly would have seen things differently. But it became increasingly clear that Jack was making Molly's personal life a professional issue; Jack viewed non-parents one way, and working parents, particularly mothers, in a different light.

Molly served on a committee to select a new Baroque expert. Reviewing one applicant file, Jack told the committee, "Well, this woman's got three kids, she won't produce much original work." Molly mentioned that she, too, had three kids and that her second book was coming out (Jack had produced only one book in his career). Clear on how Jack saw the world, Molly left to join a faculty where she could be respected for her work—independent of her parental status.

Karen, a highly placed executive at a large technology firm, was a working mother for many years before she felt some ominous rumblings. She'd held positions in the same company for seventeen years, and during that time she'd successfully returned from two maternity leaves and continued to advance at the firm. Out on her third leave, Karen learned that her department was being totally restructured, and her job was in jeopardy.

When Karen returned from leave, she still had a job, but on very different terms. Karen's new supervisor was based in Asia. "He told me I would need to be available during his full business day," Karen says. "That meant that from 4 p.m. until midnight my time, I'd be participating in conference calls." Facing the night shift to keep her full-time job, Karen took a part-time position her company offered. Would this change have occurred if Karen hadn't taken a leave? Maybe. Maybe not.

Note that not one of these women asked for anything special. No one requested flexible hours, a day to work from home, or reduced travel. Yet, these "team players"—hard workers all—were subject to what amounts to postnatal hazing: Their jobs got harder, the ante was upped when they became mothers. We can't know for sure what their bosses believed. But if women let workplace decision makers continue to think that mothers are distracted with their home life and are no longer capable of hard work, many successful careers will get crushed by the maternal wall.

F is for "flexibility": The new scarlet letter

Magazines praise companies who put pro-family policies on their books. We salute their progress, but these programs won't do the trick alone. "Most of these policies haven't helped as much as people expected they would," says Frank Dobbin, a professor of sociology at Harvard. Tracking outcomes from eight hundred employers over thirty years, Dobbin and his colleagues found most pro-family efforts aren't raising the numbers of women in management. Programs that officially reduced a mother's time in the office (like part-time hours and working from home) did not improve the advancement of women.[8]

Harriet, who made it to the senior ranks of a major corporation, tried to change her sixty-hour-a-week schedule to something more family friendly. "Even you? This diversity thing is a joke," said her boss, referring to the millions her company spent to recruit and retain female employees. Harriet was deeply committed to a job she'd loved for a long time, but she wanted more leeway in her workweek to address her kids' needs. Her boss (a man in his forties) concluded that even a "tough" woman like her couldn't hack it because, unlike her male counterparts, she wasn't able to fully off-load her family.

Noreen had successfully worked Fridays from home in her job as an editor. For years, she found her one day at home was often more productive than her time in the office. She could make phone calls, edit copy, and meet deadlines without interruption while her child went to his regular full-time sitter for the day.

Noreen's boss had okayed her remote Fridays informally—and then he moved on to another job. The new boss had a different view: "It's not corporate policy." Working from home was common in other departments and Noreen was known as a productive editor. But the new boss made it clear that she didn't take Noreen as seriously as colleagues who were in the office five days a week. The fact that Noreen's coworkers took longer lunch hours, lingered in doorways for gossip, and came in late was apparently irrelevant.

So Noreen gave up her work-from-home Fridays, got less work done due to more commuting and office interruptions, and realized that her fifteen-year run at a company she loved had to come to an end—thanks to the narrow thinking of one particular person who happened to be her boss.

Ashley was a highly regarded grade school teacher. When she realized that her salary wouldn't cover the cost of full-time day care, she went to the headmaster and asked if it would be possible to "team-teach" with another working mother. His response was "full-time or nothing." She found a team-teaching position at another school, but her old school lost a great first-grade teacher.

When you ask for flexibility, it's not just bosses who give you a hard time. Julie worked as a public defender in a court where the trials routinely began at 10 a.m. "My kids don't start school till nine and I've got a forty-five-minute commute," Julie explained, so for her, this schedule was ideal. But then a judge moved start times to an hour earlier, noting that most courts across the country convene at 9 a.m.

"A lot of public defenders are mothers responsible for dropping their kids at school," Julie said. So the judge reconsidered and gave these women an exception: Employees with school drop-off duties could start their work at 10 a.m. "They tried to be discreet about how they handled it but it didn't work," says Julie. "Now we have court reporters rolling their eyes at ten a.m. asking why I can't be there earlier. It's not as if I'm keeping them at work longer—I'm a prompt and responsible person. So there doesn't seem to be any reason for this attitude and I really resent it."

Policies are powerless without good bosses and (your) good judgment

Research also shows pro-family policies work *only* if your immediate managers fully support them. All it takes is a few bad apple bosses (and attitudes) to spoil a lot of careers. Shelly, a lawyer, told us, "The chairman of my firm would say, 'let us know what you need.' But the environment never felt safe. It requires someone to *really* care, with power and empathy, to break the culture." Shelly switched to a law firm where she became a partner and had time for her kids. All the partners at Shelly's new firm have working spouses.

"My male bosses all have wives who don't work. When I think about asking for flexibility, they are the ones I worry about," says Rose, a media executive with young kids who continues to work full time. "Asking to shrink my hours feels like a values statement. You get classified as 'not the right kind of person.' They think it's a question of character, that it's your first step out the door."

An HR professional in Silicon Valley told us that her company's all-male board of directors thinks few mothers stay the course at work. She's been asked to seek replacement candidates for pregnant women even before the babies are born. It may not be entirely legal, but she says her company is hardly alone in doing it.

We've both been blessed with our share of great bosses (many male) who did not buy into the myth that women with kids are some special, unreliable group. If you can't find someone like this where you work, you may have to pack your bags. Good bosses *do* exist—and it's worth the effort to find them.

If you use good judgment and know your employer's needs, you raise the odds that you can engineer flexibility in your job. There *are* legitimate limits to how much you can shrink your hours (and how many people can do it at once). The head of a nonprofit, a mom who works full time, said, "Women tell me they want to work sixty to eighty percent. We have *so* many part-timers that our board asks me to hire more full-time people. I'm happy for two women to split one job—but I need them to take responsibility for the *whole* job. They need to think through who is going to cover and make sure the work gets done." Trish works a four-day week at a large firm and ran a group where one-fifth of her team of twenty-five people did the same. "People working a reduced schedule can be very productive but you need boundaries," she says. "Having twenty percent of our team part time was the limit. I don't think we could have managed any more part-time people. As a manager, you end up giving part time to your top performers."

We aren't out to wreck the work ethic. No one seriously thinks you can work from 10 to 2 and get paid for full-time work. But how about leaving at 4 p.m. on Fridays because your son's after-school program ends early? When your husband shares the load, you each leave early two times a month. Is this a big deal? If husbands are doing half at home, moms and dads aren't so different and require just one thing: enough control to duck out for a school play and work through lunch to make the deadline, to get home for dinner and do e-mail after bed-time stories.

Unless you're in charge of the president's briefcase (the one with the nuclear launch codes), not every minute is critical and you can find breathing room if you look for it. What's "reasonable" depends on what kind of work you do—you can't walk out on a cardiac arrest or a corporate crisis either. It's up to you to read the culture and determine what's valuable to your employer and do as much of that as you can—and as little of everything else. Hard work is the cornerstone of most achievement and we are great believers in it. The trouble is many bosses have gotten used to confusing hard work with make-work (more on that in Chapter 5).

TELLTALE SIGNS OF A 50/50 EMPLOYER

Gus is the CEO of a consumer products company and likes to make din-ner with his kids. When his cell phone rings, "I try to let it go. Otherwise, it detracts from the whole purpose of being home early. You go and check messages later." How does this translate into how Gus thinks about his employees? "In the interviewing process, I screen for people who don't need the structure of a nine-to-five-defined day, punching in and punching out. The expectation is that people can figure out how to get their job done. The results are what matter." Another marker to look for: Evidence of working spouses—Gus's wife is an engineer.

While good managers do matter more than what's said in the

employee handbook, there are *some* policies that seem to help working moms more than others. Professor Frank Dobbin finds that employers who allow moms to work the standard volume of hours with creative supports (like on-site day care or the option of coming in early) *do* raise the number of women in management.[9] Myra Hart, one of the founders of Staples, mother of three, and a professor of entrepreneurship at Harvard Business School, shares this view. To retain more women, Hart worked with Ellen Mahoney in the business school's HR group to develop a suite of services. With on-site day care already in place, they added the convenience of takeout meals from the school dining room and introduced a concierge service.

In 2008, researchers at Brigham Young University found something dramatic: The happiest working parents get home for dinner *and* have long hours. Surveying 1,580 IBM employees living in the United States with dependent children, this study explored how much missing family dinner aggravated work/life stress. Turns out that having to work through supper makes the stress much worse—employees working long hours who often skipped dinner at home reported 25 percent more work/life conflict than their peers who worked the same hours but got home to eat with their families. Interestingly, women were significantly more distressed about missing dinners—and much happier when they could get home.[10]

So when you are looking for a place to work, beware when everyone knows dinner takeout menus too well.

WHAT HAPPENS WHEN WOMEN DON'T TELL THE TRUTH

We have overseen many female employees as both managers and board members. In our experience, most moms do remain committed to their jobs, especially if the workplace accords them the respect they had before becoming parents. But many men seem to think that women want to leave their jobs because they enjoy work less and love their babies more. (What do these guys tell their *own* kids—"Sorry, I love you less than your mom does—I'm a man"?) Motherhood, in their

opinion, has these workers hankering for home, and they are less ambitious and more risk-averse. With these views, men aren't surprised
and don't look for more answers when female colleagues downshift or
stop altogether.

Randy worked for a start-up and had her first child two years into
her job. "While I was on leave, I had a sense that I'd never get back on
the fast track—the only track I wanted—and it made me depressed.
And I was mad at all the men from my business school class who
weren't dealing with that problem. I had not expected any of these
feelings," she told us. "My boss told me, 'We need to change your responsibilities since you probably want to work part time.' He just assumed this because his wife stayed home. So I said yes to part time,
less status, and less pay. I ended up miserable and not being taken seriously. Then a headhunter called me about a more intense job, full
time, and I took it. If I was going to go to work, I wanted to have a job
I enjoyed and felt passionate about." Not wanting to burn bridges,
Randy never told her boss his assumption was wrong—and a key reason that she left.

We understand her reasons, but it's a big problem that women
aren't candid when they quit. It means employers may never catch on.
A large professional services firm hired Stanford researchers to solve
what seemed to them a mystery. Top-performing women were quitting in high numbers, saying in their exit interviews that they wanted
to spend more time with their kids. But the employers later learned
these women had returned to work, some starting their own firms and
working longer hours. In anonymous interviews, the women who had
quit explained the disconnect: Most said they'd left their jobs because
"they could not see a future for themselves there." The "more-time-
with-kids" story was just cover—so they could maintain good relations with their former bosses.[11]

In another study, Korn/Ferry, the international recruiting firm, surveyed 425 women and found that women's desire for "opportunity"
was the primary reason they left traditional firms and started their
own. Although half of them were mothers, these women reported
working an average of fifty-five hours a week.[12] You can't blame
women for wanting a smooth exit. However, their failure to be honest

and state the real problem, that they want more respect and upside, leaves employers holding fast to a bad old saw—that women (particularly moms) won't put in the hours.

It's going to take a lot more straight talk to help men over another hump: Men often *want* to believe women leave voluntarily. It's more convenient to believe that it's all okay, that women gladly depart, so nothing needs to change. The Stanford researchers found that, for reasons of comfort and competition, both old and young men embraced the belief that women "choose" home over work. "When older men hear from a woman that she is leaving 'to spend more time with my family,' they are relieved," the researchers wrote. "Their notions of what is 'proper' for women are reinforced and they need feel no guilt... Younger men, despite their different upbringing, often have much the same reactions... They have learned from these older men the value of the male systems of segregation. Many are pleased that, by leaving, senior women have helped lessen the competition among remaining men."[13] Note: It's not just the dinosaurs, it's the guys you went to college with, too.

We *do* have to work harder than men to get ahead, whether or not kids are in the picture. You've heard the old saying about Ginger Rogers: She did everything Fred Astaire did, but backward and in high heels. But don't expect sympathy from all your male colleagues; they often don't see it. In surveys women consistently say they need to "work harder" and be "smarter" than men to get the same respect— in a 2007 poll, 71 percent of women felt this way while only 36 percent of men agreed.[14] Yet, the more we persevere, despite those bosses who think no working mother can produce at the level she used to, the further we'll travel.

Let men talk (even when it hurts to listen)

At family bingo night (or flying to your next conference), ask the guy seated next to you what he really thinks about women at work. Often, you'll find that there are a lot of men who want to help working moms but just don't know how. And often you'll learn that when women don't voice their hardships, men infer a lot of things that just aren't helpful. Men develop theories that say female underperformance at work makes perfect sense.

One man told us about his old girlfriend who was at the top of her law school class, a Supreme Court clerk, and an associate at a prestigious law firm. After having kids, she quit to stay home. "She didn't quit for her kids," the man told us. "She just didn't have the right stuff. Yeah, she could get what she needed one on one, she could do the things that get you good grades. But in the hurly-burly of a big law firm, where you have to influence groups of people, you have to take risks. She just lacked that skill set."

Speaking of his daughter, a strong math student, another man said, "You know, I'd love it if she could be in business like me, but I think we've ruined her. While we'd let her brothers stomp in mud puddles and get scratched up, our daughter's nose was always clean and her clothes were never dirty. Now she cries for hours over little things her friends do at school. How will she survive in business? Maybe she should be a doctor."

"Do you really think women are as ambitious as men? My wife really isn't. I'm the more ambitious one in our family," a progressive man told us. "Do women really want success as intensely as men do?"

Try talking about mothers and work and you'll learn even more. "Women never return from maternity leaves. I have to protect my business and move on," a forty-year-old male boss told us. Why aren't there more part-time jobs? "When women work part time, they have unreasonable expectations—they think they should be paid ratably, eighty percent for four days at the office," a new dad told us. "These women don't understand that they are creating big costs. Someone else has to cover for them. We have to make a much bigger effort to communicate and that's a drag on productivity." (Caution: It's easier to engage men in this topic on the playground on a Saturday than at the office, where the stakes feel too high.)

The problem is not that men think these things; they have plenty of reasons to do so. The problem is that we need to help men see more subtle truths—like when women *think* they can't win, they quit trying.

Workplaces today pride themselves on being data-driven on every topic but this one. We need the space, and the words, to get out of our single-sex silos and talk. How many companies publish their numbers on the performance and pay of women who return from maternity leaves? Who shows their math when they say they can't "afford" to sponsor child care? Who has done a profit-and-loss analysis on people who job share? Yes, these are tricky topics but it's not productive when these issues are only discussed in hushed voices, behind closed doors. Men and women need to hear each other's views, look at the facts together, and find solutions that can suit us all.

PUT YOUR BOSS IN YOUR SHOES: HOW CANDOR CRACKS THE CODE

In his book *Leadership,* management guru Tom Peters describes how he was transformed by hearing women speak candidly. Attending a meeting of women business owners, Peters said, "I listened as one powerful woman after another described the torturous struggle against male-dominated hierarchies that had marked her personal and professional life. Listening to these stories, frankly, made me feel like a spoiled brat (at age fifty-four!)." Peters now challenges business leaders to look more closely at their assumptions and to draw on the strengths of women (rather than trying to make them conform to male models—which are frequently unproductive).[15]

When he was CEO of Deloitte & Touche, Douglas McCracken said he was skeptical when his firm first decided to put five thousand managers through two days of diversity training. It cost the firm more than $8 million and tens of thousands of billable hours. But when he attended himself, he saw the workshops as a turning point, because of the dialogue between women and men these events inspired.

"It wasn't enough to hear the problems in the abstract; we had to see them face-to-face—sitting across a table from a respected colleague and hearing her say, 'Why did you make that assumption about women? It's just not true...' Many of us had little exposure to dual-career families but did have highly educated daughters entering the workforce. A woman partner would say to a male counterpart, 'Sarah's graduating from college. Would you want her to work for a company that has lower expectations for women?' Suddenly," McCracken said of his male colleagues, they'd "get it."[16]

Silence doesn't solve many problems. Talking (the two-way kind) does.

BEFORE YOU CHANGE JOBS, CHANGE YOUR ATTITUDE

Tearing down the maternal wall is our generation's challenge, but as long as it is standing, we need to find protective gear to lessen the blow when we run smack into it. When we clearly see what we're up against, we can spare ourselves the pain and blinding frustration. We can find ways to move forward. In our experience, most walls have a door somewhere. Once you've nursed your bruises, you can walk through them—staying with your current job or going elsewhere.

Stand up for what you need

Standing up for yourself is the best way we know to protect your morale. Women often hesitate to take a stand. When you just want to belong, you never get good at drawing the line, especially if you look different and stink at basketball (as we know from personal experience).

Elena, a surgeon in her thirties, put it this way, "You get ahead by being a team player. As a woman, even more so. Never say anything about sexist comments. Work harder. Always be there. Never complain. I took what they gave me and I kept my mouth shut. But gradually, you can't keep feeling you have to work harder than everyone else and deal with a family. And I had no experience standing up for myself. Saying, 'No, I can't participate on those committees' or just 'No, I can't do it.'"

Before kids, women try so hard to assimilate they tend to minimize their needs, even for nonfamily support that employers happily give to men (who voice their needs). "Men are not afraid to ask for more resources. 'Where's my administrative person to do this?'" Elena points out. "Women say 'I'll find a way to make it work' and we do it on our own time rather than having a secretary to delegate to."

"You have to stand up for yourself," says Ann, the political science professor. "I have male colleagues who get parental leave even if they aren't taking care of the child. But I didn't get maternity leave with my first pregnancy here; the department chair said she would let me use some credits I'd accumulated but didn't give me an actual leave. I didn't know the policy so I didn't object. When I had my last child, I realized that I should have been allowed a leave on the prior pregnancy. I wrote a memo explaining why I deserved not only one maternity leave but something retroactive for the leave I was denied," Ann says. "Life's too short to be quiet."

So claim your fair share of resources and know you still have dibs on prize assignments. If you're feeling sidelined when colleagues make unhelpful assumptions (working moms can't commit to big projects or travel, for instance), call them on it—nicely. When you see important work that used to go to you get handed out to other colleagues, ask why: "'My experience working on X might be useful on this new project. I'd like to be considered for the assignment.' Actively expressing your concerns, or your interest in new work, as questions suggests a spirit of cooperation, and may elicit useful information," suggests Cynthia Calvert, deputy director of the Center for WorkLife Law. "It's helpful to take a low-key approach that's nonconfrontational and funny. If it's a job involving travel, maybe you say: 'Gee, Joe, I know you're looking out for me, but when you have an infant, you sometimes *need* a night away. It might be the only good sleep I get for weeks! I'd like that assignment and I'm fine to travel for it.'"[17]

Stand up for what you think

How clear are you in your *own* mind that you can really perform well? No matter how free-thinking you are, studies say most women absorb widely held beliefs—even when they may be false and bad for us personally. For example, when women take math tests, research shows they do worse if asked to check a box indicating "male" or "female" before they start. That tiny act recalls the idea that "girls aren't good at math." Experts call this "stereotyped threat," getting psyched out by reminders that others doubt you. On the other hand, when women are primed to focus on a positive self-image (or a useful stereotype), like "I'm really good at tests" or "I'm Asian," they do well on the same math tests.[18]

In her book *Tempered Radicals,* Stanford professor Debra Meyerson says that "learning to reject negative self definitions is a crucial psychological step," part of a process experts call "armoring." Seeking out people who defy the stereotype (e.g., highly capable working mothers) allows you to replace toxic bunk with a view that's more accurate—and healthier for you.

The next step is to find effective ways of standing up that seem *doable,* ways that won't get you fired or consigned to the loony bin.[19]

Jean Kahwajy runs Effective Interactions, a leadership consulting firm that works with large employers. "Many women remain in their jobs begrudgingly. They are losing. They are getting beaten up every day," Kahwajy told us. "Some women never learn to stand up and their unhappiness makes them less effective." Kahwajy shows how women can clear the air, making it easier for themselves (and often for others) to breathe.

Kahwajy smiles often and her voice is always warm. "You have to know what you want and you can't succumb to outrage," says Kahwajy. "You have to see that you are misusing your own energy by getting angry. Assume that men are doing the best they can without your help. Think: 'He's blind to what he's saying. I have to *help* him see.' What you control is how you *receive* what's said to you." So when someone makes an off-base comment, catch it in a way that builds muscle and train yourself to be an expert receiver.

"Wow, you're leaving your kids with your husband for two days. You must be really nervous," a colleague said to Zoe. She could feel her defenses rising. "Travel is part of my job and this guy seemed to think that was something I couldn't do as a mom. He might as well have said, 'Can you really *do* this job?'"

But Zoe took a deep breath and said: "Actually, my kids love time with their dad. He's as good with the kids as I am."

Or perhaps your colleagues have planned a meeting in the middle of your family dinnertime. Debra Meyerson suggests you "interrupt momentum" by pointing out that everyone's free at 10 a.m. tomorrow. If it's too late for that, being funny never hurts. Try: "Oh, well, good thing my kids ate a big lunch." Meyerson points out that humor is a great way to make your point.[20] "You want to respond in a way that is encouraging and helps men *want* to learn," says Kahwajy.

PROTECTING OTHERS TO PROTECT YOURSELF

Standing up for *others* is even more doable—and good for you. "When I stop a bad behavior, even when it's directed at someone else, I'm acting for my own benefit," Kahwajy says. Every time we let bad behavior pass unchecked, we gradually acclimate ourselves to accepting it. "If I let a man interrupt another woman, I reinforce the view that 'women are supposed to be interrupted,' " says Kahwajy. "Instead, say, 'Hey, I want to know what she's saying. Can we hear her out?' Every time I do that, I protect my own values," Kahwajy says. "All it takes is one supporter to stop an interruption. And it's easier for me to support *you* than myself—with a positive tone and an open mind."

"The senior guys I work with didn't want to promote Lynn to run a small, local business," Angela told us. "They said she didn't have enough experience. But at the same time these guys were putting a fellow named Jack in charge of a big global business that he knew nothing about. So I just said, 'I guess Jack is *a lot* smarter than Lynn.' They stopped, laughed, and gave Lynn her promotion."

In this way, "you stand your ground without pointing fingers. When you respond in a way that cleans the environment, you yourself win, as does the organization," Kahwajy says. And so does your employer. "People who have limiting expectations about women are hurting themselves (and their work) because they lose their ability to take in information women have. When you respond thoughtfully, you aren't only helping these people relate to you, you are helping them consider input they'd otherwise miss. When we let these low expectations go unchecked, women stop wanting to contribute and employers often mistake deflated morale for proof these women had less to contribute in the first place."

When women stand up for themselves and others, "very quietly, they rock the boat," says Meyerson. "They help others by encouraging them to stay in the game, even when it looks hopeless."[21] And they help themselves stay, too.

Stay in the game—there are many ways to play it

"I had difficult managers at one point and I kept thinking, 'I want my children to be in good hands and I'm not enjoying this. Let's move to Nebraska or someplace where we could live on one salary,'" says Joan, a journalist with small kids. "But I know myself. If I quit, I would have looked at the paper in the morning and said, 'Gosh, why isn't *my* byline on that story?' I worked ten years in journalism to get this job and it's one of the best. I feel like I still haven't gotten my money's worth out of this job yet. I want to do some work that only a paper like this can allow me to do."

Most women we interviewed faced bad deals at work at some time in their careers. But they saw the light and kept going by asking the right question: not "Should I quit?" but *"How* do I keep working?" Some simply waited out the naysayers, others changed the "rules" where they work, or struck out on their own, or made wholesale career shifts.

Though they took a wide variety of paths, all of these happy working mothers shared a mind-set that made their lives possible. They saw they could be committed to both their families and jobs by exercising more control—deciding for themselves what deserves time, both at home and at work. "It's unrealistic (and crazy-making) to think that you need to be on the hook for every single event in your child's life; learn to pick and choose, and to share responsibility with your spouse," one mother said to us. "It's also unrealistic to think you need to work sixty hours every week. If your team's weekly meetings really must start at 5 p.m., well, you can call in from the car."

When you take a job, you owe your employer one thing: good results. When you're part of a team, producing strong results can get harder if you work different hours in different places. But if you've ever worked with colleagues in different locations or time zones, you know that syncing up is feasible—you just need to plan more. It's the same if you're working alternate hours or from home; with a little bit of strategizing, you can be very productive. It's up to *you* to figure out how to get your work done—really well.

Having control over how you do your job lets you get home in time for dinner on most nights, and manage your travel schedule most of the time. One couple (both parents are partners at a big accounting firm) said they could count on one hand the number of times they were *both* out of town the same night in the *twenty years* they had kids at home. Having control means you can take your child to the doctor when you need to and so can your husband. Having control gives you the courage to attend back-to-school night or the swim meet knowing that it's the right thing to do and you'll get your work done later. With two parents on tap, you can do that most of the time.

How do you get control of your job and still keep your coworkers, clients, patients, suppliers—and your boss—happy? Here's what successful working parents told us.

Show no fear—don't apologize

Helen and her husband teach at an all-boys boarding school. When their first child was born, the couple arranged their schedule so they could trade off watching their son—and when that didn't work, they brought him to class. "More traditional faculty might have been a bit ruffled. But they are the kinds of people who are ruffled by changes in anything and they knew the headmaster supported us," Helen said. With her kids now off in grade school, the logistics are easier for Helen's family, but, she says, "The trick is not being afraid. When someone tells you, 'Well, that's never been done before,' you say, 'Okay. So how can we do it?'"

While some women can change the rules of work enough to continue working full-time hours, others opt to change their hours at work. "Call it an 'experiment,'" says Mark, a headhunter who has placed many women (and men) in part-time positions. "When a new arrangement is an 'experiment,' it feels less risky, less permanent. It's all about how you pitch these things—and the results that you show."

Keep showing up—you'll convert most doubters

Sometimes, if you just keep showing up and doing your job, things can settle back down. "I was a sales manager at IBM and my boss had me on this fast track. When I got pregnant, his perspective changed," says Laura, who has spent most of her career at large high-tech companies. "But as soon as I came back to work, it was fine, he didn't care. I didn't let it bother me that he had different assumptions. I just thought, 'He doesn't know me—he just has a different perception of the world.' I just ignored it. The second time I was pregnant, I was at another big firm and they promoted me to the next-level job, a real primo job, before I went on leave. I already had a child, and they knew me. So they made things work so I could have the baby and come back."

Be flexible about flexibility

"Being at one place for so long is sort of unheard of in my business, but I've been at the same company for eighteen years," says Susan, a software engineer. "I've looked for ways to keep the job interesting and new opportunities within the company instead of moving jobs like most engineers in this industry. I'm lucky that I really like the people I work with. But I'm also not excited about going to another firm and having to prove myself at a new place, where I wouldn't be as efficient. I have a lot of capital with my employer and that gives me leverage and lets me have flexibility.

"There are no women at my level or above who are mothers. I was nervous about asking to do something different," said Susan. So she proposed an experiment while she was pregnant, in the name of efficiency, not kids. Susan told her boss she'd work full time, but three days from home. Cutting three two-hour daily commutes would give the company six more productive hours. "Some senior people didn't think it would work. 'You're a manager. Can you really do your job from home?' I pointed out that I'd successfully managed people in Germany, London, and India remotely. Managing my colleagues at our main office, in the same time zone, *had* to be easier." Susan's boss said, "Let's try it," and Susan has successfully worked most days from home for eight years—while continuing to advance at the company. "I really invested a lot to prove to them that it was going to work, trying to make it feel like I was in the office—tons of phone calls, checking in with my manager, coming in to the office more days when the work just demanded it. I think when you get flexibility, you have to be flexible in return."

Laura also points out how having an open mind about what "flexibility" means to you can help a lot—that a job may not be family friendly in all dimensions but can still give you what you need. "When I was VP of business development, it was bad in the sense that there could be a lot of travel, but it was great in the sense that I could work from home when I was in town—no one cared where I was, as long as I produced," she says.

Part-time hours, full-time commitment

If you've been a full-time worker and now want to ratchet down to part time, remember that the work has to go somewhere.

" 'Oh, it's such a pain in the ass, we can't do that here.' That's the response from a lot of people here about part time," says Trish, who became the first part-time professional at a hard-charging firm. "We have kind of a heavy meeting-based culture, because you're often sitting down looking at a whiteboard, you're looking at designs and sketches, and you're working with designers, you're working with an engineer to try what this product is going to look like. Sometimes you just have to come in on your 'off' days. And if you call in from home, you have to be as low-burden as possible. You can't slow people down."

Trish has worked her four-day week successfully for five years, and her example has made part time possible for many of her colleagues. But, Trish cautions, you have to take the time to build buy-in—every time you get a new set of colleagues. "I always walk into it really carefully. You can't do what I do unless you have a great team and everyone supports how you are working. So I sit down with the key people and say, 'Here's what I do, and here's how I do it, talk to people who've worked with me before. I want to make sure you're on board before we all jump into this.'"

Trish, like other successful working moms, accepts that there are just times when you have to work more hours. "But the jumps in my workload have always seemed reasonable in the scheme of things. I could see where it would end. For instance, when we bought a new company or we have to get a product out." And when she knew she'd be working more than her 80 percent for many months, Trish told her boss, "You're going to have to pay me one hundred percent for the quarter, because this is a two hundred percent job." Trish has now managed a number of part-time people on her own team and she strives to set expectations the right way. " 'This is a high-performing company,' I tell people starting part time. 'There are going to be times when it's extreme, where you're working as much as you would on a five-day week.' However, I make sure that this isn't over extended periods of time, because ultimately it has to be fair."

Carmen, an internist, spent years adjusting and readjusting her part-time job until it felt right. It took a long time to craft a good outcome: arguments with her boss, competing job offers, managing her own expectations, and lots of soul-searching. What did Carmen learn from all of this? "That you need to have enough specific parts of your job that you really *enjoy*. As one female colleague told me, 'Ask for the world. They give things away all the time. You just never hear about it.'" Carmen loved helping weight-management patients and seeing their progress. So she asked her boss to remix her schedule—to include more of that and less of work she disliked. That added satisfaction made Carmen's job rewarding enough to stay. "Since then, I've been so happy."

Become an expert—then a free agent

But in some fields, at some firms, part-time work is so stigmatized that women choose to strike out on their own so they can keep doing the kind of work they love. "When I resigned," says Grace, who has spent her career in advertising, "they said 'you can work part time here, we'll put you in charge of special projects.' Like most ad firms, mine had a play-to-win culture. Special projects weren't strategically important work. It was not a real job.

"I said, 'There's got to be a different way for me to do this.' I got on the train, bought a beer, and wrote down what I wanted on a cocktail napkin: 'strategic work for smart people that I like.' I laid out the value equation—is this engagement worth my time? Will it give me back something I'm proud of? I decided that's how I would judge the work I take. If it fits this bill, I'll take it. I framed my cocktail napkin so I'd remember and when I stick to it, things are great," says Grace, who continues to do important work for important clients—but now as the head of her own consulting firm. She also makes more money than she did as a partner at her old agency.

Julie, the public defender in the court that moved start times to 9 a.m., set up shop as a private investigator, photographing crime scenes, talking to witnesses and friends of the accused to ensure a fair trial. She points out that doing her old job part time would have been hard; the crisis element of criminal defense makes the hours unpredictable. Now, helping disadvantaged people find justice in a different way, Julie continues to serve a purpose she believes in—on her terms, with hours that usually work for her family. "I think a lot of people would be happier if they could think outside the box. When female colleagues hear about what I'm doing, it's like a light bulb goes off. 'How did you think to do that?' they ask. Reaching out for new ways to pursue your goals you can create jobs that are very rewarding."

Find a "hidden passage"—uncharted paths still lead you forward
If you don't want to hang out your own shingle (or it's not an option in your field), there are other paths. Carol Muller is the founder of MentorNet, a nonprofit mentoring network for the science and technology professions. "There are lots of ways to stay in the game," says Muller. "The question isn't 'How am I going to work eighty hours a week.' It should be, 'How am I going to keep a hand in?' People who get to the top take some very interesting turns in their careers. It's not one step after another in some linear order. In fact, unusual career diversions can create opportunities, open up new networks, provide great experience, and offer freedom—making one a better and more skilled leader and a standout in one's field."

Muller uses the example of someone in science. With a little creativity, we can picture how her advice applies in many fields. "Do a fellowship where you are away from the day-to-day politics of your regular job. Ask for a special project or a consulting assignment...Or you can keep doing your job part time. You can teach three courses and not six in the same space of time. On your résumé, you never have to say this was a part-time job. You do have to do something of substance, something that you can describe to your next employer, but how you gain that substance is up to you. You see guys do it when they have a new relationship or a divorce or a parent is ill or they don't like their boss. They change their jobs or they go play golf, but they do it in a way they can recover from." Muller calls these routes "hidden passages" and you can use them, too.

"I wasn't sure I'd like it," said Elena, the surgeon, about her decision to leave academic medicine for a county hospital. "It was very different from what I'd been doing. Taking care of a much more diverse patient pool rather than just becoming more and more expert in one part of surgery. But the money was good and the hours were a lot better. My husband said, 'You can always quit if you really don't like it.' I thought, 'I can do this for the next seven years and keep up my skills. If I can just keep going, I won't be out of surgery for life.' It's turned out really well." In addition to operating, Elena now participates in a major project to help hospitals share best practices across the United States—something she could not have done in her old job.

Ann, the political science professor, worked as a management consultant after she got her PhD. At the time, she lived in New York and was pregnant with her first child. "I worked for a client in California, so I spent my pregnancy on a plane. After my son was born, I was working like a dog. I would get home 'early' at eight and find that he was already in bed, day after day. I cried every night. It wasn't sustainable. But I never thought about not working. Luckily for me, I'd continued to publish while I was a consultant and landed a job back in academics." It wasn't luck—it was attitude. Keeping your mind (and options) open is what it takes to keep working.

Live the Apple ad: Think different

You can keep your head in the sand, popping up for air to see if your parental status has been forgotten, hoping that your boss thinks about your results more often than your motherhood. You can fight back and charge the newly erected barricades by staying late, coming in early, and forgetting what your family looks like. You can try both tactics until you get bored, exhausted, demoralized, or quit.

Or, you can do something that is more effective than going underground or going ballistic or going away. You can keep working—on your own terms.

Chapter Five

Success Does Not Require 24/7

We started our careers in two time-intensive fields—Joanna in law and Sharon in finance. We each looked around our offices and saw men working 24/7, and women doing the same thing—until they became parents. In our mostly male professions, long hours were not only a badge of honor and a sign of status, they were a necessity for anyone who wanted to get ahead. It was clear who the working mothers were (a handful of women who tried to keep more normal hours), but it was hard to tell who the fathers were. Single or with four kids at home, all men arrived at work early and went home late—or so it seemed. Talking to men and women in all kinds of jobs, we heard the same story. As young people starting out they, like us, got this message: To succeed, you need to work all the time. To work all the time, you need to be (or act) childless.

We've been lucky to learn this is not true—but only after many years of laboring under the delusion that it was. We've all been duped into thinking that more is better when it comes to our jobs, that somehow the more time we spend at work, from offices to hospitals to test kitchens to newsrooms, the more productive we'll be. It starts from a belief that's largely right: That hard work is good (which it is), that we can do a better job if we put in more hours (which was true when we were talking about bringing the harvest in before the crops froze). "It didn't used to be this intense," says Bill George, who ran Medtronic and now sits on the boards of global companies like ExxonMobil. "It got much worse starting fifteen years ago."[1]

Compounding the problem, some of the most hardheaded leaders romanticize 24/7 life. "I used to show up at the office Saturday morning," writes former General Electric CEO Jack Welch in his best-selling book *Winning*. He had plenty of company, all men, on these weekend mornings he describes as "a blast." "We would mop up the workweek in a more relaxed way and shoot the breeze about sports.

"I never once asked anyone 'Is there someplace you'd rather be—or need to be—for your family or favorite hobby or whatever?' The idea just didn't dawn on me that anyone would want to be anywhere but at work."[2]

We've created a breed of managers who think 24/7 is a matter of pride and the only path to success. The overfocus on hours can lead even bright bosses to stop measuring things that matter more, like results or the inputs that drive them, which take more effort to track. Consider the management maxim that "what gets measured gets done" and it's no wonder we're all at the office ever longer.

Studying a large firm, Harvard Business School professor Leslie Perlow heard one boss excuse a failing worker this way: "I think we would have lost faith in him a long time ago. But he works so hard, you just have to assume he's working on something really challenging." Bosses at this firm (as in many) were so focused on hours that they would cut a poor performer slack but pushed out successful workers who put in less time.[3]

Something happens to our sense of time when we become parents. Time becomes a prized commodity, something we'd rather not waste. When our time is being misused—by either ourselves or others—we want to punch the clock, literally. It's always aggravating when the person who called the 2:00 meeting shows up at 2:15 and then blows another fifteen minutes off topic. It's even worse when you'd like to leave by 5:15, not 5:45. That's half an hour your child will be waiting for you at day care (accruing those infuriating late fees).

" 'This is the dumbest meeting I've sat through in my life.' That was all I could think. It was an important client but we weren't using our time well and I had to leave to make my daughter's event," said Grace, the advertising executive. "Before kids, I'd bought into this idea 'I'm a partner at this big firm and this is what we do.' But when there are kids who need you for specific things, you acknowledge the truth—that we spend a lot of time doing stupid things at work."

It gets harder to see 24/7 as heroic when you know how much it hurts the well-being of kids (and of your marriage and spouse). You can't get good results unless you put in good, hard work, but as Doug, a professor of psychiatry, says, "Sometimes I think we overdo it. When people feel they're expected to be at the office for twelve hours a day, they spend a lot more time bullshitting at the watercooler."

While it's easy to think that the workplace is kinder than it was a generation ago, we are in fact being asked to work longer, harder, and faster, all in the name of the global competition. If we're really interested in winning, our addiction to midnight oil is a danger. Productivity, efficiency, innovation should be our focus—all more easily achieved by alert minds *not* working 24/7.

How 24/7 hurts profits, and why smart bosses say, "Go home"

From the moment we get our first jobs, we're led to believe that more is better—more billable hours, more orders from customers, more time with clients, more meetings to set more goals, more tasks learned, more e-mails sent, more products produced, whether it's cherry pies or radial tires. More, more, more is the way of sending the signal that you're good, better, the best at what you do. Working all the time says you're tough, you're tops, you're macho (even if you're biologically female). The old way of being macho was to play basketball on a sprained ankle for hours on end. The new way of being macho is to work nights and weekends.

But competing when you're not at your best is always a mistake. "Businesses need to be 24/7," says Xerox CEO Ann Mulcahy. "Individuals don't."[4]

Not only do we not need to be "on" all the time, but for the good of our employers, we shouldn't be. It's no secret that when we work while exhausted, we often do more harm than good. Sleep experts have studied truck drivers and nuclear plant workers and have concluded that it is downright dangerous for them to work more than a six-to-eight-hour shift. The medical field is an infamous hotbed of sleep-deprived workers. Comparing hospital interns on a "normal" thirty-hour shift with those working shorter hours, one study found dramatic differences in performance. Interns on thirty-hour shifts misdiagnosed patients six times more often and made almost 60 percent more errors compared with interns who got more normal amounts of sleep.[5]

While most of us aren't doing jobs that could kill other people if we work past our peak, we can still do a lot of damage. Consider that e-mail you fired off to the Big Cheese at 11 last night (you misspelled his name), your after-hours voice mail to the supplier who's late again (you said something bad, but what was it?), being abrupt with the rookie who screwed up the numbers after working all night.

A guru to Fortune 500 CEOs told us, "If you can't get your job done in ten hours a day, there is something wrong with you." His point: No matter where you sit in the food chain there are only so many productive hours your brain can put in—after that, you'll make mistakes, you'll make a gaffe, you'll make a mess. "Your priority list should be short and very focused; you have to say no or delegate to others."

When Joanna began her first career, she joined a large corporate law firm. She'd worked hard in law school to build what she thought were the relevant skills: studying precedent, learning to gather evidence and build legal arguments. But, for junior lawyers, a crucial part of the job was late-night proofreading, with the stamina to do it again and again, night after night, patiently shepherding hundreds of pages through a multiday, round-the-clock production process, often twenty hours at a time. Sitting at the printers until 2 a.m., Joanna knew she and all the other associates were expected to be at their desks the next morning to begin again, minds as sharp as the day they were hired. But Joanna couldn't do it and didn't want to. Doing deals was her thing, proofing vigils weren't, so Joanna left for a job where she could contribute (mostly) during daylight hours.

U.S. economic power is second to none, but it turns out that our actual productivity per hour lags behind that of many other countries. (In hours logged by the watercooler, perhaps we're first.) When faced with a need to expand capacity, we throw more people and more hours at the problem, rather than figure out how to work more productively. We call more meetings. We generate more e-mails. We get busy—but in the wrong way and for the wrong reasons. Martin Baily, former chair of the Council of Economic Advisors, says, "There is probably not a productivity penalty to shortening hours in the U.S., and there may even be a benefit."[6]

Researchers know too much 24/7 causes serious problems, that workaholics, who incidentally develop stress-related ailments that drain employee health-care benefits, have compromised decision-making and problem-solving skills, as they become uncreative and forgetful. The Chernobyl disaster, the *Exxon Valdez* oil spill, and the explosion of the *Challenger* space shuttle were all the result of too much 24/7, according to Martin Moore-Ede, physiologist and author of *The Twenty-Four-Hour Society*.[7]

Most bosses don't see the problem of pushing employees to the max because they get the results they want—short term, at least. The 24/7 ethic is a gross perversion of the good old-fashioned work ethic and it costs us a lot in productivity. In her book *Finding Time*, Harvard Business School's Leslie Perlow conducted a nine-month study of time management at a Fortune 500 firm. She found that "those who work hardest do not necessarily contribute the most to the corporation's productivity, and, in fact, that often no one benefits from this behavior, not even the corporation... if we had the incentive to get the work done in less time, we could create alternative ways of working that would be more efficient and effective."[8]

CLOCKING THE WORKDAY

Leslie Perlow has devoted her career to exploring how people use—and misuse—their workday. Since the early 1990s, Perlow has been clocking workers in a variety of demanding fields from software programming to consulting. Among her key findings: We can do more in less time if we help each other and interrupt less.

Studying a Fortune 500 technology firm, Perlow asked workers to wear a watch that beeped on the hour, reminding them to record what they'd done with that unit of time—both at the office and at home. Then she asked the engineers to review their time logs and reflect on what did (and didn't) help them get work done. What Perlow heard was dramatic: Even star workers felt much of their twelve-hour workday (sometimes close to half) was lost in activities that were either needless or ill planned. Straining to meet a product-launch deadline, many engineers complained about stress and overwork. So Perlow suggested an experiment: "Quiet time" three mornings a week when interruptions would not be allowed. The goal was to permit workers to rethink how they used their time. By the end of the experiment, 71 percent of engineers said that creating these blocks of focused time made them more productive. The project's leaders were impressed, too—the team successfully launched its product on time and managers credited Perlow's experiment.[9]

Why do we perpetuate so many ineffective patterns of work? We're often convinced that our way is the only one. Even when it's clearly not true. It turns out that the very same task—at the same level of quality—can be done many ways. To discover just how differently people produce the same thing, Perlow looked abroad. "We asked a large U.S. company to identify joint venture partners that were highly productive and equally productive," Perlow told us. This sent Perlow and her colleagues to three software firms—in China (we'll call it "Cco"), India ("Ico"), and Hungary ("Hco")—to observe one top-performing group in each of these places.

In the United States, it's common for programmers to work twelve-hour days and longer—plus weekends. It's assumed that this work style is required to produce top-notch results. But in Perlow's study, only the Ico programmers believed they needed to work long hours like their U.S. peers.

At Cco, the workday was 8 to 5, with an hour for lunch. How? Programmers sat in a single room, quietly performing individual tasks, consulting the manager—and only the manager—as needed. Apart from the one-hour lunch break, there was no fraternizing, no team meetings. "We judge engineers based on how hard they work (while at work)," a Cco boss said, "and their native talent."

At Hco, engineers had significant latitude to decide when and how they worked. "I don't evaluate people based on long hours," said an Hco manager. Work varied with the firm's needs—normally, programmers worked a nine-hour day but, in an occasional pinch, they would stay as late as needed. Meeting time was used for group collaboration (not the perfunctory status updates that are common in U.S. office culture). Many Hco employees chose to work from home without fear it would count against them. In fact, the Hco project leader explained, "I get a lot more done at home. I work at home whenever I can."

Hco managers encouraged engineers to help each other so that individual workers could leave the office without letting down their team. Hco engineers developed overlapping expertise so that if one programmer was out—running an errand, tending to a sick child, or on a long vacation—someone else would fill in and work would progress at a high level of quality.

For the engineers on these three equally productive teams, the different work cultures drove very different results for family life. One Cco manager explained, "The government is concerned that it is not healthy for the workforce to overwork," and his employees openly expressed their desire to maximize family time. At Hco, work hours rose and fell with the demands of the project and engineers were comfortable saying that they needed time for "rest and revival, as well as for family needs."

At Ico, with its culture of long hours and individualism, programmers made a point of saying their work came before all else.

Intrigued by these findings, Perlow has brought her research back home to the United States. "Can we rethink the norms in places that are the toughest?" Perlow asks. She is finding some encouraging news in her work with highly competitive professional service firms. Time can be treated as something valuable that should not be wasted, not as the sole currency to prove you're committed to your job. "Work naturally has its peaks and valleys," Perlow says. In the United States, it is standard to work at peak level all the time—the culture does not allow us to work *less* in the valleys—unless we are willing to challenge our assumptions and experiment. "We can do things differently. What we discovered in our cross-cultural work is bearing out in the United States. That it is possible—not unrealistic—to think you can reorganize work in a way that's good for both family life and the bottom line."[10]

More focused effort, less wasted time

Best Buy, the electronics retailer, which is at the hub of global competition, saw that too many talented people quit due to their long hours. Best Buy is now three years into a program it is calling the ROWE ("Results-Oriented Work Environment"), where thirty-five hundred employees are allowed to work when and where they like, setting their own hours. With the employee discipline encouraged by ROWE, some divisions posted double-digit productivity gains, and virtually all groups gained lower turnover, and much higher job satisfaction.

How did Best Buy do it? They changed the culture—and made it clear that formerly admired work habits are now bad form: two-hour staff meetings, drop-by interruptions, long e-mails. They've also made productivity standards explicit.[11] At Cisco Systems, managers are being urged to find effective ways to evaluate an employee's performance. "If hours worked or face time is the criterion used, employees who can be very effective and organized may get penalized," says Noni Allwood, Cisco's senior director of worldwide diversity and inclusion.[12]

You don't have to have a big corporate program to find bosses who look at your output more often than your hours. Rob took over a failing staffing firm and made it highly profitable by recruiting the right people to help him run it. Two of his seven top people were mothers who worked part time. "It would have been very easy to fill those jobs with men willing to work full time," says Rob, "But we didn't want to *not* hire the best person for the job just because they wanted to work less than five long days a week." Valuing talent more than hours, Rob turned the firm around, made it a leader in its field, and sold the company for a handsome profit.

Even if there isn't a results-focused program or a Rob where you work, there are plenty of things you can do on your own. First, let's consider what gets in the way when we try to talk about efficiency at work.

The forest for the trees: How hidden agendas lurk in the 24/7 woods

Our 24/7-loving culture provides cover for a lot of ineffectiveness—and other unattractive practices. Julie, the former public defender, told us that some judges feel pressed to push trials through because the backlog of cases is so high. "Judges set schedules so aggressive that defense attorneys, caught racing from trial to trial, don't have time to prepare fully. A lot of these cases have a natural life span and they need time to progress—time for evidence and witnesses to be identified," says Julie. When the wrong guy goes to jail, the bad guys roam free—keeping the cops (and our tax dollars) busy. These judges, like their peers in many fields, get blinded by the idea that lots of work equals good work. Worse, "These judges make you go to trial because they can; you sense that often it's just a power trip," says Julie.

At 5 p.m., a sales manager named Kirk tells his junior colleagues what they need to do for the next day's meetings: long lists of things to prepare, to be completed after they eat dinner at their desks. He seems untroubled by the fact the young people on his team are underemployed during the day. This is Kirk's standard operating procedure. Kirk spends his own days meeting with more senior colleagues and clients. "Kirk isn't any more productive than the rest of us—we brief our teams as early as we can, and our folks get home," says his colleague, "but Kirk seems to think he's entitled to use his team's time however he wants." In a well-run firm, Kirk won't last too long. But there are plenty of places where people like Kirk, and the judges in Julie's court, use other people's time as a way of demonstrating their own dominance.

Face time versus family time

In some workplaces, one person's BS is another person's path to glory, that holy grail known as "face time." Once there was a time when you put up with it in its many forms: unproductive meetings, mindless chitchat, power breakfasts, business lunches, and celebratory drinking and dining, or simply coming in early and staying late to be "seen." When you are an active parent, you see these things in a different light. You see them as wasteful.

Lan worked as a portfolio manager and was considered a great investor, one of the best in the firm, and gifted at working with clients whom she often traveled to visit. But during a review her boss told her, "You're not integrated enough into the office culture. You need to spend more time in the office so other people see you here—you're not in the football pool, you don't hang around and shoot the shit."

"But I try to be efficient—that's why I work through lunch—so I can get home to see my kids," she told them. His response: Act like everyone else. "We want you here," Lan's boss said, "but you won't get promoted unless you spend more time being visible."

"The guys in my department decided that our weekly divisional meeting should be at 7 a.m.," says Linda, the medical professor. "That was a huge hardship," Linda recalls. "I could not do the morning routine getting the kids ready for school. I showed up without complaint, but it was really annoying. The meeting took an hour and a half but had only about twenty minutes of substance. Everyone else in the meeting was male and it was sort of their breakfast club—they were having a grand old time." If Linda's male colleagues had been doing their half at home, would things have been different?

Building teamwork does take face-to-face interaction and that does take time. Lan and Linda (and working parents generally) just want some rigor around how hours are used when they cut into valuable family time: 8 a.m. (vs. 7 a.m.) meetings, business lunches (instead of dinners), efficient (rather than inefficient) off-sites. Small tweaks make a big difference. If we can spot the agendas (displays of dominance, conformity, and machismo) hiding in 24/7, it's easier to uproot them.

CAUTION:
Men at Work

"If women can't work 24/7, they just shouldn't do important jobs," a male business school student said to us. "I'm on the road twenty nights a month," one father told us. "I'm the go-to guy for my boss. It's a real man's job." When did lots of hours and travel become a marker for manliness? Twenty-four/seven has gotten tangled up with masculinity in an odd way. How many moms do you know who boast about their long work hours? Some men worry that anything less than all-the-time work calls into question more than their job commitment. "I was at Starbucks at 8:30 getting my preschooler some milk before drop-off. I saw an important guy I know and I was really embarrassed," another dad told us, "like, what's he going to think of me, hanging out with my kid when other guys are already in the office?"

The good news: What's macho changes all the time. Two hundred years ago, the world's most powerful men expressed their manhood by wearing lace and stockings. The sooner we can help men see 24/7 as an unfortunate male fad, the sooner we'll have more practical talk about how to take fat out of the workday.

Eighty percent of mothers in our survey agreed with this statement: "Men think success requires that they appear to prioritize work over family." On a family vacation, one working mom told her husband, " 'You know, they'll survive if you don't check e-mail every two hours.' But he looked offended, like I was implying he wasn't important if he wasn't needed all the time." Another woman said her husband wants to be more involved with the kids but "he thinks he'd be looked down on, he worries he'd look like a failure if he weren't seen at work on weekends."

When you question the usefulness of working long hours, some men get quite emotional. Sharon was telling a thirtysomething couple about the research on efficiency she'd read for this book. The wife asked what Sharon planned to do in her next job. Before Sharon could answer, the husband said, "Well, with a work ethic like Sharon's, who'd hire her?" Seeing she'd stepped on a raw nerve, Sharon resisted the urge to compare her many years of twelve-plus-hour days with the more limited demands of this man's job. It's hard not to be proud of our hard work and harder still when someone infers our sacrifices sometimes just aren't needed. But we *can* rise above this knee-jerk reaction, and some far-sighted men are joining women and leading the way.

The founder of a fast-growing, publicly traded firm strictly limits business travel. He sees that often you can do as much business over the phone as in a face-to-face meeting. A lot of business trips are, well, boondoggles and a (not terribly productive) way of keeping score. "I used to be proud of working all the time," says Craig, the CEO of a technology firm. "Now, I feel like a loser if I'm in the office past 7." Or as another dad, a successful investor, told us: "I don't know why some men feel they have to work eighty hours a week to deserve their pay. They must have low self-esteem."

What sane man would tell his kids "My job is more important than you"? Yet that's basically what 24/7 machismo requires. When airline miles and hours logged are used as measures of masculinity, cutting back on them feels harder than it should. We'll have more rational talk about what's really needed to do a job well when we acknowledge that 24/7 weakens men in their most manly of roles—fatherhood.

The cult of 24/7—how we got sucked in

During the post–World War II boom years, when lucky homemakers were given "modern conveniences" like dishwashers and vacuum cleaners, the idea was that women would spend less time on housework. A self-cleaning oven! A washer and dryer! Yet, in 1960, women spent just as much time on housework as they did in 1920.[13] Now that moms could do laundry faster, the family bought more clothes and thought less about getting them dirty. Electric irons and fancy vacuums failed to net mothers more spare time because standards were raised—more was expected.

We know the clean-versus-dirty-house pendulum has now swung back in favor of the dust bunnies—we're spending less time on tile grout and more on our kids. Several decades into household gadgets, we finally realize they can give us something more valuable: a little more time with our families. The same thing needs to happen at work. We have reduced paper memos, but they've metastasized into thousands of e-mails. Mobile phones, laptops, and BlackBerrys have become blankies for grown-ups. But how are we doing as the most wired (and tired) generation yet?

All these devices give us a world where "the marginal cost of interaction is falling toward zero," says Lowell Bryan, a partner at McKinsey and Company, the consulting giant. "The volume of interactions is headed toward infinity and infinity's winning."[14]

We all have our entries for the Pointless Meeting Hall of Fame, but have you ever calculated the hours you've spent in them? In 2005, Microsoft surveyed thirty-eight thousand workers in two hundred countries. The average worker spent nearly six hours a week in meetings, and rated 71 percent of those meetings as unproductive.[15] That's veering toward an entire weekday taken up with useless activity.

Another study found that 80 percent of top management talent is spent on work that represents less than 20 percent of the organization's long-term value. McKinsey's Bryan points out that many jobs are actually undoable if we expect people to participate in all their meetings, and respond to all their calls and e-mail. "We have created jobs that are literally impossible," says Bryan. "The human cost is profound and the opportunity cost is also great in terms of organizational effectiveness."[16]

TAMING THE TIME BEAST

It's hard to change how you work if you don't believe there's another way to do well. At work, many women see the listed price (all or nothing) and think that's what you have to pay, that it's nonnegotiable. "I wanted to be great at my job and the only way to be great was work all the time—so I quit," one woman told us.

Part of the problem may be finding the right job for you—where you can excel efficiently. "Too many people don't ask themselves what their strengths really are, so they get into jobs that are wrong for them," says Laura, who raised two kids while serving in senior roles at big firms. "There's a whole set of stuff I'm really bad at. But if you do what you're really *good* at, people will recognize your talents and you'll get the respect on your terms."

Another factor may be that many women (like men) see long hours as a sign of character. In the *Harvard Business Review,* a recent study of "extreme jobs" showed that women get the same high from throwing themselves into jobs as men do.[17] You feel needed (ten voice mails while you were in your morning meeting), you fit in (remember high school, when you wore the same shoes as everyone else?), you feel like you are achieving something (exactly *what* you are achieving is sometimes unclear, but you're too pooped to notice). Giving it your "all" is the stuff of movies; anything less seems B-team.

It's hard to shut that worry out, especially if you kept 24/7 hours in your pre-kid life. But, as Carol Muller of MentorNet points out, "Guilt is a useless emotion. It keeps us from setting boundaries and makes us worry needlessly if we do. Women have not been in the workplace in large numbers for long enough for there to be lots of good role models. But if you pay attention to the work habits of both men and women you can find some answers. Women tend to focus on the man who works eighty hours a week because we assume that his way is the only way to be productive. We often fail to notice there are some equally successful men who actually have a life and spend it with their families." And they don't make a big deal out of carving out the time—they just do it. We should, too.

Carmen, the internist, says that she's learned a lot from her husband's guilt-free work style. "His self-preservation instinct is much better. He says 'no' and nothing bad happens . . . It is so easy to get sucked into thinking you have to do everything to be successful. No one tells you how to say no—how to stop throwing yourself in front of the bus."

"All the moms in my group leave at 5:30. I keep shorter hours and I get my job done," says Darcie, the ice-cream executive. "But it's an internal struggle for me. How much do I have to worry about showing my face? I still wrestle with that. My husband doesn't have this problem. He gets his work done and he's totally comfortable with leaving early to coach our kid's soccer game."

The journey may be (a bit) longer, but you'll get there

If you do your job, and you do it well, you will still get ahead even if you don't get to the office at dawn and stay until your wastebasket is emptied. Your own biggest enemy may not be your boss, your meeting schedule, or the pinging sound of your e-mail inbox. Instead, it may be the little voice you're hearing that warns you'll be penalized for going against the grain—you know, pursuing that radical wish to see your kids for dinner.

When (and if) there is a cost to leaving on time or cutting your hours, it's worth it. Just ask the experts—the parents who've been successful doing these things.

"It does have a cost," says Henry, a law partner who decided to work a four-day week when his child was small. "The peace of mind you get from doing things like everyone else." But, he adds, "It was the most wonderful decision I ever made. It gave me the magic of being with our daughter and being more involved than most men get to be." (His wife rearranged her schedule to work four days, too.) Senior colleagues— men—took him aside and said, "You're doing the right thing. The rest of us will lie on our deathbeds wondering why we spent so much time in the office." Decades later, Henry heads a practice for his large firm.

You may worry that in addition to being viewed as "different," you'll also get docked on the promotion and salary front. But actually, while you may pay a small price, in the end things can even out—if you stay focused on the goal and continue to perform. Economist Robert Drago at Pennsylvania State University surveyed over 4,188 academics at 507 colleges and universities to explore the costs of using family-friendly policies (and signaling a commitment to family). How *much* did family-oriented academics pay in career terms? About one year on the tenure clock—on average, these people got their professorships about one year after peers who did not make use of these policies. The parents we've met who readjusted their hours say the same: The price for saying no to 24/7 is surprisingly small and often negligible.[18]

Shirley Tilghman, now president of Princeton University, has had a long career as a pioneering research scientist in the field of molecular biology. Her work at the National Institutes of Health on the cloning of the first mammalian gene is considered groundbreaking, and she's made numerous important discoveries in the fields of human genetics and biochemistry. She is also a mother of two now-grown children, whom she raised while working hard to advance in a field where few women make it to the top levels. Tilghman says she avoided late-night "macho" labs, noting that the extra hours on the job "are mostly spent socializing."[19]

"I chose to go to a great company but not one with an eighty-hour week," says Laura, who started her career at IBM and later ran several start-ups. "I said, 'Okay, I'm gonna have my children, and I'm going to try to build my management credentials in an environment that would be conducive to making that possible.'" Laura notes that a lot of her peers took Wall Street jobs but found that "business has a macho culture that's not even productive. But that's not the culture in every place. If you know that there are better cultures out there, you can make a point of looking for a culture where you can have a family and succeed."

"I took a financial hit for cutting back my hours, but I thought it was fair and worth it," says Don (another law partner), who lowered his hours by about 25 percent after his last child was born. "I really wanted to get home by 6:30 p.m. so I could read to her." Don later took his hours back up to the normal range at his firm. "Now, I probably work ten percent less than I did before we had kids," but he says he's still regarded as a high performer. How much more smoothly would your week go with just a 10 percent margin of added time? A nice picture? According to one Catalyst study, dual-career couples don't want radically less time on the job—they just need a few extra hours per week to get things in order.

"I have always seen work as a hairy monster at my front door," says Henry, the lawyer who worked a four-day week. He loves his job, but he says, "You have to slam the door to keep it out. Lots of people don't see it that way. They're slaves to the hairy monster. They think, 'I can't say no or I'll get fired.' That is the unexamined attitude that keeps people from controlling their work."

Do the math: pro-parent is pro-profit

There are jobs that need huge numbers of hours (at least for a time): being CEO, launching a product, running for office, stopping a forest fire, saving a patient. In some jobs, you get more money or promotions the longer you work. But, interestingly, some of the country's most successful law firms—who compete on "billable hours"—are on the cutting edge of getting hours under control. Paradoxically, it's all about profit.

Lawyers are doing better math than most of corporate America and quantifying just how much it costs when women who are active parents quit. And there is good reason for that. Young lawyers are leaving firms in record numbers—more than 75 percent of associates quit within five years, and work hours lead the list of complaints.[20]

What does this cost? The price is $1.5 million for every ten declarations of "I quit"—and that's the low estimate. Experts say turnover costs one to two times the quitting person's salary. Bosses, peers, administrators—they all drop what they're doing to take over work that's left undone, find a replacement, and scramble to figure out what knowledge and contacts are walking out the door.[21]

Women are now 70 percent of all CPAs so there's no lack of supply, but allowing women to take half the big-firm leadership spots will take an attitude shift. In her book *Mass Career Customization*, Cathy Benko says we need to mainstream the idea that careers can move forward in many ways—not just the single way that leaves scarce time for family. Benko, vice chairman and chief talent officer of Deloitte, LLP, points out that people who use flexible work arrangements suffer some: Only half think these arrangements will work and all say they have no idea how working differently will alter their promotion track. "We need to replace the career ladder metaphor with a career lattice—where, from time to time, you take a step sideways but don't fall off the structure entirely."

Change comes slowly, and a lot of managers start by saying, "Wow, we can't do that," Benko told us. "But this is becoming a cross-gender issue. Some of the Boomer-age male partners at Deloitte have said to me: 'I want this, too.' So I think a lot of people, men and women, want to be able to explore dialing down and dialing back up. If we can mass-customize M&M's, why not careers?"

"MODIFIED HOURS"? MORE MOMS AT THE TOP

George is a senior partner at a large midwestern law firm that has made impressive gains retaining talented female lawyers. At George's firm, women have been roughly half the new hires for many years. But the ratio of women fell to 29 percent at the senior associate level, the group considered for partner. And the share of female equity partners, as in many large law firms, seemed stuck around 13 percent. "Two-thirds of Phi Beta Kappa are now women," George said. "Women are half of the law school students. We see this as a matter of institutional survival. We want the biggest brains and women represent the largest part of the talent pool. Women comprise fifty-two percent of our senior associates—they are sticking around in dramatically higher numbers. And the ratio of women in the partnership is edging up, too—now eighteen percent.

"We had tried a lot of things before that had not worked," said George. "We realized we needed to get very granular, to figure out baby steps that would actually work." For concrete advice, the firm looked to the Project for Attorney Retention (led by Joan Williams, the University of California law professor). The biggest change: a "modified hours" program. The firm calculates that attorneys can be profitable working at 75 percent of "standard" hours. So "modified hours" lawyers pick a percentage down to that floor for a two-year, renewable period. Many partners feared that there would be a rush of lawyers opting for shorter hours. But four years into it, fewer than 5 percent of the firm's attorneys have chosen modified hours. They include some female partners and one man. As George says, "It has had a disproportionate effect on the number of women who are choosing to stay. They now know 'if I need it, it's there.'"

What about the fear that people working different schedules are a big administrative burden? "That's crap and wrong," says George. "One of our colleagues said, 'Hey, I need my associates working on my case one hundred fifty percent of the time,' but then another male partner pointed out, 'None of us have any associate working for us full time—each associate works with multiple partners so actually all of our associates work part time from the perspective of any one case.'" Lawyers with modified hours know there will be times they have to surge—to work more than their percentage on an important case or to meet a tight deadline—but that they will get those hours back. Seeing how lack of clarity derails many retention efforts, the firm put out FAQs and formulas to make the program transparent. "We did not want to leave this program to the vagaries of the judgment of an individual office manager," says George. Instead, two active partners oversee applications and make sure managers across the practice are effective using the program to keep talent at the firm.

The goal itself is not reduced hours. The goal is to have a critical mass of women partners in a reasonable period of time, to get women evenly distributed across the partnership so that women's issues are institutionalized as firm issues. "Making these programs work is a matter of management discipline," says George. "The question is how you enforce discipline in your top management." Beyond modified hours, George's partners have taken a number of other steps, like placing women in key governance positions—leadership of practice areas, business cultivation, the compensation committee (female retention impacts partner pay). "We think it's possible that the leadership of our firm could be forty percent women in ten years," says George. Can your employer say the same?

FOCUS THEIR EYES ON YOUR ACHIEVEMENTS—
NOT YOUR HOURS

How do they do it, these people who win in defiance of round-the-clock work demands? Even Jack Welch, GE's former CEO, concedes, "Most bosses are perfectly willing to accommodate work/life balance challenges if you have earned it with performance. The key word here is *if.*" MentorNet's Carol Muller puts it another way: "Many jobs are really demanding but you deserve to be evaluated on what you accomplished, not how many hours you were behind a desk. When you know your job well, you find efficiencies and reap the gains. You get to decide whether you turn that gain into more money or more time."

"I don't sit quietly and do e-mails when I come in to the office. I use that time for things that need to happen face-to-face," says Susan, the engineer who parlayed her long tenure at her firm into the right to work from home three days a week. "I definitely spend time managing my manager—letting him know what I'm doing and what my results are. But what it really comes down to is getting good products out on time and on budget."

A woman who'd worked full time for a large security firm decided she wanted to work four days a week when she had children. Her boss didn't like the idea though she'd been a strong performer for many years. "I'll make you the same money in four days as I did in five. If that's not true, the deal is off," she told him. Outperforming her peers in fewer hours, she proved her point and her boss got what he wanted.

Producing a lot gives you leverage to work differently—so does producing something unique. So specialize. An employment lawyer we talked to made herself an expert on an obscure part of the federal code. She's the go-to person for that at her firm, and her knowledge brings in a lot of business. She'd be hard to replace and her partners know it. So she gets latitude to do her work when and where she wants. A 2006 study of women on Wall Street found that successful women were those who were expert in a specific technical niche—their results were quantifiable and clearly attributable to them.[22]

If you're the only person who still knows how your firm's creaky accounting system works, if you're the one who got your nonprofit the biggest grants, you have unique value, and you can call more of your own shots.

How confidence beats the clock

When we are young, we think we're doing a good job if we do exactly what we're told. A lot of people never graduate from that way of thinking. Your job is to do what's needed, which is often different from doing what's asked for. But you have to take the risk of making those judgments yourself.

Many 50/50 dads told us stories showing how a little gumption has always gone a long way. Ed, a successful physician, worked in a large practice when his children were young. "When the kids were in preschool, we had a car pool and, several days a week, I picked up. Back in the 1970s, all the other drivers were women—I was the only man," says Ed. "I'd race out of my office at eleven-thirty, get the kids home, and be back downtown at one. I did this for four years and I was never late for the kids and never late back to the office. I never made a point of saying what I was doing and no one asked. I found it amusing and was proud of the fact I was able to do it."

Shelly was an associate at a large law firm for most of her career. When a judge said, "I need this brief tomorrow," Shelly had been trained to say "Absolutely." The result: She and her colleagues would toil all night to meet the deadline. At her new, smaller firm, she saw her partners would simply say, "Your honor, we need five days." The judge would agree, clients were fine—and her firm was just as profitable. "When you convey to your clients that you are 24/7, you train them to abuse your time," says Shelly.

No matter where you work, you can do this, too—it just takes courage. As one working mom said to us, "If I'm asked to do a meeting that conflicts with something important at home, I simply say, 'We're not available then. How about Tuesday?'" (Gumption alert: Listen to your male colleagues—how do you think they find so much time for midweek golf?)

Vicki, a salesperson, told us this: "When I was more junior, I did whatever my customers asked. I thought I was doing a good job for them by just hopping to it. But then you realize that clients, people in general, aren't good at telling you what they really need. If you want to be great in sales, you have to probe, to figure out what's really key for the customer and what's not. That often gives you a chance to give a better result with more control over how and when you work."

"I get as much done as a person working fifty-five hours a week," says Meg, who runs a strategy team for a Fortune 500 company on about ten hours less than that. "I schedule twenty-minute meetings. People know that they have to be quick because I'm on to the next thing when time's up." When others ask her to come to their meetings, she asks them to articulate their goals for the meeting and then asks, "Do I really need to be there?"

"I move to end meetings. I keep things short. I drive for conclusions and demand clarity. 'By when will you have that finished? Let's decide now,'" another working mom told us. "Before I'd let things work themselves out. I don't have time for that now."

"Become dispensable," advises Robin Wolaner, who ran several businesses at Time Warner. In her book *Naked in the Boardroom,* Wolaner writes, "At some point in [your] career or particular job, if you have to work a lot of hours either you don't know how to delegate or you are in a business that's not healthy enough."[23]

Use your clout to change the culture

Trish had been working only a few years when she went part time, rising steadily through a tough organization. Trish says, "People on my team get different kinds of opportunities working with me. When I'm out on Fridays, I let them take over and junior folks get much more exposure than they would working for someone else.

"'Oh, I had no idea you worked part time,' other managers here would say to me—they were shocked. I had a high-profile job and the perception is that you can't do part time in a job like mine. But now that's changing," says Trish, who has also helped a number of her direct reports go part time. "It costs a lot when people who have expertise leave. You go for months trying to hire someone, and then it takes frankly six months to get the new person up to speed and adding value. Turnover at our company is about eighteen percent, which is in line with our industry. In my group, attrition is less than five percent. You gain more than you lose when you let people work part time. In my experience, someone working and getting paid eighty percent is usually producing about ninety percent as much as their full-time peers—they tend to be high performers and very effective with their time."

"If you are a manager and you talk about balance but you don't do it yourself, you don't have a lot of credibility," says Meg, who leaves at 5:15 each day. "I manage fourteen employees and I've recruited a lot of great people to my team. Women really like it," she says of her commitment to work efficiently so that she—and her team—can leave on time, "and most of them aren't even married. Men are surprisingly admiring of it."

Susan has led successful engineering teams for almost two decades. "I have a top-performing team because it's been steady for years—no one has left voluntarily for a very long time." Why? "People like working for me. When there's a new task, I ask myself, 'Does it really have to be done? Is there someone else that can do it?' I think there are win–wins—something's not a good use of my time but it's a great growth opportunity for someone else in the company. If you always ask yourself, 'How can I have the biggest impact on the company in the most efficient way?'—that's a valuable question for every employee to ask whether they are parents or not."

Enlist the real men: How active dads turn the tables on 24/7

"A lot of people talking about family values are the same guys running the companies that make valuing families virtually impossible," says Doug, the psychiatry professor. Worse, as a female executive points out, "A lot of senior men make such a wreck of their families they don't even want to go home. And they dictate the rules to the rest of us who want to do right by our kids."

If work were a democracy, the 24/7 mess makers would be voted out of office. Dual-career homes are now the single largest group of families in the workplace. Factor in single-parent families and you have most of the labor force.[24] In a referendum, pro-parent reforms would win in a landslide.

We can't evict the 24/7-ites by recall, but we can populate leadership with people more like ourselves: moms who are fully engaged at work and dads who are fully engaged at home. When there are enough of us speaking up together, we can build a new model of productivity and help people who represent us move higher, or we can move into management ourselves. "Revolution needs to start from the top," says MIT professor Lotte Bailyn, a pioneer in work/life research and author of *Breaking the Mold*. "If those with the most power—both men and women—demand change, organizations and social institutions will have to respond, for the benefit of all."[25]

In 2000, a study polled over one thousand key executives at big companies like Citigroup, Marriott, and Dow Chemical to learn about work/life patterns and success. All respondents were at the top of their firm, reporting directly to the CEO or to the CEO's direct reports. "How many times in the last year have you put work before family or family before work?" the survey asked. Turns out, 32 percent of these hard chargers give family life equal priority with commitments at work—they are not work-centric or home-centric. They are "dual-centric."

Who are these leaders who prioritize family equally with their work? "Dual-centric people were as likely to be men as women," says Ellen Galinsky, who developed the study. "They work five hours fewer per week. They are more likely to take full vacations." Most surprising: Dual-centric executives feel most successful in their careers (more than even work-focused men).[26]

"A lot of people are supportive of family in theory but they've never done any of this themselves so they don't know the subtlety," says Carol, who worked at the same big accounting firm as her husband, Eric, while their kids were young. "Eric was actively there doing his part at home, rather than just talking about it, even when he had a leadership role in his practice," says Carol. Eric not only set a better tone in the group *he* ran, he also helped Carol triage her own workload. "When I was managing partner, I would say yes to too much. Eric was great at helping me say no," Carol recalls. "I would overcommit and Eric would say 'you need to say yes to half and no to half.'"

In 2007, Gary Newman and Dana Walden became chairmen of Twentieth Century Fox Television (part of Rupert Murdoch's famously pro-profit NewsCorporation). Newman and Walden had served together as presidents of the studio for a decade, thanks to a boss who saw that two (complementary) minds were better than one. Sharing this top job made Newman and Walden far more productive—and more available to their respective families. When Walden's child broke an arm, she could get to the emergency room and let Newman take over for the day. "I have a greater freedom," Newman said, "to be a participant in life."[27]

Working full bore no longer guarantees a job-for-life, a raise, a bigger bonus, or a promotion. It does guarantee that a father won't see his family much. As more working moms find ways to stay in the workforce, and as more dads get hooked on the benefits of being equal parents, we can stop viewing 24/7 as the path to glory and see it for what it is: a big waste of time.

The 24/7 chink: A weakness you should exploit

The hairy monster that is 24/7 has one weakness: It needs warm bodies to stay alive. You and your spouse can choose to feed the beast—or starve it. "It's getting harder to populate our jobs with only workaholics," says one high-level executive who cut back his hours for a while when his kids were young. "I talk to clients all over the country—whether they are plant managers or executives, people in mainstream America are running around like crazy and have no time to see their families. At some point, people say 'enough.'"

In 2001, Neil Patterson, CEO of a software firm called Cerner, sent a scathing e-mail to his managers: "The parking lot is sparsely used at 8 a.m.; likewise at 5 p.m.... NEVER in my career have I allowed a team which worked for me to think they had a 40-hour job. I have allowed you to create a culture which is permitting this. NO LONGER..."

Patterson warned that the parking lot would be his gauge, that it was to be "substantially full" on weekdays at 7:30 a.m. and 6:30 p.m. As for Saturdays, he expected it to be half full.

Someone leaked the e-mail to the press and Cerner's stock tanked. Investors saw Patterson's call for longer hours as what it was: a weak form of management and a sign there might be other trouble at the firm. You may not be ready to blow the whistle like the Cerner employee who hit "forward," but recognize that you—and your husband—can advance the ball by bringing 50/50 to work with you (and taking it home again, at a reasonable hour).[28]

" 'Nobody's here at ten p.m. anymore, they leave at seven—or five!' That's what the older men at my lab said ten years ago when the young men started going home to their families," says Carla, a mother of grown children who leads a medical research team at a large institute. "The young men I work with have wives who expect them to share—to take care of the kids and the meal planning."

Carla's male peers grumbled a lot. "But they couldn't do much about it because this was true of virtually all our young people—men or women," Carla explained. "I'd say to these men, 'Look, I have kids and this is what they're going through, too. The old days aren't coming back.' And that's a good thing."

A better workplace: It all starts at home

When you and your spouse are both in charge of making money and caring for your kids, you find the confidence to tame the hairy work monster. You'll give each other a great gift: perspective. Men are less likely to get swept away by the 24/7 storm when a working spouse provides ballast. When you share responsibility with your spouse, patterns emerge that stop that monster in its tracks, because you simply can't do 50/50 and work 24/7.

Chapter Six

It's Not a Fair Game—but You Can Improve Your Odds

"Lots of women just don't *like* their jobs. They don't find work as rewarding as their husbands do. When they become moms, these women cut back." We encountered this refrain often in our research. So we asked a lot of moms who quit just how it was they came to like their careers less. They didn't start out that way. Women we talked to leapt into their first jobs with the same gusto as their male peers. But slowly their excitement for working dimmed. "I didn't like the culture." "I didn't fit in." "It wasn't rewarding."

We know what these women are talking about; we've had moments when we felt the same way. And as managers, we've spent many hours counseling female peers fighting the same malaise—a slow-growing realization that something doesn't feel right.

Credit for their work seems to go to other people, they don't feel included. Yes, our male colleagues have their issues with work, too. But the frequency and scale of these challenges for women is greater. Because most employers claim to run on meritocracy, women have a hard time seeing what the problem is. The discontent piles up. And when the stress of new parenthood comes, it gets even harder for women to gut it out and keep working.

Biases remain in the workplace for everyone who is different. Social scientists show that both men and women suffer from an inability to see the talents of women as clearly as we see those of men. If you're looking for a job as a waiter, hand in a résumé with a male name and you are 50 percent more likely to get the job than if that same résumé has a female name. If you're a woman musician, you are far more likely to get an orchestra job in a blind audition with a screen.[1] Across the spectrum of jobs, the research is clear: Few bosses can measure performance as cleanly as our teachers or coaches once did. We like to think that things like revenues, sales, patients seen, hours billed are equivalent, but they're really not. Students get the same test; athletes the same ball. But at work, the picture gets a little murky when you think about how clients are allocated, who gets resources, how office politics work, and so forth.

"Yeah, it sucks," a female boss said after listening to Sharon's list of things that felt unfair at work, "so what are *you* going to do? Give up, or get in there and do your best to fix it?"

For us, when the odds feel uneven, it helps to remember how much the people we love win from our jobs. Our husbands gain control of their lives and don't have to make up our lost earnings by working more hours. Our kids get dollars for college and the chance to see a proud mom. We win, too, by showing ourselves that it can be done.

Recall that studies show that when women are 25 percent of an applicant pool, they are more likely to be negatively evaluated. But if women represent more than one-third of a group, they will be seen favorably as often as men are.[2] More women need to stay in the hunt to reach critical mass where it counts—in good jobs where we have clout enough to make work a fair game.

THE GENDER TAXES (WORSE THAN FICA)

If a man and a woman leave a starting point at the same time, with the same destination, driving the same kind of car, can't they arrive at the same time? They would, except that one of them keeps pulling over to pay little tolls while the other car drives right on by. Women get hit with extra costs—"taxes," as we think of them—just for being women. Some of them don't matter. We spend more time and money on our hair than men do; someday we'll worry over wrinkles while men go without sunscreen. That's just life (and gravity), and a few minutes lost in front of a mirror won't crash your career. But the taxes we'll discuss here do matter and most affect all women, whether or not they have kids. Added together, these taxes deplete morale and make it harder for women to stay the course when children enter the picture.

Some of these taxes are levied by others, but many are self-imposed. And it's easy to overlook these tariffs or believe they don't apply to you. But once you can spot a Gender Tax, you can do something much more fun: Give yourself a tax break.

Each of the seven taxes we discuss below has at least one loophole. Find it, and you can free yourself to enjoy work more.

The Little-Me Tax: "No really, you take it, I don't deserve it."

Even strong women—as in pro-athlete strong—can get sideswiped by the Little-Me Tax. Beginning in 2006, players at the U.S. Open were allowed to challenge judges on a limited number of questionable calls, thanks to video replay. When a player challenged a call, the video supported the player's view about 30 percent of the time. This held true whether the player was male or female. So all players had a strong incentive to challenge calls: 30 percent of the time they got back a point that they had otherwise lost. You'd think every player would make use of the right to challenge. But here's an amazing example of unforced error: Female athletes, women engaged in one of the most important competitions of their professional lives, challenged calls half as often as men did.[3]

Maggie Neale, a professor of negotiation at Stanford Business School, uses this story to illustrate female fear of taking what's called "interpersonal risk." Neale notes that women often prefer to keep their heads down and work hard (believing that eventually the boss will notice). Women worry about appearing "demanding" because they don't want to risk being disliked.

This means we often don't embrace our own power—even when we clearly have it. Peninah Thomson, executive coach and author of *A Woman's Place Is in the Boardroom,* observes that even at very senior levels, women can be excessively self-deprecating. "We describe it as the 'little me' syndrome," Thompson says, describing women who succeed in their jobs. "It's almost as if a woman doesn't quite believe her job (even though it may be at the highest level) can really be a serious, 'big' job—simply because she's doing it."[4]

Men don't seem to have this problem. They may be capable of holding the door open for you, but don't act surprised when they walk past you and grab hold of something you thought was yours. Kelly was an editor at a large publishing house. "I was sitting in my little cubicle and fuming. A nice guy named Jack was taking over the big windowed office I'd wanted for years," Kelly told us. "I told a female colleague how I felt, that based on tenure and performance that office should have been mine." "Why are you wasting your time talking to me?" the woman told Kelly. "You should have said something earlier. Don't blame Jack. And don't wait for someone to hand you the prize you want. Because they won't." Kelly knew her colleague was right.

Tax Break #1: Keep score for yourself and share the results

It's easier to speak up for yourself when you know how valuable you are. When you see the success of the 24/7 guy who spends Saturdays brownnosing the boss, it's hard not to get psyched out. You might even start to wonder if Mr. Brown Nose isn't really more useful than you. If you've just had a child and feel like you're dragging, your self-confidence can plummet, even if your results are as strong as ever.

In her book *Naked in the Boardroom,* former Time Warner executive Robin Wolaner advises, "Since most bosses are woefully bad at praising your achievements, you will be a much happier employee if you judge yourself—rigorously, but pausing to note the successes…learn to be your own evaluator, and find the benchmarks to know how you are doing, even when your boss won't tell you."[5]

If you take the time to calculate your "points," you'll either learn you have work to do or that you should be proud of the value you add. You'll know where you stand. And you can stop paying the Little-Me Tax.

Margaret Heffernan, a woman's business expert, describes a female Microsoft employee who cleverly tracked her own worth at work. Each week, she logged what she'd achieved in a notebook. So before her review each year, she could see for herself all she'd accomplished—and walk into her boss's office with the confidence that comes from having facts and figures.[6]

Sharon had always worked in her firm's New York headquarters until she transferred to the company's San Francisco office. "You want to stay on the radar," a very successful woman told her. "Get to New York every six weeks and see your division head when you can. Have three bullet points—two big pieces of business you've done, and one request for something that will help you do more business. You'll be giving senior people information they don't have, you'll focus them on how much you're producing, and they'll be more invested in giving you what you need to be successful."

It's up to you to do your own "accounting." You can apply this advice to virtually any workplace. In every job, some types of work get you more points than others and knowing your metrics always helps: the number of patients seen, grants won, or crimes solved.

As another female executive told Wolaner, "Never look to the left, never look to the right. Look at your own career. If you're doing okay, you don't have to give a shit about anyone else. Tend to your own business and you'll do fine."[7]

CRYSTAL CLEAR:
What *Real* Meritocracy Looks Like

Lehman Brothers hired Jack Rivkin in 1987 to turn around a failing research department. In three years Rivkin's team was ranked number one in the industry, stunning rival firms.

While Rivkin was driving his group's epic rise, an even more astounding story unfolded for the women who worked for him. When Rivkin took over, 20 percent of his research analysts were women and very few had high standing in their field. Three years later, in the same year Lehman cracked the number one spot, the women on Rivkin's team were flourishing. Not only had Rivkin attracted more women to the team but *80 percent* of the female analysts were recognized by *Institutional Investor* as tops in their field. What's good for women is good for excellence, too: relentless focus on objective results. (Side note: When Rivkin retired, Lehman's research group slid back to number 12, women fell to 11 percent of the team, and none achieved industry accolades.)

Transparency—the ability to *see* how you are evaluated next to everyone else—helps a lot. "Anything that he could, Jack wanted to measure," said one of Rivkin's analysts. "Number of calls, trading commissions, written reports, client visits. But there were no secrets. The numbers were out there for everyone in the department to see."[8]

Metrics and clarity are even more important when people work nonstandard hours. Don, a lawyer, says his firm hands out a spreadsheet where every partner gets to weigh in on what every other partner makes. That leaves little room for private agendas on what constitutes commitment. "If your billings drop and it's related to a leave, I've never seen anyone penalized for that. We know it's a temporary issue. Our system handles personal choices very well."

A woman who runs her business with three other owners says, "Among the partners we know which of us brings in the business and the revenue. We also very carefully figured out how much of a cut we'd take for reduced hours, etcetera. But I realized that the young people in our office didn't know this. They think when a senior person is working less hours, that they are getting away with something. So I sent out a memo on how it worked and everyone seemed happier."

"What is good for women is good for all employees," according to Catalyst, the research group. This includes skilled line managers and practices "that are objective, competency-based, open, and inclusive."[9]

We all want to work in a place that's fair. It's not just that it feels good. As Rivkin showed, it helps us focus on what we really need to produce (so we can waste less time trying to impress our boss with things that are irrelevant). Meritocracy motivates us to be our best selves.

The Girl Scout Tax: "Don't worry, I'll take care of it."

When we were young, we wondered why the Girl Scouts visited the elderly and learned macramé while the Boy Scouts built cabins and got dirty climbing rocks. These days, the Girl Scouts spend more time building skills and taking risks, yet we still put a premium on the "goodness" of girls. We communicate to girls a host of things they "should" be: nice, neat, well-behaved. These are fine virtues, but why do we make them a bigger priority for our girls than our boys?

Kara, an executive at a large bank, hosted a mentoring lunch for women and was enjoying the discussion on cultivating clients and closing deals. Then, a younger VP raised a different kind of challenge—holiday cards.

"The guys in my group are all slobs," she complained. "Every year we send out holiday cards and lots get returned because no one checks the mailing list for accuracy. Our secretary doesn't really know the clients so she can't help that much. So I spend a good day's worth of time going through it myself. I can't believe the guys just don't care about this stuff." Two other senior women had one simple answer: Don't do it. If the guys can't be bothered, let them live with "return to sender." "No client ever pulled their business over a missed season's greetings," one said firmly.

The VP's tale got Kara thinking about herself. "How can it be that housekeeping habits from home, like sweeping up for the boys, have made it into the workplace? I had to ask myself, am I much better? My male peers never deal with deferred maintenance—they're out doing business with brakes that don't work, until they crash. I'm the idiot who takes the car in for quarterly maintenance. And because I can't stand seeing people who report to me crash, I take their cars in, too. How much time do I waste providing infrastructure—housekeeping!—because the guys think it's not their job?"

Studies show women are, in fact, looked to as the merry wives of the workplace. Female employees are often assumed to be "happy to help" and this may be one place where a can-do attitude is not in your best interest. At Columbia Business School, professor Frank Flynn studied how these expectations play out. Flynn engaged the employees at two companies to find out what women win (or lose) from their image as willing helpmates.

Flynn found that women were more likely than men to be asked for favors and were more likely to grant requests for help. When the recipients of help were asked how "indebted" they felt, they appreciated the help of women less than the help of men; people felt entitled to female help, it was taken for granted. Worse, the more "agreeable" the woman seemed, the more the value of her help was discounted by the person she assisted (as if they assumed "she just *likes* to help"). In fact, women who were rated as less agreeable were more appreciated when they provided help, and so were men.[10]

The bottom line: We do our daughters (and sons) no favors when we support the belief that "women are happy to help."

Tax Break #2: Let someone else take notes, even if his scrawl is terrible

It's hard to go from being Miss Congeniality to all but hollering "Get the %*&! out of my way!" but sometimes the demands of working motherhood force you to focus on your own needs and those of your family.

The key skill: Learn to say no. If you *must,* say "no, thank you," when asked to do things that take you away from your core job. Beware especially if requests come to you because people think you are "nice" or "have good taste." When she was starting her career, Sharon spent many weeks one year organizing a conference for her boss. Tracking guest lists and name tags by day, Sharon had to work into the wee hours of the night to make deadlines on her regular client work. The next year, her boss left her a note: "You did such a good job last time. Can you run the conference again this year?" "The girls *do* always get stuck planning the menu," a male peer told Sharon sympathetically while when she voiced her frustration.

Sharon walked into her boss's office and said, "Hey, on the conference, I have an idea." "What is it?" asked her boss. "Well, I'm swamped working on two big projects for you and this seems like a great job for Cole," said Sharon, referring to a freshly minted PhD who had just joined their group. "Cole's not staffed on anything yet and running the conference would help him meet people in the firm." Sharon's boss looked confused. "But Cole has no social skills," he said. "Then running the conference is perfect for Cole—he'll have to learn." Sharon's boss smiled broadly. Cole ran the conference, Sharon got to focus on money-making work, she lost nothing from saying no—and maybe gained a few points for pluck.

The next time your boss comes over with a big smile and a bad assignment, say, "I know who'll do a wonderful job" and point to the guy in the adjoining cube.

The Gal Pal Tax: "She's sooooo nice . . . I really like her."

Out soliciting business for her consulting firm, Randy met with the sole female executive at a company. The two women had an efficient discussion for twenty minutes. Then Randy's prospective client stood up, thanked Randy for her time, and left. There was a good chance Randy would get some new business since the meeting had gone well. Yet Randy felt let down. She realized she'd been looking forward to sitting down with another woman, but there'd been no friendly banter, no female bonding.

Then a question occurred to Randy. Would she have had such high hopes for warm conversation if the meeting had been with a *man*? No, she concluded. We accept abruptness from men but not from women—even if they are saving us time.

There is nothing wrong with wanting friendship from people we meet in our jobs. Sometimes, the relationships we forge at work become friendships that get us through. But women don't help each other (or themselves) succeed when we demand more "friendliness" from female colleagues than we do from male ones.

After getting promoted, Peggy heard that the younger women saw her as "scary" because she didn't spend a lot of time socializing with them—chatting, going to lunch, sharing personal information. She was a little surprised. Peggy had mentored lots of young women and she thought everyone knew that. "Do I go to the office to focus on my work, or hang out and tell my life story?" Peggy says. "I was trying to get my footing in a big new role. I had to stay afloat if I was going to be of any use to any of those young women—or myself."

"Treading the fine line of appearing competent, ambitious, and competitive, but not at the expense of others, is a tall order," psychologists at Rutgers University point out in a 2001 study. As in other research, participants demanded "niceness" from women in a way they did not from men they were evaluating. Seeing the scale of this tax, the study's authors noted: "Individuals who believe women should be nicer than men undermine women's ability to achieve economic parity."[11]

Tax Break #3: Familiarity breeds acceptance (you needn't be "ladylike" to be likable)

Howard is a successful entrepreneur in Silicon Valley. He started his own software company, worked at Apple Computer, and now serves as a partner at a venture capital firm. Howard's career is described in a business school case study that reveals how he uses his "vast personal and professional network" to achieve his professional goals. Leveraging his "outgoing personality," Howard builds relationships that help him do deals and give him a reputation as a "catalyst" and a "captain of industry." Students who read about Howard rated him as effective, likable, and someone they would hire.

Howard does not exist, but Heidi—Heidi Roizen, a venture capitalist and veteran of the microcomputer industry—very much does. In 2006, Columbia Business School professor Frank Flynn and his colleague, Cameron Anderson at New York University, wanted to test how much someone's sex matters in the way they are perceived. Flynn and Anderson changed Roizen's first name in the copies of the case study they gave to one class and left her as a woman for the other class.

How did students rate Heidi versus Howard? While they saw Heidi as equally competent and effective, students felt Heidi was significantly less likable and worthy of being hired than Howard. Why? Students saw Heidi as more "selfish" than Howard—though she was described as identical in every way (except that she'd been a cheerleader in high school and he'd been a football player). Flynn calls this a "backlash" effect. When women don't behave in a way that conforms to standard gender roles, even young people can get uncomfortable and they express their discomfort by viewing the woman negatively.

So once again, we find that being female is pretty expensive. But here's a loophole in this perception tax. Flynn and his colleagues ran another experiment on the relationship between the students' *familiarity* with their peers and how they rated them. When raters didn't really know their classmates, they responded just as the students in the Heidi/Howard experiment. More assertive men were seen as more hirable while more assertive women were seen as less hirable. But when students were more familiar with the person they were rating, the "backlash" vanished. Assertive men and women were seen as equally hirable. And more assertive women were more likely to be hired than their less assertive female peers (just like men).

You'll do yourself a favor if you help male colleagues see you as a person. And it's often easier to find common ground if you start by asking questions. Ask men about their childhoods, their pets, hometowns, vacations, cars (if you drive a fast one, can change the oil, or have ever caught a marlin, definitely bring that up). The quicker you become familiar, the lower your tax bill will be.[12]

The Pocketbook Tax: "About this raise you want..."

The numbers and reasons vary but the bottom line seems set in stone: Men outearn women, even when they do the same work with the same results. In 2003, the General Accounting Office, the federal government's audit arm, published an exhaustive study and found that for every dollar a man makes, a woman earns 80 cents. Still—even after accounting for differences in hours, experience, and job types. Without those adjustments, women made 56 cents compared to men over the period 1983 to 2000.[13]

In paycheck terms, this means that if a man makes $50,000, his female peer takes home $40,000. Factor in raises (when men start at a higher base salary, the number of dollars they get for a 5 percent raise is bigger, too) and do the math over the course of a career—it's over $664,000 more for the man.

"Women do not realize the enormous price that they pay for gender wage discrimination because they do not see big bites taken out of their paychecks at any one time," economist Evelyn Murphy told members of Congress in 2007 in her testimony to support the Paycheck Fairness Act. "Little nicks in a woman's paycheck—a promotion delayed because she is pregnant and her boss guesses (wrongly) that she intends to shift to part-time work, a sales call she misses because her boss assumes she has gone home to cook dinner for her family, a request she makes for reassignment to escape a sexual harasser, leaving the bonus she earned behind—all add up, over time, to become $700,000, $1.2 million, $2 million."[14]

Don't we have rules against this? Turns out women often rely on a statute that is the Model T of discrimination law. In 1963, Congress passed the Equal Pay Act to protect female wages. "The law's teeth are not very sharp," says Jocelyn Samuels, who works on pay equity at the National Women's Law Center. "In too many cases, courts have said that if there is not a man doing your exact job, the Equal Pay Act can't help you," Samuels told us. Bogus labels alone can be enough to render this law useless. For example, one manufacturer paid female "light assemblers" less than male "heavy assemblers." Though industrial engineering experts said the men and women were doing substantially the same work, the court said the jobs were not equal—so women could legally be paid less.[15]

Most women end up seeking protection under the broader Civil Rights Act. Under that law, you don't need to find a man who is doing your same job. You can win with evidence that you'd likely make more were you a man. How do you show that? Pointing to comments that denigrate or stereotype you is one way. This is why most suits tend to focus not on paychecks but rather on egregious conduct.

"First comes love, then comes marriage, then comes flextime and a baby carriage," a manager at Novartis, a major pharmaceutical company, allegedly said, explaining why he was not eager to hire young women. The employees filed a class-action suit.[16] The good news is that there are fewer and fewer employers dumb enough to say these things. The law has succeeded in shrinking the volume of insensitive comments but not the pay gap. Muzzling loose cannons is just not the same as getting women paid fairly.

No one wants to think they're the victim of discrimination. We start our careers in a position of relative equality, so it looks like the pay problem might, in fact, be gone. Studies show that in certain industries women are paid just as well as men starting out. But by age 45, a mother of two will have earned about 25 percent less income over her career than her female peer with no children. Even if the mother works full time, the numbers look similar.[17]

If you don't think the Pocketbook Tax exists where you work, you're probably not looking. Even in nonprofits, women executives make 18 percent less than men do, according to a 2005 survey.[18] Women in the clergy fare no better. Comparing male and female pastors at midcareer, a recent big study found that men were almost twice as likely to be in charge of larger congregations (with larger paychecks).[19]

The Commercial Real Estate Women Network (CREW), a national networking organization, surveyed nearly two thousand real estate professionals. CREW found that even women with more than twenty years of experience were more than twice as likely to be in the bottom income bracket compared to their male peers (even those with twenty years of experience). Only 16 percent of long-tenured women had taken big breaks from work (compared to 11 percent of men), so the difference wasn't due to time on the job. And the pay gap was worse for more junior women. But despite the pervasive problem, the majority of survey respondents thought women were paid no differently than men.

To close your own wage gap, you need to open your eyes—and ask for more more often.

Tax Break #4: Show me the money—help me help you

The law won't save your paycheck and you can do something more effective than going to court: negotiate. Yet, most women don't. Studies show the majority of men negotiate salaries while only a tiny fraction of women do (remember who challenged line calls at the U.S. Open?). Though men and women are now offered similar starting salaries, men negotiate even their first-year pay while most women do not.[20]

Linda Babcock, Carnegie Mellon economist and coauthor of *Women Don't Ask*, offers a way around this. At Harvard Business School, Babcock found that male MBAs were negotiating up their salaries about 6 percent and their bonuses a whopping 19 percent relative to their female MBA peers, after adjusting for field, functional position, and geography.

Then Babcock and her colleagues intervened. They gave students of both sexes the same information, including data on the range of salaries and bonuses that alumni had negotiated. Armed with numbers and the knowledge that they *could* ask for more, these women bargained their way to parity. The male/female pay difference vanished.[21]

How do you begin if you don't even know that "more" exists—and you have no friendly researchers helping you out? You can find an employer with highly transparent benchmarks for promotion and pay. Or do something easier. Go talk to the guy down the hall. Not your boss, not your peer, but the guy just ahead of you. Knock on his door late in the afternoon, when meetings are done. "You know, I want to buy a house. I'm trying to figure out when I can do that. What should I be making five years from now?" You don't have to ask him what *he* makes. You're not asking for a raise (and he can't give you one). You're just fishing. Go fishing a lot and you'll have a whole basket of data—estimates of what your job should pay, now, tomorrow, next year.

When Sharon started on Wall Street a female colleague told her, "I don't care what they pay me. I really enjoy the work." This seemed like a dangerous attitude. Sharon got an invitation to join an interesting book club—all males, all working in finance, all ex-wrestlers. Sharon joined, knowing she'd get some insight, if not the literary kind. "Hey, did you hear what he got paid last year?" "No, no, I heard it was more." These guys reveled in trading inside information about something very legal—who makes the most, who pays the most, and how you get it for yourself. (Many employers stipulate that compensation data is confidential, but no one's going to fire you for asking how you'll pay your mortgage.) Between trawling your hallways, talking to friends, and using the Internet, you can find out plenty.

Sometimes, you need only ask the person you married. Lydia and her husband, Rick, both worked in TV, starting at the same time at the same base pay. Rick's salary jumped annually while Lydia's rose slowly. "Rick moved around, talked to headhunters, and knew his market value. I'd stayed at the same place. I worked just as hard but, by the time we were ready to have kids, Rick was making fifty percent more than me. I knew I had to fix the problem before I got pregnant since things just weren't going to get any easier," said Lydia.

Rick gave Lydia some coaching and an article from *Esquire* magazine on how to ask for a raise. "It was advice I'd never heard before, on what language to use, how to make my case, how to document my accomplishments and show how I was contributing to the bottom line," said Lydia. "When I went in to see my boss, I was sweating but managed to ask for a sixty-percent raise." Lydia got 40 percent—in a time when 4 percent increases were standard. "I still find it ironic that I got my salary on par with a man's because I read an article from a men's magazine," said Lydia.

If you and your husband work in different kinds of jobs, he can still help. Even if you're a zoologist and he's the police chief, your spouse is tapped into that famous club you're not part of, the one for "boys." When your husband values your career success as much as his own, he'll help you gain admission, and you can get the salary scoop that is sadly missing from the ladies' room.

Men often complain that women depress wages when they enter a field in large numbers. As a male photographer told us, "Women keep the fees down for all of us." If we want to be part of the club, we can't always (however unknowingly) be the low-cost provider. Your male peers will likely cheer you on if you help boost their pay scale, too.

GIRL-POWERED NEGOTIATION

Plenty of research shows that women aren't nuts for ducking when negotiation is called for. Studies say that women often get a harsher response (and lower results) when they ask for more.[22]

But don't despair, there are loopholes here, too—some that take advantage of sterotypes others have about us (and that we may have about ourselves).

Backlash against women decreases when women frame their requests in a way that says "help me to help *you.*" Stanford's Maggie Neale tells the story of a female professor who got a job offer at another college that would mean a lot more money. The woman went to her dean and said, "I really love working here. I want to stay but I have this offer and I can't turn down such a big raise. Is there anything you can do to help me?" The dean didn't want to lose a talented professor. So while he didn't match her offer, he got close. Make sure to focus the other side on what *they* win by giving you what you ask for.[23]

Neale observes that women create a better mind-set for negotiation when they consider all the other people who benefit when they bargain well. Your raise isn't merely for you, it's for the good of your husband and kids. We can tell you, as bosses of plenty of men, guys don't think twice about trotting out their need to support a family. Neither should you. If you approach a negotiation as a parent, you come from a more powerful position (think lioness with hungry cubs to feed). You aren't just asking for yourself; you are asking on behalf of the community you support—your kids and spouse, perhaps even aging parents.

Neale also points out how much women gain if they can see negotiating as something they are perfectly good at. In a recent study, men and women were "primed" before a negotiation game. One group was told "good negotiators are tough, competitive, bold"—words typically associated with men. The other group heard that "good negotiators are good at listening, they problem solve and try to see the other point of view"—qualities often considered "female." When female traits were the ones touted, women in the group not only outperformed men, they performed just as well as the men in the group who were primed to believe men were "naturally" better.[24]

The Fanny Grab Tax: "Is that an iPhone in your pocket, or are you just happy to see me?"

A rookie at her new law firm, Joanna was working on a pro bono litigation. During a routine phone call about the case, the male lawyer representing Joanna's opponent lowered his voice. "So, what are you wearing?" (He wanted to coordinate outfits?) Joanna knew the guy had an agenda. She just didn't expect *she* was on it.

Didn't sexual harassment of women go the way of the typewriter? Unfortunately, some classics never go out of style. Lucky for us, we started our careers just when employers got religion about stopping day-to-day butt pinching. For the most part, we heard about the wild times secondhand (from traumatized assistants who survived them). What's left today is the residue from the bad old days. We've gotten some tax relief, but the "fanny grab" ethic—the idea that sex belongs at work—remains. And it will cost your daughter much more than your son.

" 'You're too beautiful,' this man told me. 'I can't work with you,' " a young woman in her twenties told us. "I was assigned to work on a project with this guy, we were going to have some late nights to get it done, and he was freaking out. I felt like saying 'I'm married and not remotely attracted to you. Get over it.' But instead I went to the assignment manager and said I needed a different project."

Most of the things that go on today don't get reported to HR—women like their jobs, they don't want to make waves, and frequently the "issue" is just a man playing bonehead. Sometimes it's totally innocent, he doesn't really want to jump you, and he is oblivious to the fact he's making you squirm. "The problem is that, when there are not enough women, you get some weird behavior," says Kathy, the physicist. An older male scientist at her lab who seemed to genuinely respect her work felt moved one day to pet her hair.

"I wear braids to keep my hair out of my face," says Kathy, who was presenting in a meeting and sitting next to this man. Suddenly, "He just reached over, grabbed my braid, and said, 'Your hair is really pretty.' I don't think he meant anything by it. But do I reach over and stroke a man's face and say, 'Gee, I really like your mustache'?"

We're all in favor of the male sex drive, particularly when it's focused on a loving wife (with matching drive) in the comfort of the conjugal bed (behind the locked bedroom door). But what's the point of revving male libido at work?

EMC Corporation, the $40 billion heavyweight in data storage, is facing suits from its female employees. In a 2003 complaint, one EMC saleswoman tells how a stripper appeared at a large company meeting in Chicago. The female employee stepped out of the room as her "boss licked the whipped cream off the stripper's breasts," according to the *Wall Street Journal.*[25]

In mostly male fields, low or no-clothing jollies remain common enough. Managers are still signing off on expenses from Gigi's Go-Go for reasons that may be clear to them. One EMC boss, in fact, said a woman was unfit for a job because she wouldn't "smoke, drink, swear, hunt, fish, and tolerate strip clubs."

Beyond flare-ups in sexual tension, there's a steeper tax that women pay—limited access. There are plenty of great male bosses who, like their female peers, know that work is not about sex (unless you work for Playboy Enterprises). But do some senior men ever hesitate to take promising young woman under their wing because they fear what others will think? Do they happily invite young men out for dinner to talk shop, but stop cold if the employee is female? Do young women balk at approaching senior men for guidance, or even the casual banter that makes work life more fun, because they worry they could be seen as flirtatious?

If you think moms are exempt from the Fanny Grab Tax, think again. Yes, as women gain clout in their careers, predatory men are more likely to avoid them and look for more vulnerable prey. But we have been surprised at how this sex-in-work tax never fully goes away. One fortysomething mother of two told us about her experience trying to start her own business. After months of work, she found that her lead backer wanted something from her that was unrelated to turning a profit. She felt so betrayed, she dropped her plans and returned to work she knew.

When we don't have clear rules (like "put a lid on it"), even women bosses get confused. Carolyn, trying to build up a new client base, was taken aside by her female manager. "Listen, you're doing too many dinners with male clients. Someone's going to get the wrong idea." It's not ambition or enthusiasm for the job that women lack—what women lack are connections with male mentors, colleagues, and clients, and the opportunities that come from them. And it's all because no one tells men to focus their pheromone detectors where they belong—at home, not at work.

Tax Break #5: "Rated-G"—making work culture healthy for general audiences (particularly you)

The business rationale for sex-at-work is something we don't understand, though we've both tried to be broadminded (Joanna went strip-clubbing with her clients once). We've learned that channeling sexual energy is an age-old employment problem and that armies found a solution long ago: saltpeter, putting something in the mix that takes sex out of the system.

Earlier in her career, Sharon covered a hermit-like portfolio manager who would not do business with her team. According to hearsay, the hermit only did business with people who took him to "gentlemen's" clubs. Sharon and her teammate Doug joked about who'd get stuck "entertaining" the hermit with some topless dancers. But it never got to that. With enough persistence, meeting repeatedly over milk and cookies (yes, really), the hermit broke down and became a good client for Sharon and Doug.

"This is an industry of men—building design and construction are mostly guys," says Larry, who runs a team of architects in Texas. "Sometimes what's said out on building sites can be really off color and it's often directed toward women. Sometimes it bugs me a lot and I can't imagine anyone who wouldn't be offended. On a lot of construction sites, there aren't any women for long periods of time so no one really thinks about it. It doesn't mean it's okay but it's an issue we need to talk about openly."

Larry finds that women often bottle up how they feel when the culture starts to wear on them. And then something sets them off—a random event that might not even be sexist. "Be direct," Larry advises.

"Don't go to HR or the boss, tell guys to their face. You can say, 'Hey, what's that on your desk?' and be funny about it. You have to do it in a way so guys don't feel threatened but you are making your point."

A G-rated workplace is just good business, and making that point often helps. "She can say, 'We're a growing company, we want to be more professional, we want a good image. I understand this is just the industry. There may be an appropriate place for photos and jokes like that but it's not on our sites, not in the work environment,'" says Larry.

Larry's rule of thumb: "If you can say it to your mother or your wife, it's probably appropriate. If you can't, don't say it here. Most guys will say, 'Yeah, that's cool.' Sure, some men will get mad and say they don't want to change but they are the minority."

The Velvet Glove Tax

Stanley has been a senior executive in media companies for most of his career. "I make it a point to balance my management teams half women, half men so we get diversity in dialogue—in line with the audience we address," he says. "But too many women don't get real feedback from their bosses," Stanley points out. One reason is the very way we talk about managing people. "'I kicked *his* ass and I turned *him* around'—that's what you say when you're responsible for improving someone's performance," says Stanley. "How many people say 'I kicked *her* ass and I turned *her* around'? No one. We're afraid women who work for us will get upset or consider the use of time-tested theatrical 'tough boss talk' a personal threat."

Absent from the football team or other all-boy experiences, most girls grow up unfamiliar with this part of the game. "You know, just as many men have cried in my office as women," he says, "but the men go wash their face and move on, you never talk about it again. It's like getting in a fight on the basketball court, you clip a guy with your elbow in practice, he hauls off on you, you get pulled apart and then shake it off and play again, you don't stay mad or you can't play well."

"Women can be really embarrassed for crying at work," Stanley says. "They keep apologizing for it. It makes upsetting a woman feel like a bigger deal. They reference it years after you have forgotten about it, and then you feel badly all over again. So if you see tears coming in a meeting with a woman, you're likely to back way off rather than let her have the full dose of the medicine you'd give to a man. Many women on the rise don't get honest feedback from anyone," says Stanley. "When you go to management meetings and people complain about a woman in your group, you just say, 'I've talked to her about it. We're working on it.' And it's just understood that it will be a long, indirect—and probably unsuccessful—discussion."

The same laws that aren't fixing women's pay problems are doing something else effectively: stopping a lot of men from saying things that might help women succeed. "Every single individual in the workplace should be protected from sexual harassment and discrimination of any kind, our humanity should ensure that," says Stanley. But the way lawyers and HR departments deal with discrimination complaints leads to some unforeseen (and unfortunate) consequences.

"Very early on in my career I was advised, 'When you do a review with a woman, particularly one not living up to her promise, leave your office door open so your secretary can overhear the entire conversation,'" says Stanley. "Tell me, how much real candor can you offer with your door open and your secretary listening? You just say as many nice things as you can and end the meeting quickly. You are more worried about your own safety than getting that person to rise to her own potential, fearing she might not like the way you say it."

Should women toughen up? Or should men tone it down? We think there's lots of room to meet in the middle. But the real answer is there should be one standard for what's okay and everyone should know it. Is it: "You screwed up. Your sales numbers suck. If they're not up ten percent next month, you're fired"? Or: "I know you tried hard. But it seems like things aren't working very well for you. Maybe we could get someone to help you improve over the next year"? Smart leaders can spend fewer dollars on legal fees if they clearly communicate a single standard.

"Every senior male executive I know has been threatened with discrimination charges regardless of the goodness of their track record. Charges almost always get dropped or negotiated, but the process itself is terribly embarrassing, even debilitating. Simply having an employee who says you're not paying her enough because she's a woman can get you caught up in the company's HR vortex. There's an investigation. You tell your wife—at first she's sympathetic, then she starts to question you herself. Your own wife! It's a nightmare," says Stanley.

"I've seen it make cynics out of a lot of men who started out very differently—men who championed diversity in the workplace and in their hearts truly embraced egalitarianism and meritocracy."

Here's one place where men and women are completely on the same page: We all want clarity. When women and men agree on a common language at work, we can throw out the velvet gloves for good.

Tax Break #6: Straight talk and the single standard

Maybe the biggest kindness we can show other women is to give them the unvarnished truth. As a business school dean said to us, "Men are very clear with other men about what the standards are. Women need to do that for other women." Like Stanley, a lot of men think (with some cause) that they can't be the messenger.

Sharon had been working for almost seven years before she got her first female boss, Amy. "Russ does not like you, Sharon," Amy told her, "you need to get on that right now." Amy minced no words, pulled no punches, and gave Sharon the best feedback she'd gotten in all her career—cumulatively. Amy demanded high performance but let every member of her team, including Sharon, know clearly she was on their side. "You use too many words," Amy told Sharon. For years, Sharon's male colleagues had obliquely said the same thing, noting that she was "articulate" and "gave a lot of detail." But Sharon saw these comments as semi-compliments, not the complaints that they really were. Thanks to Amy, Sharon got on the brevity bandwagon (though she frequently falls off it).

Tessa hired a new woman for her team, a mother of two young children. Two days into her job, the new woman's colleagues came to see Tessa. "You know, she's going around the office telling everyone she has a cold. And she wants to know which of us gave it to her," the coworkers said. "I can't afford for my kids to get sick," the new hire told Tessa when confronted about this odd behavior. "No. What you really can't afford is for everyone in this office to think you're a nut," Tessa told her. The new hire has since become a star performer.

A male boss told Vickie, "A lot of people have a hard time giving feedback. When you come out of a meeting, right on the spot, say, 'Hey, please tell me two things I did well and two things I could do better.'"

Related to ending the Velvet Glove Tax is blunting the effects of the iron fist inside—the double standards that are not at all soft on women. The research group Catalyst points out that the "corporate environment includes built-in assumptions that create a higher burden for women than men" and that "women need to join together to bring these assumptions into the open."[26]

Kara recalls sitting in a hiring meeting a few years after joining her firm. She was the only woman in the room. Her top pick was Gwen—the person with the most relevant experience and best grades from school. "But Gwen giggles a lot," objected one of the guys on Kara's team. "It's not professional. I think we should hire Chuck." Kara thought for a moment and asked, "Did Chuck tell you what he did last night before his interview?" "Yeah," said Kara's teammate, "he said something about being chased out of a bar at two a.m. by a bunch of models who thought he was cute." Kara let that sink in. "Okay, I get your point," said Kara's colleague, "Chuck doesn't win points for professionalism either." Both Gwen and Chuck got offers, and both did well at Kara's firm.

"My job is holding up a mirror and helping women see how talented they are when they stop feeling that way," said a woman who's spent many years at the same company. "We hire a lot of smart women from good schools, everyone expects a lot from them: And these women expect a lot from themselves. When they don't get ahead at the same pace as their male peers—and this is way before kids—these bright young women get demoralized. They don't feel they can say anything in public: They think they'll sound like whiners. But they do need a place to vent, so they can get it off their chest and move on."

The I-Don't-Know-How-She-Does-It Tax: "You're *still* working?"

No one ever asks men these questions: "Are you going back to work after the baby is born?" "Wouldn't part-time work be a better option, given your family?" "Do you realize how much more time you'd have for your child if you quit?" Fathers are never grilled by friends or coworkers on how they plan to "make it work." They're never told, as Joanna was, "My wife really loves staying home. You'll come back after your maternity leave, but you'll probably wind up wanting to stay home, too." Only women get the flurry of questions and second-guessing (more than ever, it seems, as women who "opt out" continue to be misunderstood when they quit).

On the verge of taking a new job, Sharon met with a lawyer to discuss the terms of an employment contract. "You know," he told her, as they ended their meeting, "I'm not sure you really want to do this. I don't know any couples where there are two real careers and the kids turn out okay. My wife was a lawyer but she quit." Sharon had asked the lawyer for his opinion on a contract, not her life. But this man felt no qualms about lurching into personal advice (all while charging hourly). And out of the blue one day, a male friend told her, "Sharon, don't you know that combining a demanding career with being a mother—well, it's so passé?"

Like many parents, these fathers were absolutely certain that because they themselves had failed to maintain dual-career households others would surely fail, too. "If *we* can't figure it out," they seem to be saying, "then you can't either." On the popular show *Grey's Anatomy,* a senior male doctor regrets neglecting his family by working too hard. So this man decides to "protect" another doctor (a working mother) by denying her a big promotion, wanting to save her the personal losses he has experienced. He doesn't want to believe that he did a lousy job managing his own work/life situation; instead, it's easier for him to believe that failure is inevitable.

From our own lives and our interviews, we've seen many ways women (and some great men) create fairness where it's lacking. But unwritten rules lead too many people to give up. At those moments when your stamina is flagging, just remember our favorite line from Ari, the talent agent on the Emmy-winning show *Entourage*: "You fire a guy, you create a rival. You fire a woman, you create a housewife."[27] Don't prove him right.

Tax Break #7: Bridge the gender gap, end the Gender Taxes

Remember the boys who ran around kindergarten making rude noises? In our Girl Scout days, we felt pretty confident that *we,* not the boys, had the more useful skill set. But then a lot of rude-noise makers grew up to be the men running companies, branches of government, universities, hospitals, and the corner grocery.

Maybe the real way to achieve meritocracy is to drop the girls-versus-boys superiority contest, to stop reveling in how we are different, and focus, instead, on common interests and the many ways men and women are, in fact, similar.

Janet Hyde, a psychologist at the University of Wisconsin, is the author of an article titled "The Gender Similarities Hypothesis." She has analyzed the massive body of psychology research on gender differences and has concluded this: Almost 80 percent of these studies show that gender differences are small. However, she observes that "over-inflated claims of gender differences carry substantial costs in areas such as the workplace and relationships." When we insist on being gender extremists, we can't see how easily we can escape a polarized world of male versus female standards at work (and at home) and meet in the middle.

One study that Hyde examined looked at gender and aggression. Participants played a fighter pilot computer game, defending home base and attacking enemy targets by dropping bombs. Half the participants were asked personal questions, wore name tags, and knew they were being observed. The other half were told they'd be entirely anonymous and unobserved. Who dropped the most bombs? In the observed group, men were the standout aggressors. But in the anonymous group, women dropped more bombs than anyone—even more than the men in the observed group. So, if we know that someone's watching, we play to our stereotypes. Are women as ambitious or competitive as men? While the expectations about men and women muddy the picture sometimes, the facts say we're more alike than different.[28]

But while research has proven that we can widen the gap by keeping our differences front and center, it has also shown that we can close the gap if we want to. For example, one study looked at the subset of math tests where male scores exceed female ones by the greatest amounts. The researchers showed that while the gaps were meaningful, they could also be closed with relevant training.[29] Hyde suggests we might refocus our attention on bridging supposed sex differences so that men and women can work together more happily. Good communication, decisiveness, nurturing, risk-taking: There is a single standard, a common list of qualities we all need to be effective workers and parents, whether we are male or female.

MERITOCRACY IS HARD WORK—AND MAKES US ALL BETTER AT WHAT WE DO

Not enough bosses understand how meritocracy and diversity are linked—if your workplace rejects people who seem "different," employees really are not competing on merit. Allowing diversity is a precondition for meritocracy. Absent this understanding, progress is slow. At a corporate conference on diversity, one participant asked, "What solution can you share for retaining women?" No hands, we are told, went up. "What is the actual evidence that diversity makes firms more effective?" another female executive asked us. "That it's more than just a nice-to-have or protection against lawsuits?" The good news is that there are good answers to these questions. The bad news is that so few people hear about them.

Meritocracy at the office takes a lot of work, including setting aside stereotypes, tradition, and precedent that block the way for all women. "There's a preference for self-similar individuals," Steve Jurvetson, a venture capitalist, explained to the *New York Times* in an article about the dearth of women in his field. Jurvetson says if you ask one of his peers what it takes to be successful, "you'll get a description that sounds a lot like himself."

"It's a logistics issue," he went on, stating that in his business there's just not the infrastructure to comb through lots of résumés. Attempting to diversify its talent pool, Jurvetson's firm has gone to the length of hiring an outside contractor to screen candidates.[30]

With the same goal, the University of Michigan launched an effort called STRIDE (Strategies and Tactics for Recruiting to Improve Diversity and Excellence). While one third of the PhDs in medicine and science were female, women candidates landed only 14 percent of the new faculty jobs in those fields. Five years later, women win more than 30 percent of those jobs at Michigan.

What got STRIDE such fast results? Just the facts. "There's been a lot of really, really good research . . . these studies are fantastic," said a male hiring committee member. STRIDE enlisted a team of senior faculty—five male, three female—to educate the hiring committees, sharing in simple terms the sea of data that says women are held to a higher standard for hiring. We can learn two things from Michigan's dramatic success. First, numbers speak for themselves: Standard management training should include STRIDE's kind of objective data that helps all of us hold our bias in check. Second, progress toward meritocracy accelerates when men and women team together to make it happen.[31]

So what's the payoff from making all the effort and gaining more diversity? Higher levels of innovation and performance. While some studies say diversity may interfere with the speed of completing a standard task, if you need to come up with new ideas where you work, heterogeneous groups do better. Why? When there is little disagreement, no one is forced to think hard and explain themselves. Researchers say that when people deemed different join a team, they change that dynamic. Psychologically, "different" people, such as women at a conference table dominated by men, force everyone in the room to recognize they can't assume uniformity. Even the "good old boys" feel more free to dissent. There's more fresh thought, more useful debate, and stronger decisions.[32]

A fair game, real meritocracy, is what women need to happily stay at work. More women in boardrooms and more men in classrooms will bring better results to our economy and our kids. If we, as employees and bosses, embrace the three truths we've discussed in Part II, if we understand that meritocracy takes some elbow grease, if we know that the effort is worth it, we'll all know that getting to 50/50 is more than something that's good for our families, it's good for the world, too.

Part Three

The 50/50 Solution and How to Make It Yours

Chapter Seven

The Great Alliance: How Your Husband Solves the Work/Life Riddle

The mother-to-be was glowing in her last trimester, but when she opened her mouth to speak she exuded anything but inner peace.

"I don't know how I'm going to do it. I'm having my second child but where will I find time for the first? It's already hard enough with just one toddler. I need a good day care, but how am I going to pay for it on *my* salary? Or manage the commute, keep the house together, and have any time for my husband? I have a great job, but something has to give."

"I don't know how *I'm* going to do it." How often do we hear that from pregnant moms? How many times will she wake up at night, not because a baby is doing midnight flips, but because she's thinking about all the work at home and at the office—and all the people who've told her she won't be able to cover both fronts? Does she feel it's okay to ask for help from her baby-making partner, to tap that reserve of manly talent lying right next to her?

You can do many things by yourself, but getting pregnant isn't one of them. (If you adopted, did the man you live with sign the papers, too?) "I don't know how *I'm* going to do it"—if that's what you're thinking, hit the brakes hard because you're backsliding. Replace the "I" with "we" and you'll see a clearer path before you.

If you both value both of your careers, you'll build a life where you can both be breadwinners—you know that's good for your family. If you *both* see yourselves as *equally valuable* parents, you will build a life that allows your kids to know you equally well. Along the way, you'll learn to talk (early, often, and with as many jokes as possible) about all the crazy things that get in the way of 50/50 life, so that you'll get around them together.

THE 50/50 MIND-SET: FROM "I" TO "WE"

You start out in marriage with a noble intention: You will be partners in all things. Your jobs, your families, your leisure time—neither his nor yours will take precedence. It's a pretty easy bargain to keep when you're sharing the expenses and upkeep of that one-bedroom apartment or cozy starter house, taking turns grabbing takeout or whipping up Sunday breakfast, picking out a movie, folding laundry together while you deconstruct a difficult boss or plot out your next vacation. You work late, he works late, so you split a pizza for dinner and afterward he washes the wineglasses while you dry. And then—through extremely precise planning or the whims of Mother Nature—you conceive a child.

"We were young; we were smart; we were looking forward to the world of work...why did we get it all so wrong?" Michael Elliott, a journalist, started out in his marriage thirty years ago with a firm commitment to share family life and chores with his wife. In his essay, "Men Want Change Too," Elliott writes, "My wife and I...thought we'd have it all. We'd both have successful, satisfying careers. We'd share in our kids' upbringing and divide the chores. We were convinced that the world of stay-at-home moms and job-trapped dads had ended, oh, sometime around 1969."

Elliott says his wife "gave up a high-powered career as a government official to have children. Consciously trying to balance work and family, she took part-time jobs that in some cases were enjoyable but that never gave her the recognition or professional advancement that you get if you're in full-time employment. Meanwhile—first for fun, later because the extra income helped—I allowed work to take over my life." Their life became "nothing like what my wife and I imagined it would be," he writes. "It's not just women who are disappointed that modern life has not accommodated their various needs. So are millions of baby-boomer men who wanted their marriage to be a genuine partnership of equals."[1]

Elliott's story helps us see the compound effects of small-in-themselves choices. It's these *little* things that add up to one big result: a life that will or won't let parents stay equal. When you don't deal with the little things—the everyday demands that come with blending family and work—in an equitable way, if you don't share the task load fairly, you both risk straying from the path you set out on.

(Self-) perception is reality

While some men may need an attitude adjustment to do their fair share, women say it's often their own views that have to shift first. The key to how we are perceived by the men in our lives is *how we view ourselves.* As wives and mothers, do we make an assumption (or allow it to creep up on us) that it's our job to do most of the work when it comes to taking care of the house and the kids? That we are more biologically equipped or otherwise more capable than our spouses when it comes to these tasks? That we need to ask for flexibility in our jobs so that our husbands can continue to work as if they were childless? That our husband's career is more important to his self-esteem? If we buy into any of these beliefs, we're setting ourselves up for a division of labor that grows more skewed over time.

Who's on first: husbands, wives, or both?

We've watched many couples we admire give up the struggle to manage both careers. Listening hard, we realized that the women in these couples usually believe that a man's career goals come first. Mothers with promising careers stepped back so their husbands could go full throttle. "We just couldn't make it work any other way," they told us.

Women often fail to fight for their careers because of their desire to be a supportive spouse. Hanna, a CFO, was talking about quitting her position at a rapidly growing company. "My husband really wants to be on a fast track, he needs to travel two weeks a month to impress his boss, so I am essentially a single mom. I hate it but his career means so much to him." Hanna felt she should scale back at work because her husband's dreams seemed to demand it. Was she happy about it? No. But she was scared to ask him to rethink how he pursued his career goals to allow room for her own job.

Couples can conquer that fear and start talking if they focus on the price tag, how much it costs to pare back a wife's career. The landmark 2003 GAO study that we discussed in Chapter 6 found that the biggest reason women earn less than men is time out of the workforce, followed by fewer hours on the job. Even sanctioned policies like maternity leave, reduced hours, and telecommuting turned out to cost a lot in terms of future promotions and wage progression.[2] In 2005, a study in the *Harvard Business Review* showed that 93 percent of mothers who'd stopped working in professional jobs wanted to get back in. But if they'd taken more than two years off, these women faced a 40 percent pay cut when they returned to work.[3] What about staying current with part-time work? If you are lucky enough to find a part-time job, know that you'll earn 21 percent less per hour than your full-time peers.[4] Hopeful note: Many women who went out on their own as consultants (and chose to work part-time schedules) told us they made more per hour than when they worked full time.

We're not saying that these penalties make sense. But they will likely remain until there are enough women and committed men in positions of power to deal with the workplace issues we discussed in Part II. Couples are more likely to hold on to two work lives—and stay on a more attractive part of the time/wage curve—when they embrace the idea that both careers count.

Make no mistake—it can take guts for women to give their professional dreams the weight they deserve. "This job will make my career," Perry told his wife, Leslie, explaining why he needed to move the family from New York City to Minneapolis—the fourth move for his career in their marriage. Leslie, who was working for Johnson & Johnson, arranged to keep her job, part time, long distance. But after two years in Minnesota, Leslie suggested the family return home to Washington, D.C. Perry objected: "I earn more money than you, and I think we should stay a few more years."

Leslie began to add up the reasons things had to change. "I'd begged my husband to come home in time to read the kids a bed-time story," Leslie said, "and he'd replied he couldn't because of a meeting with 'someone really important' (as if we weren't)...I had been in a terrifying head-on collision with our daughter in the back-seat; when I called to tell my husband we were okay he asked if he could finish up some paperwork before he came to get us. It was sud-denly, horribly clear that he was oblivious to the reality of my life and what I'd given up for him. And I'd helped create this monster, by moving for him, by keeping quiet when he worked late month after month, by playing the role of supportive wife just like...my mother," Leslie concluded. "I was so furious that for the first time in our marriage I was speechless."

On the advice of a friend, Leslie took charge. She found her own dream job working at the *Washington Post*. The starting salary wasn't huge, but her savings from Johnson & Johnson would allow her to rent her own place and pay for child care in DC. "I didn't break all our china or stage a three-hour fight. I told my husband it was his turn to move for me. And then I shut up," says Leslie. Days passed. Then, "One morning at breakfast Perry cleared his throat and said, 'I've been thinking about what you said about moving back home. I guess you're right. I'll start looking in DC right away.'" Leslie Morgan Steiner went on to edit the bestselling anthology *Mommy Wars,* and Perry has found rewarding work, too.[5]

How committed is each of you—to your job?

A lot of the 50/50 couples we interviewed had never talked explicitly about staying equal. But almost all of them shared one thing: a hus-band who is devoted to his wife's career. Whether their wives worked for little money or lots, 50/50 men said similar things when they talked about their wives' work. "Her success is our success." "She comes home with so many things to talk about." "Her job makes her happy. That's good for our family."

Many 50/50 men don't start out that way. They become enthusiastic about what their wives do for a living because their wives are excited about their work, too. "If I continued in the traditional way that I had been brought up," said Frank, an entrepreneur, "I'd have thought: *The man provides and the woman does not. If the woman has a career or not, it doesn't really matter and it's secondary.*" But that all changed when Frank met his wife, Vera, now a partner at a large law firm. "I'm very competitive—on her behalf," says Frank, a big backer of Vera's career and full participant in family life.

But a lot of men have not made Frank's conversion yet. In Chapter 4, we told you about the 2004 study of high-achieving professional women who "opted out" of their careers—the one in which 84 percent of the women said they would rather have stayed. Then why did they leave? Two-thirds of those women cited their husbands as a key driver of their "choice" to leave the workforce; many said their husbands "preferred" an at-home wife. Despite their often high incomes, these women saw their financial contributions as "secondary to their husbands' and/or unnecessary to family welfare."[6]

In our survey, one woman stated: "My husband and I have the exact same job and salary. I cannot say, therefore, that his job is less flexible than mine. Rather, he is less flexible *about* his job than I am about my (same) job. He feels that the demands of the job come first and that tasks at home are less important; I end up trying to balance them equally, which is impossible, but results in my treating the job as one of several demands on my time that I must balance regularly."

"A man's ego is an important factor," says Frank. "In the traditional setup, if I wanted to set up business dinners every night of the week to advance my career, I wouldn't worry about the effects on my family. I'd think *It's okay. My wife will cover.* If a man chooses an inflexible job and keeps that traditional kind of ego, the couple loses a lot of options."

But simply blaming the male ego can end up reinforcing the status quo. It may be that many wives don't make it clear to their husbands exactly how much their jobs mean to them. And if they have been affected by the workplace issues we discussed in Part II, they may have lost some of their own conviction about their careers. Research done by psychologist Janice Steil suggests a more constructive approach. Steil found that men and women attach equal importance to their own careers, and they are equally likely to believe family comes first. The challenge is what wives and husbands believe about *each other.* Wives, on average, overestimate how much a husband values his career while husbands underestimate how much a wife values hers. "There is no mal-intent. We just have these assumptions, sometimes outside our awareness," Steil told us. "Unless men and women sit down and discuss these things, it's easy to be guided by these unmonitored beliefs. So maybe the best thing a couple can do is open a dialogue."[7]

BUILDING A 50/50 MARRIAGE: YOUR GUIDE TO CHARTING A BETTER COURSE

No matter how many children you have (or don't have), the first step toward building a 50/50 marriage is the same for all of us: Talk about who will do what as soon as you can—and make it a lifelong discussion.

POPPING THE QUESTIONS
(NO RING NEEDED—THOUGH A SMILE HELPS)

"At our wedding, we read that Kahlil Gibran poem—about how love is letting each other grow strong and not standing in each other's shade," says Maggie, the ICU nurse, married to a 50/50 guy for eighteen years. "Things have worked pretty well because I married a man who shared my beliefs."

You'll only know what he believes if you ask. "But isn't it awkward to start a relationship with a lot of probing questions?" one young woman asked us. Maybe. But, in our experience, most guys (like women) want to share the way they see the world—and sometimes just helping men voice how they feel opens them to new possibilities.

- Tell me about couples you admire: What do you think they do well?

- How did things work in your family? What did you like or dislike?

- How old do you want to be when you have children? How many do you want?

- What was your dad like? How much time did you get with him? What will you do when you are a father?

- What are your favorite memories about your mom when you were little? What kind of a mother do you want your children to have?

- How much career success do you need to be happy? How do you measure it? Do you think your wife will want an equally rewarding career?

- If a wife makes less money than a husband, how should that affect how family chores are shared? What if the wife makes more money than the husband?

- How much money do you need? How much money would you give up to have more time for your family?

Sharon's father is a psychoanalyst. His dating advice to her: "Let people talk. They'll tell you everything you need to know." His other advice: "You have to kiss a lot of toads before you meet a prince."

So, after asking these questions, feel free to let a few dates hop away. And if you're already married, know that many 50/50 princes are made, not born, as many couples have shown us.

Redefining "I do"

"I do" is not merely the response you give before the ring goes on your finger. Ongoing negotiation about what "I do" and "you do" often determines the fate of a marriage.

Psychologist John Gottman, who has studied thousands of successful marriages, says that what counts in a relationship changes over time. Specifically, when you are dating, good relationships are defined by the number of good feelings the couple shares. Once you are married, something else matters more: how well you handle conflicts.

Dodging tough topics does not bode well for couples. Religious leaders have long advised couples to explore differences early and learn to resolve those conflicts. Churches, temples, mosques—they all offer premarital counseling on how to talk about the hard stuff constructively.

"How about Pre-Cana?" relatives asked the newly engaged Sharon and Steve, referring to premarital counseling from the Catholic Church. Sharon and Steve liked the idea, went an alternate route, and took marriage prep so seriously it became a bit of a family joke.

While they shared many values, Sharon and Steve came from different backgrounds and had some big differences to resolve. On their first date, Steve said he thought women were "naturally" more nurturing and should probably stay home for a few years as primary caregivers. Sharon's view was that any man she'd be willing to marry could equal her as a caring parent. "I want my kids to have more than one 'primary' parent—I want my husband to be my equal, a real partner," she told him.

After weeks of debate, Sharon and Steve found a bridge: two concepts they agreed on. The first: *What is natural is not necessarily good.* They'd both taken a college biology course where the professor had pointed out that murder, cannibalism, and rape exist and serve a purpose in nature, but that doesn't make them good. It is up to us, as human beings, to decide what parts of nature we deem good and what parts we'd like less of. The second: *Fair deals are better deals.* This idea came from a shared civics class: A social contract like a marriage will last longer if it serves each party equally well, if there are no resentments. So they came to share a goal: a marriage that gave them an equal chance to enjoy both their children and their careers.

"Is this *romantic*? Will it *work*?" friends asked. Egged on by the skeptics, Sharon and Steve found a marriage counselor and family lawyers to help them ask (and try to answer) the key questions. Q: "What if one of us makes most of the money?" A: "We're each still on the hook for half the work at home." Q: "What if one of us wants to stay home with kids?" A: "If we can afford it, we'll each have the *option* to take turns staying home. And we'll both have the *obligation* to return to work and make money." All this research became a multipage agreement. Steve and Sharon's bet? They'd find more long-term romance by getting on the same page, literally.

Did they think of everything? No.

Their agreement sits quietly in a file drawer, but Sharon and Steve still rely on skills they learned in their everything-but-the-kitchen-sink approach to marriage prep (see box on dirty socks near the end of this chapter).

A written agreement isn't for every couple. Joanna and her husband, Jason, started working on their list of premarital questions given to them by their rabbi.

Question 4: How much money can each of you spend without asking the other?

"If I want to spent a few hundred dollars on a dress," said Joanna, "that should be okay."

"How often?" Jason wanted to know. "How *many* hundreds of dollars? Why should *I* be okay with that?"

The ensuing discussion (fight, actually) lasted so long that they never finished the list of questions.

But it turned out that the hard questions for Jason and Joanna weren't about dresses and they weren't really apparent until they had been married a few years.

When Jason graduated from business school, he was really excited about the emerging world of the Internet and the companies he planned to build. Joanna was a not-so-happy second-year lawyer, not even sure that she would want to keep working after she had kids. So at the beginning of their marriage, Jason's career really did come first, in large part because Joanna was not passionate about hers.

But then Joanna left the law and rose to become a partner in a venture capital firm. She found she really *loved* her job, but that made things more complicated with Jason. When their daughter was born, she couldn't make it home each night at 6 p.m. to relieve the nanny. Joanna started to need (and want) to work later in the evening, so she asked Jason to take his share of early nights. In her old law job, Joanna had been willing to move her meetings when they conflicted with

Jason's. Now, the stakes were high and the work was fun for Joanna. If, on a given morning, they both had breakfast meetings, "I was less excited about being the one to accommodate," said Joanna. While Joanna's blossoming career put a strain on Jason's (a few male colleagues thought it odd that a *husband* might be the one to go home early), Jason really valued the fact that Joanna worked, and did his part so she could be successful.

Over thirteen years and three kids, sometimes it's Jason's career that comes first and sometimes it's Joanna's—but always there's the idea that they will both be active parents, each with an active career.

One couple we interviewed, Sara and Jamie, have now been married for twenty-three years. Their eighteen-year age difference caused them to talk a lot early on. "My friends were saying 'he's too old' and his friends were telling Jamie 'she's too young.' So there was more intensity in figuring out if this was the right relationship," Sara says. "We'd sit in the car talking for hours—'here's why this relationship shouldn't work.'"

Talking about why relationships won't work early on is, in fact, how to give yourself a better chance the union will work for a long time. "We have friends who've been married for years and they haven't talked about all the things we did in our first months of dating," says Jamie. Whether you are dating or toasting your tenth anniversary, what keeps a relationship vital (and fair) is talking about what's hard to discuss.

More romantic than roses: a to-do list

Get oil changed, buy swing for backyard, pay mortgage, assemble swing, buy milk, renew health insurance, fix swing that kids broke, plan birthday party, scrape out gunk in sink.

It may not be the stuff of a Shakespearean sonnet, but how you deal with these lists can strengthen a marriage, or punch holes in it. Chores and children make up most hours of a parent's married life. The tone of your family script depends on who gets which lines (and how many) off the checklist.

As unromantic as your to-do list may seem, focusing on how you divide the load is an act of love. Some women tolerate stepping over mountains of Legos and newspaper, but apparently most of us can't: When women start arguments at home, it's about division of household tasks 80 percent of the time. (We were surprised to discover that women initiate two-thirds of all divorces after age forty—perhaps they have spent their twenties and thirties mopping up too many spills.)[8] Couples therapist Terrence Real says, "Few women who back away from their needs manage to bury their resentment...And even if women try to accept and forgive, eventually passion drains away from the marriage." In his book *How Can I Get Through to You?,* Real says that young women today still capitulate too often and eventually resent it.[9]

Jill has two young children and an architecture business she runs from her home. "It was driving me nuts, I had so much to do and my husband thought he was so helpful. So we wrote down all the things he was doing for the family and what I did. There were five things on his list—and they were all important. But there were about thirty things on my list," says Jill. "My husband looked at my list and said 'Wow.' He just didn't realize how out of balance things had gotten. And then he took over a lot of stuff."

The ideal is to start out as equals and stay that way. The reality is that things change, and it takes a conscious effort to hold on to equality in marriage. Jobs are lost. Babies arrive. Raises are handed out. Houses get dirty. Go into married life with your eyes wide open, know that the power dynamic will likely shift from time to time, and be ready to rebalance the load so that it's fair for both of you.

As Terrence Real says, falling in love is spontaneous, but "staying in love demands craftsmanship"—and often some lists.

FAIRNESS 101

Myra Strober, Joanna's mother-in-law and a labor economist at Stanford Business School, teaches a popular class called Work and Family. One assignment asks the students to role-play with a ten-item list of everyday parental tasks. Pairing her students as "husband" and "wife," Strober asks each team to negotiate who does what on the list. Each "couple" decides if one person will do more, if outside help will be hired, if a task will be shared equally.

Before the students start allocating chores, Strober assigns each pair a different background for their imagined life. In some couples, husbands and wives have equal resources (e.g., jobs with similar pay); other couples have resources with varying degrees of inequality. Besides the economic scenario, Strober also tells each pair whether their relationship is "solid" or "shaky."

Strober gets her class thinking about how equality of resources, or lack thereof, shapes how task lists are split. For instance, when a wife earns much less than her husband she may feel that she should take on more child care and housework because she literally "owes" it to her spouse. Since her work at home has no dollar value, both husband and wife may begin to underestimate the worth of what she does—to take her contribution for granted. This can end up destabilizing a marriage. (Recall the study in Chapter 2: Even when one spouse outearns the other, marriage is more stable when the high earner keeps doing a meaningful share of housework.)

The shift, the drift, and the rift

While inequality can seep into marriage in many ways, the birth of children is the most common cause. Studies have long shown that infants are a marital stress test. Noted marriage expert John Gottman writes that women undergo a transformation "of values, roles, and goals" when they have children but that "only some men will go through an equivalent transformation and stay connected to their wives."[10] In their research, Gottman and his wife, Julie Schwartz Gottman, observed couples making the transition to parenthood over more than a decade. The Gottmans found that two-thirds of couples experienced a significant drop in marital quality in the first three years after a baby is born. (If you think it was easier in a more traditional time, don't—a landmark 1957 study found that 83 percent of new parents experienced some amount of crisis in their marriage.)[11]

A key problem is that men miss the boat and don't keep up with their wives on the journey into parenthood. But don't just blame the guys. Often it's their wives who pull up the gangplank and sail off without them. Women can either invite their spouses to participate as equals, or they can claim that women are born superior parents. In 1998, psychologists Ross Parke and Ashley Beitel studied three hundred couples to explore the impact of these kinds of beliefs.[12] "Women who endorsed the view that women are biologically better prepared had husbands who were less involved than women who did not. Most interesting: It was the mother's attitude that mattered most," Parke told us. Repeat: Your attitude is what *really* counts.

In Parke's research, a man who thought he was biologically equal to his wife was less involved as a father if his wife believed she was "naturally" better. The lesson is clear. If you want your husband's company in the odyssey of child rearing, you have to value *his* parenting views as much as your own.

In the 1980s, Berkeley psychologists Carolyn Pape Cowan and Philip A. Cowan tracked ninety-six couples over ten years as they made the transition to parenthood. They found that 92 percent of couples fight more about household obligations after their first child is born. Even in marriages where husbands wield dish towels and know how to vacuum, the wife ended up doing more of the housework when the baby came—there seemed to be a slide backward toward unequal roles at home.[13]

In a 2000 update to their research, the Cowans say declining job stability and less public money for family support make "the risks for marital strain even higher." Reviewing more recent research, the Cowans conclude that couples continue to suffer "without models of how to create a new kind of family they had dreamed of."[14] As Gus, a fortysomething father, told us, "There is a belief held by many people, an expectation that women are going to be doing the child care. And that means a significant break, if not a departure, from the workforce. I'm shocked as I look around at our friends and find that a majority have done that."

In our survey and interviews, being "transformed" was something mothers talked about—but some felt like they were "demoted." On maternity leave, the wife takes on more housework (she's the one at home) and more child care (she's the one at home). After weeks of training, Mom does develop some expertise and starts to believe she's better suited to run family logistics. She may decide she should cut back the hours of her workweek, setting up a tough cycle where she's ever more valued at home while her workforce value, the kind you get paid for, *deflates.*

But there was a way out of this. One group of study participants got coaching on how to talk about their unspoken expectations and hopes for family life. Among the control group that got no such coaching, 15 percent of couples divorced within three years of becoming parents. In contrast, none of the couples who were part of the "coached" group got divorced in that same period (more on the merits of outside help below).[15]

Creating an equal partnership

We want to be very clear with our women readers here. You may be the one with the stretch marks, or the one who stays with a baby in its first months at home. But the minute you start thinking about "*my* child" instead of "*our* child" you are setting yourself up to be in this alone.

The 50/50 mind-set means that you have an equal partner—and *treat* him as an equal. Really. No matter how many baby books you marshal to support your view, if the evidence does not sway your partner, remember he has half the votes. Let him cast them.

Joanna didn't think she was a fussy dresser. Yet, when her daughter was born, Joanna learned she had strong opinions about fashion, at least about the baby's wardrobe. Jason would take charge of getting their daughter ready in the morning but Joanna never liked his clothing choices. Joanna would criticize Jason for his efforts, take the baby back to the changing table, and redo Jason's work so their daughter wore outfits Joanna chose. "I'm not doing this anymore," said Jason after several months of this. "If you want to be the clothing director, be my guest."

Karen came home from a business meeting and saw her husband on the floor with their eight-month-old son, playing, and both of them were eating Honey Nut Cheerios. "What are you doing giving our son honey?" she asked in alarm. "Don't you know he can't have honey until he's one? I told you what to feed him. Why didn't you do that?" He thought, *I was having a great time with my son—until you got home.*

When you are working with a peer at the office, do you tell her how to do her parts of a joint project? You know to keep your mouth shut even when you'd like to offer some "advice." You won't be a very popular colleague if you intervene on her turf. She'll resent you (even if—particularly if—your way *was* "better"). And then she'll ask for a transfer. When husbands stop helping, that's what they're doing.

Marriage expert Joshua Coleman, the author of *The Lazy Husband: How to Get Men to Do More Parenting and Housework,* told us, "When moms have rigid standards, dads walk away from the bargaining table." In fact, research shows that women with perfectionist expectations have lower satisfaction in their marriages overall.

We know, very personally, that easing up is tough to do. Our feelings about our kids are stronger than any other emotion (and *that* may be both natural *and* good). Even 50/50 moms confess that it's an epic struggle to cede control. "The burden disproportionately falls on the woman," says one of our survey respondents, "maybe even by her own choosing."

Rose has a demanding job in TV and a deeply involved husband who handles as many diapers and feedings as she does. "When we are at home together we are equal, but when we go to work, I'm the one who tends to worry. Like when it's raining outside, I worry about how the nanny is going to get our kids around town. I make the doctors' appointments, Mark goes. I get the preschool application, Mark helps me fill it out.

"Mark would do more, but usually I want to do it. I want to be part of everything my kids do when I can. I guess it comes from the model of a family you hold in your head," says Rose. "I like to complain about how hard it is. But I'm not complaining about Mark. I'm just complaining about the strain on me."

How do you build a life that looks different from the one you knew growing up, where you feel good about yourself as a mom but let your husband enjoy the freedom to be a parent in his own distinctive way? This is a challenge for many of us.

"Having the right mind-set is really important," says Sara, who learned this when her husband, Jamie, retired from his career in sales to spend more time with their kids. "A lot of women say, 'Well, my husband helps.' What do they mean 'helps'? It means that the women still feel accountable. You really have to let go of ownership. If we tell men they have to do it our way, or correct them all the time, that's not going to work.

"When Jamie first started staying home, I was treating him like the nanny. I'd say, 'Here's the plan, go follow it.' Jamie just said, 'Wait a minute. I have my own way I do things.' I had to step back." We all need to embrace the idea—and encourage our husbands to remind us—that sometimes moms just need to get out of the picture. If 50/50 is going to work, when it's your husband's turn, you need to gracefully butt out.

Unless you're successful at fighting the "I'll just do it myself" urge, you have to make a conscious effort to give your spouse some breathing room, especially if he's as new to parenting as you are or if he's taking over a new task. You may intervene if the baby's diaper is slipping down to his knees, or if your husband mixes bleach and ammonia while cleaning the bathroom, but every time you correct your spouse's "errors" or criticize his way of doing something, you're dealing a blow to 50/50.

LET GO AND LET DAD

"Let go and let Dad." This is the motto we'd like to suggest to all mothers. To make 50/50 work, you have to remember that taking on more than your share as a parent (even though you're the mom) will skew the division of labor, interfere with your husband's experience as a parent, and shrink the common ground you have as a couple.

Resist the urge to take over and do it all (or most of it). Resist the instinct to be a control freak. It's normal (particularly among new mothers), but if you don't encourage and support your husband in his efforts to do his share, then you're undermining him and setting yourself up for a difficult solo journey.

Dad's way is the "right" one at least half the time

Care for inanimate objects is hard enough to split. The car—clean it weekly or quarterly? The dishwasher—pack it tightly, save water or load loosely, get spotless plates? But when a crying baby sounds the alarm at 2 a.m. or the school nurse calls the office about your feverish first-grader, it's far more emotional and you have to decide quickly who's on point.

If you haven't fully committed to letting your husband do half, these are the moments when it all goes wrong—when exhaustion or worry leads Mom to huff and say, "Oh, I'll do it." Women have a harder time sharing, either because they *don't* ask for (and therefore never get) help from their husbands, or they *won't* ask, because for whatever reason they think they'll do a better job (the "biologically better prepared" belief that Ross Parke highlighted in his study).

This attitude is the biggest 50/50 deal breaker. It doesn't matter if your spouse takes charge of all house-related chores; if you're doing all the kids' stuff, you've got some recalibrating to do. You know that school emergency form? List your husband's number first—and help the school know that Dad's just as much on call as you are.

"I think there is a female mother instinct," says Carol, a mother of two. "When your child is sick you feel like you *should* be there." That may be natural—but what is natural is not necessarily helpful, if your goal is to have a father who's fully involved with his kids. Fathers can comfort their children, too, if you give them the chance, as Carol did for her husband, Eric.

"Today is Mom's day for a big meeting," Eric would tell their kids when it was his turn to take over. Carol, who rose to partner at a national accounting firm, credits her husband (also an accounting partner) with helping her succeed at work. Many other women we've spoken with also are quick to point out that unless they'd asked—or allowed—their husbands to help with the kids, they could not have achieved as much in their careers.

"When our daughter was born, I'd get up at night to help Sara with the feedings," says Jamie, a former NFL player. "But when nursing was over, Sara didn't get up anymore. I'm a light sleeper and I'd be the one to hear our kids. So by the time the kids could walk, they'd show up on my side of the bed when they had a bad dream. It was very rewarding for me to have that connection with them."

Jamie's connection to his kids remains strong and healthy—they are approaching adulthood themselves now. As with many fathers and their children, this lifelong bond began simply enough, when this dad got involved with the day-to-day work of parenting.

"I think a lot of women are very persnickety about exactly how the child care gets done once they hand it over to the dad," says Joan, a journalist. In fact, Joan feels she's learned things from "stylistic differences" she once thought were her husband's parenting faults.

"I respond to every question my daughter asks. Paul will answer every fifth question—he skips the other four. 'Water, please?' our daughter would say, and Paul would wait until she'd asked several times. I'm like, 'But she's thirsty. That's terrible,'" said Joan. "Then someone said to me, 'You know, the second you give your daughter the water it's going to be something else she asks for.' And I started to see that Zoe didn't nag Paul the way she nagged me. Paul and Zoe have a very different dynamic and a good dynamic—in part because he doesn't pay attention to every little bit of minutia."

Even when you're convinced that your way is right, it often pays to keep that to yourself. "I'm the person who does the homework with the kids," says Kathy, the physicist. Her husband "lets the kids take homework to school without really checking it. But you can't micromanage. You have to accept how your husband does things or you end up doing everything yourself."

There's a range of opinion on virtually every choice in parenting, and your husband will sometimes be on the other side of the spectrum. Pacifier or no pacifier? Co-sleeping or separate bedrooms? Computer games or no computer games? The choices keep coming.

Some of them matter more than others—it's worth finding the time (and tone) to share views about schools and limits and friends and all the big decisions in raising kids. But in the end, you have to trust that you married a man with a good head who loves your children as much as you do. If you intervene when he's helping your daughter learn to read, or ride a bike, or resolve a conflict with a friend, he will stop helping. And no one wins from that.

Conquering Mommy Madness

As one father said to us, "I'd love to do more. But some of the things my wife thinks we 'must' do seem crazy to me." The best cure we know for Mommy Madness—that desire to be the "perfect" mommy that afflicts so many of us—is a healthy dose of input from Dad.[16]

Perfectionism and Girl Scout instincts don't help us enjoy life or excel at work. They certainly don't help us seem reasonable to our husbands if we have a gift for turning simple tasks into complex ones.

Worse, we often think we are "right." "My husband is useless, he gives the kids Cheetos." "He doesn't know their friends, or where we keep the school directory." "He cannot put the kids to bed on time." How often do we walk into conversations like this? "A lot of women *like* to think men are incompetent at home. It's part of female bonding—we even joke about our husbands in public and the men play along," one woman commented. "If a man questions natural female aptitude at work, he's likely to get in trouble. But everyone thinks it's okay to make fun of men for being inept at home. No wonder guys want to stay at the office."

In our own lives, we find our spouses have a gift for spotting a faster route. When we get a notice from school, like "Bake Sale on Tuesday," our first instinct is often "Let's go buy butter and eggs!" In contrast, our husbands say, "Let's go buy cookies!" What we moms often forget is that bake sales are to raise money, not to prove that you can operate your oven.

Sharon spent many days designing a multistep treasure hunt for her three-year-old's birthday party, until Steve told her it was overkill. "A three-year-old feels special having hats, horns, and cake. He'll have fun if you have fun—not if you're overfocused on your nifty treasure map." Sharon got the point, contained her inner impresario, and got a husband who does party invitations.

"I would clean the house before the cleaner. I used to cook dinner every night until my husband said, 'Why? Takeout is great,'" says Alexandra, the corporate executive with three kids. "It probably took me ten years before I realized that doing these things was not important."

EXTRA HANDS ARE WORTH EVERY PENNY

In our interviews, husbands were often more willing to get (or pay for) help to shrink the size of the home pie. When it comes to child care, 50/50 couples do the math differently. They don't ask if a wife's salary will cover the expense. They see these costs as an investment with big returns to the family over time.

Doug, a psychiatrist married to a scientist, says this: "You want to pay anyone to do anything you don't absolutely have to do so you can spend time on your kids and your work." Doug's kids are now successful adults and the strain of child rearing is over. But Doug notes that people aren't totally logical on this topic because they're uneasy about paying for things you could—in theory—do yourself. "Besides financial constraints," Doug says, "we have this pseudo-equality in this country—we're happy to buy takeout prepared by someone earning minimum wage but uncomfortable if we hire that person in our home for more money."

"You can't feel guilty about hiring help," says Carla, the researcher in her sixties. "Postpone other purchases—you don't need a bigger house or a new car to keep your career going. You *do* need some extra hands and you shouldn't feel guilty investing in that."

But a lot of couples *do* feel guilty and it limits their ability to see that it never pays to have a spouse quit their job. When women say, "I have to quit. My salary doesn't cover day care," they have failed to consider that this is a joint cost: Child care should be looked at as a percentage of the parents' combined incomes, not as a percentage of the mother's income alone. Child-care needs are short-lived relative to a thirty-year-plus career. Throw in raises that compound over time and it's clear that you'll end up with more savings to pay for college or your retirement if you both keep working.

"Money is tight with day-care costs," says Celia, a public school teacher. But realizing that they'll need child care only until their son starts school, Celia says, "We cut corners where we can. I no longer get my hair done at the salon—my husband does my dye jobs. It's fun, kind of romantic, and Fructis #60 actually looks better than the last brassy highlights I got at the salon. (Only $12.99 to cover my grays!)"

"Early on, my income was lower and the cost of help was really high," says Liz, who rose to become COO of a public company. "At the time, about sixty-five percent of my after-tax income went to paying for all that child care and family help. But I knew my income would grow. Over time, child-care help cost less than two percent of my income."

GETTING FAIRNESS (WITHOUT A FIGHT)

If you can agree on what actually needs to get done, it's much easier to split that list in half. Scoping the project (a.k.a. your family life) and figuring out who's gonna do what is not a one-time job. It's a weekly (or daily) discussion that can give you more (or less) equality depending on how you approach it. In Neil Chethik's book *VoiceMale,* a survey of 360 husbands said they were more motivated to do their part when women did the kinds of things that good colleagues do:

1. **Create a master plan.** Many husbands told Chethik that "things worked most smoothly when they and their wives created an overall plan for work in and around the house...Both partners usually ended up doing most of what they preferred doing, along with some chores they didn't like at all. Every few months, the tasks could be divided again if one or the other partner was unhappy with the list."

2. Give notice. One husband told Chethik that "he does housework at a different pace than his wife does...He said he's far more likely to accommodate his wife's housework desires when she recognizes this, accepts it, and, if she has specific cleaning wishes, makes them clear well in advance. This husband said, 'When she says she wants it done now, it usually doesn't happen.'"

3. Change expectations. "Several husbands suggested that their wives put too much emphasis on cleaning. One man spoke of his wife's 'vigilante attitude' about housework. This husband, and others, said they would be more interested in doing housework if their wives compromised on the thoroughness and frequency of the cleaning."[17]

Josh Coleman, the marriage expert, points out "the lyrics are rarely as important as the melody—getting your tone right is key." From his counseling practice, Coleman finds wives are most effective when they speak in a matter-of-fact way "rather than a victimized or burdened way. Her tone should be *affectionate though unmovable.*" The result? The majority of women in his practice experience success with this method.[18]

In our interviews, couples explained the many ways they sort things out. Hearing the clever things these couples do was perhaps our favorite part of writing this book. Below are five themes that stood out to us. They won't solve all your problems, but we hope they will inspire you to find couples you admire and ask them lots of personal questions. "I don't know *how* you do it" is the comment 50/50 couples (particularly wives) often get. Instead, let's make it "How *do* you do it?" and ask for details.

#1: Do what comes easy (which may mean skip it)

Darcie and Jim have two kids and busy careers. The way they share the load is to break it down. Each person gravitates to certain tasks (he does lunch boxes and laundry, she likes to cook), "but one person is 'primary' on different things," says Darcie.

Sharon and Steve have dubbed each other "tsar" of the varied fief-doms of family life. Sharon doesn't like to cook but she's the Food Tsar because she cares more than Steve about what she (and everyone else) eats. Steve is the Car Tsar. He cares about horsepower and timely oil changes more than his wife. Steve takes the lead when it's time to buy a new vehicle and is buddies with the local garage. He's not in love with Sharon's driving (with some cause), so on most weekends Steve's at the wheel. Whether it's nature or nurture, husbands and wives can gravitate to "girl things" and "boy things" and still do 50/50. But if her tasks sap more time than his, it's time to reallocate.

But what if your spouse doesn't naturally gravitate to doing his part? "I know a lot of women who enable their husbands to do very lit-tle," one mom told us. "If you are too emotionally tied to your idea of how to run a house, then you take care of everything before your hus-band even misses it. You have to get control of that part of yourself. You can't negotiate a better deal if you aren't willing to play at least a little game of chicken."

"I've had the most supportive husband you could imagine but there is a natural tendency to take advantage of resources," says Rachel, who has been married to her doctor husband for over twenty-five years. "If I had been willing to do all the cooking and laundry and errands, Don would have said 'great.' I didn't blame him for it—if I were in the same situation, I'd take advantage of free resources, too." But, Rachel ex-plained, with a very full-time job as a stockbroker and three kids, "I had to break him of it. If the laundry wasn't getting done, Don would notice it and he'd do it. Friends would come over and Don would be cooking. They'd say, 'I didn't know you liked to cook.' Don would tell them 'I don't. I like to eat.'"

If it seems beyond you to ignore dirty socks and cede control like this, consider the advice of Terrence Real, the therapist, who says, "Changing one's own behavior is a much more promising strategy than insisting on change" from your spouse.[19]

#2: Telepathy is overrated:
Ask for what you need (and be specific)

As one 50/50 dad said to us, "First, the hardest thing is to know what you want—if you can't pin it down, your spouse is unlikely to guess right. Second, you have to ask nicely, in a way that doesn't sound like a criticism. Third, you need to listen, to understand that what you want may not work for your spouse, or that they might have another way to do it. You need all three steps—if you skip one, you won't get good results."

Saying to your husband, "I want you to start doing more around the house" isn't going to get you as far as saying, "Let's agree on a list of what needs to get done around the house and divvy it up." Be clear (and nothing beats writing it down). "I want you to spend more time with the kids" is too general. If you say: "Since we agree that the kids need two hours with each of us each night, how can we make that work?" you've stated a specific goal and asked a specific question. And your spouse can respond to it specifically. Working couples who communicate successfully do so regularly, with respect, and with a sense of empathy. This means that along with your request, you convey the message: *I'm standing in your shoes, ready to listen to why this may be hard for you, but I'm asking for a good reason.*

No one's a mind reader. No matter how much you and your husband love each other, you don't get a mind meld with the wedding ring. If you want something, you need to *say* it. Nothing is "obvious" to anyone but you.

"The biggest challenge is to ask for help. Craig is not going to intuitively know when I'm at my breaking point," says Mary of her husband. "It has been a big part of my personal development to be able to ask for help. I used to wonder, 'Is he going to notice that I need help?' What I've learned is, no, he's not going to notice. I just have to ask."

It's also easier to ask effectively if you do it before you're about to blow a gasket. "Periodically we get out of balance," says Grace, the advertising executive. "I have to say, 'Yo, dude. I'm paying the bills, booking the kids for summer camp, I'm traveling my ass off. My hands are full. A little help here, please?' And Jerry will say, 'I'm sorry, what do you need me to do?' Usually I tell him: 'You choose what's easiest. But please take something.'"

"Piano lessons, food, playdates, cleaning the house are part of my consciousness, but David was oblivious," says Diane, who worked full time with two kids. "Initially it never dawned on me that he could help. I asked David to do one dinner a week and he said 'sure.' He made the same food every week, but he did it."

Another thing to communicate clearly: appreciation. "You get no feedback in parenting. The kids don't come home and say, 'You did a great job packing my lunch box,' or 'Thanks for putting me to bed early, I really needed that,'" says Eileen, a mother of four. "Your seven-year-old is never, ever going to thank his father for reminding him to floss his teeth, but you can."

#3: Be direct (not directive)

How you ask matters a lot. Couples therapist Terrence Real points out that women are socialized to complain and criticize, rather than simply requesting what they want. He quotes studies showing that the "most reliable predictor of long-term marital success was a pattern in which the wives, in nonoffensive, clear ways, communicated their needs, and husbands willingly altered their behaviors to meet them."[20]

"I was totally tied up in my career," says Dan, a successful businessman. "Liz would delegate things and I would be passive-aggressive. I would think, *I'm a more important person than that. Don't delegate to me.* I wouldn't do it. It made Liz resentful. And if you feel guilty, you start to feel victimized and become surly and uncooperative. I knew this wasn't the fair way to do things," he admits. "At one point, Liz got so angry that she started giving me checklists. I actually found that useful," said Dan. A to-do list might drive some spouses nuts, but Dan said he liked it because it gave him the latitude to make his contributions on his own schedule.

One woman told us how she used technology to take the edge off of asking. "I've always booked the kids' doctor appointments," Darcie said. But she didn't want to be the one to leave work and take the kids every time, too, she wanted her husband, Jim, to cover his share of visits. Darcie started using her Outlook software to "invite" Jim to the kids' appointments as if they were team meetings at work. Jim had the choice to accept and put the e-mailed appointment on his calendar, or reject it. Later, Jim joked to a friend, "What was I going to do, hit the 'decline' button on my daughter's dental checkup?"

Low-tech methods can also help to maintain neutrality. In their kitchen, where no one can miss it, Darcie put up a large whiteboard. "When I see something around the house that needs to get done, I write it up on the board, like 'call electrician.' It's not my job, it's not his job, but we all know it's out there. It's become our shared to-do list," says Darcie. "Sometimes things sit on the list for two to three weeks or longer, but then Jim will come along and take a chunk of five things and just cross them off. The board works because we don't have to tell each other to do things. We can just share the observation that they need doing and, when we can get to them, we do them."

#4: Barter, accrue credits, and cash them in

Most days aren't exactly 50/50—they're some other ratio based on whose schedule is more packed. But with couples who share easily, doing more than what's fair has a benefit: What you give today, you get back tomorrow (or next month).

"I try to be flexible and cover for my husband so that when something comes up for me, I don't have any guilt about it," says Susan, the engineer. "When I know I've done more than my part, it's easy for me to say, 'Hey, I'm in a bind, I need you to pick up the kids even though it's my day.' Just like you want to build credits with your boss, you want to have credits with your spouse so there's a reserve to draw on when you need it."

"Mary will send me an e-mail saying, 'I've got this date to go out with some girlfriends. Thanks for your support!'" says Craig, who knows that Mary is really asking him to deal with homework and bedtime alone. "When I see that, I think, *Great. I'm going to earn a chit.* And I actually like when it's just me and the kids."

Part of 50/50 is being able to pull back and recalibrate; to put yourself in your partner's shoes and consider what *his* work life looks like, and to appreciate how that stress impacts home life; to ask him for help when you need it, and to offer it when he does.

Grace, the advertising executive, is married to Jerry, a neurosurgeon. They both have demanding careers—though with different demands.

"Our second baby was walking birth control. We'd planned to have three children but Adam woke up at night so much that we changed our minds. We'd hear him crying and I'd turn to Jerry and say, 'Hey, can you do this? I'm pitching to the CEO of Sony tomorrow.' Jerry would roll over and say, 'I'm operating on a guy with an aneurism.' It came down to 'whose day is more stressful tomorrow,' and I tended to come out with the short end of the stick on night duty.

"But Jerry makes up for it in other ways. He helps the kids get fed and bathed and he plays with them. I have a three-hour round-trip commute to the city and Jerry has no commute, so between 4:30 and 7:30 he's on duty. He does the evening program with the kids."

Fifty/fifty parents need to become experts at bartering. There's usually a deal that will make everyone happy if you stick with one idea: Loads are for sharing.

WHEN HE'S THE NEATNIK

Men aren't the only ones who forget what hangers are for. In fact, there are plenty of women who are gifted at looking the other way when the dirty towels are piled as high as the Matterhorn. Even the smallest families make a lot of mess, and you may be fine with a more relaxed approach toward housework, but some men get stressed out by raisin trails on the carpet or Barbie shoes that crunch underfoot.

Joan's husband, Paul, was disturbed by the clutter, until they adopted a special end-of-day ritual: five minutes cleaning up with the kids before bedtime. "Paul says it really gives him peace of mind."

Steve got tired of Sharon leaving her clothes strewn around the room, so they made a deal that he'd just toss all of her things in one pile in a spot where he wouldn't have to look at them. It works—she finds what she's looking for, he doesn't need to worry about it.

When men take over household tasks, they can be superstars. Jamie (the former NFL player) liked clean laundry. Thanks to Dad's skill, Jamie's son went to baseball practice with the whitest uniform—no matter how many times he slid into base. One day, Jamie got a call from another team parent, who sheepishly confessed: 'My son insisted that I call you to ask, how do you get those uniforms so clean?' " It seemed to be a big step for this mom to call for laundry advice from a *man*.

Jamie also tells this story: "One time I called a plumber to fix a leak and the guy told me he couldn't come for a week," says Jamie. "So I said, 'Look, I need this fixed now. If you can't come today, there are nine other plumbers in the phone book.' So the guy showed up and fixed it that day. But on his way out, the plumber turned to me and said, 'We don't get this shit from the women.' " So let's admit it, a manly touch at home often gets some very good results.

#5: If you can't agree, call in the experts

As Neil Chethik found in his survey of married men, "Many of the most satisfied couples disagree on a regular basis...The key issue is not *whether* a couple argues, but *how*."[21]

Christina and George have two kids in grade school and a baby. Sharing parenthood and work over the years, they had few conflicts over managing the kids—until it came to the question of free time (which had all but vanished with a third child). George wanted more of it. Christina's view: If they weren't at work, both parents should be with the children.

One way to resolve conflict is to get more information. Christina and George made an appointment with a child psychologist and asked, "How much of our time do our kids really need with each of us?" The psychologist did more than give them an answer—she mapped it out. With a pen and paper, she divided the couple's non-work time into three-hour chunks, allocating some of that to family and some to one-on-one time with each child (one parent/one child and one parent/two children). There was also a three-hour chunk on Saturdays for each parent to go off on their own. The result: an orderly schedule where everybody won.

Embrace marriage advice books—they're a great genre and can give you both perspective and useful tips. *The Lazy Husband* is one of our favorites (tell men not to bristle at the title, it's a pro-male book). It's written by marriage counselor Josh Coleman, who says the men he sees often feel guilty about how little they do. "Despite his behavior, your husband probably really does want to make you happy," Coleman says. But "it's also likely he is confused about what's fair to do with the house and kids based on social pressures about what it means to be a man, what he observed growing up, and what he observes from his peers."

Coleman's advice to wives: Focus on what *you* control. Are you clear in your own mind and will you hand off chores without critique? Do you negotiate ("If you do task X that I care about, I'll do task Y that *you* really care about")? Do you let him live with consequences (if he doesn't do his X, you refrain from doing your Y)?[22]

Counselors, parenting classes, websites, books—new (objective) information often goes a long way to settle the kinds of disputes that get in the way of 50/50. But help—or a better attitude—can also come from the most surprising places.

If your husband recoils at the touchy-feely tone of parenting and marriage gurus, try management experts. "It takes an epiphany to get out of this cycle," says Dan, the businessman who admitted his past behavior was "passive-aggressive." After Dan sold his firm, he took a business school course that changed his whole perspective on doing his share at home. "It talked about how to recast your life after you've left one career, how to stop seeing your career as everything."

In fact, some of the best relationship advice we've seen comes not from woman's magazines but *Harvard Business Review*. In an article titled "Rethinking Political Correctness," the authors (experts in organizational behavior) recommend four steps to resolving conflict. While intended for colleagues broaching touchy topics at work, the steps below apply equally well at home (with a little elaboration from us in italics).[23]

- **Pause** to short-circuit the emotion and reflect. (*You just want him to put the wet clothes into the dryer—this is about laundry, not his love for you.*)

- **Connect** in ways that affirm the importance of relationships. (*This is your husband you're talking to, not the no-show house painter, so treat him accordingly.*)

- **Get genuine support** that doesn't necessarily validate your point of view but, rather, helps you gain a broader perspective. (*Talk to other working couples. Do they, with similarly overpacked schedules, think it's worth insisting your husband bleach the bathroom tile grout?*)

- **Shift your mind-set** from "*You* need to change" to "What can I change?" (*Hold your tongue when he puts the pillows on top of the bedspread. Try to see it as creative.*)

"WHEN I SEE DIRTY SOCKS ON THE FLOOR, I FEEL _____"

Communication tips helped us in prenuptial discussions but they help us even more in what we'll call The Post-Nup—the running log of agreements, decisions, appeals, overturned decisions, and new accords (think English common law) that make marriage work over time.

If your spouse does something that drives you nuts, there is a communications formula that couples therapists swear by (but like contraception, effectiveness depends on actual use). You say: "When this thing happens, it makes me feel ___." (How you fill in the blank is the trick. Well-considered, sincere, measured adjectives are useful. Expletives and angry words, less useful.) Breathe deep. Listen carefully. Repeat back your spouse's response—accurately and calmly. "What I heard you say is ___. Did I hear you correctly?"

If your response to this is "Ugh," know that developing these skills may have big side benefits: You and your spouse will improve your negotiation skills.

Bruce Patton is the coauthor of the negotiation classic *Getting to Yes* and the bestselling *Difficult Conversations.* Patton says that negotiation can help couples get outcomes that will make both spouses happier.

"Many people avoid negotiation because they think it's an either-or trade-off: Either you maintain the relationship *or* you get what you want. But that you can't have both," says Patton. To avoid such negotiations, many couples divide realms (inside the house versus outside the house) and pretend they don't care what their spouse decides, that they are happy to defer. "But when you do that, often you get subopti-mal solutions. Because usually you end up caring about things in your spouse's sphere."

Because of this misperception, "couples often settle for less than they could have because they don't feel comfortable negotiating. Take fur-niture. You can defer to your spouse or try to argue them out of their preferences, but it's a lot easier just to look a little longer until you find something you both like."

Patton tries to help people see that "there are ways to handle conflict when you can get what you want and at least maintain the relationship and work to meet your interests. Sometimes negotiation builds the rela-tionship because it fosters understanding and respect." In *Difficult Conversations,* Patton and his colleagues illustrate how to talk about con-flict with an open mind. Try saying: "I feel strongly about this. Do you see this differently? Can you tell me why?" And again, listen to the answer.[24]

#6: Sneak off with a special someone—your spouse

Relationship experts say that having regular one-on-one time with your spouse is vital for the health of a marriage. As much as you love being with your kids every day, it's funny how much more you love them after date night.

"We really needed that time together," says Carol, thinking back to the weekend dinner she and her husband would share without their two kids. "We'd spend the week going in our own directions and when we came home we'd be dealing with the kids."

Dana and Joseph didn't find the need to have a weekly "date night" because they enjoyed staying in on Saturdays and cooking a big dinner with their son. But midweek, they'd make it a point to have lunch, just the two of them.

"We worked in the same building so that made it easier to meet," says Dana, "but we worked for competitors so we'd sneak over to a diner where we wouldn't run into any colleagues. Somehow, that illicit quality made it more of a treat. Our conversation would range from our son to work to things we were each thinking about. We covered a lot of ground, we worked through many problems big and small, and it was pure luxury to talk without being interrupted."

"Invite us to your wedding or holiday party and we're that crazy fortysomething couple doing the 'pretzel' with such gusto we run into people," said Chip. "We love dancing with each other—just the two of us together in a sea of music. For a few blissful minutes, we can safely forget the kids, our jobs, the mortgage. And while Vicki's still not okay with the idea that men get to lead, she thinks it's funny when I dip her."

When your kids are very small, when your job feels very large (most of the time), when you feel you've got no control, that's when you get close to surrender, to giving up on your 50/50 hopes. And it's then that you most need to get away as a couple. Whether you call it "date night" or "grown-up" time, whether you get dressed up for a fancy meal or just walk around the block, all that matters is that you make time to talk—or maybe just hold hands.

R-E-S-P-E-C-T: It's a two-way street

A 50/50 man values his wife's work enough to make room for it (and raises her chance of success). Mary was just starting her own firm when she had children. Her husband, Craig, was an established investment banker. "Craig was clearly the higher earner," says Mary, "but he knew that I cared about my business succeeding and he came home early so I could stay late and focus when I needed to."

It's more than just respect for a wife's work: 50/50 men value what employment does for their wives. "Our decisions about who does what are not economically driven. Jerry's support for what I do is both selfless and selfish," says Grace. "Selfless because he wants me to be happy and selfish because he wants a wife who's engaged in the world."

A 50/50 wife values her husband's parenting enough to make room for it (and raises *his* chance of success as a father). "I may not agree with every call he makes at home," says Kara about her husband. "But he just glows when he's with our kids. He's so proud of being a great father. And our kids feel very special to have a dad who comes to their classroom. All the hours he spends on parenting, they give him more patience and humor. That makes him more effective in his job—and a fun date for me."

Money or profession may dictate if one partner's job takes precedence from time to time. If one spouse is a teacher and the other is an aerospace engineer, when NASA calls about the first manned flight to Mars, should they move to Houston? Big opportunities and bigger paychecks may drive whose career gets more room to run—short term. Maternity leaves and shorter hours may make one parent the kid "expert" for a time (more on that in Chapter 9). But for 50/50 couples, if the baton gets passed to one partner—to be primary parent or worker—it's with the understanding that it's just for the next leg of the race, not forever.

Chapter Eight

The Pre-Baby Road Trip: Mapping Out a Leave You Can Return From

A lot of women say their favorite part of pregnancy came early, when it was still a secret shared with only their spouse, then maybe with family and close friends. But then you "go public" and suddenly your private life is everyone else's business. Once you can no longer button your favorite pants and decide to tell your boss, things are never quite the same.

"I'm having a baby." When you utter those words, even in the most formal workplace, it's like an emotional floodgate has opened—for your colleagues. It's mostly a happy reaction tempered with some cautionary words meant to be helpful. Very few people will rain on your parade in those first days, but there's a storm cloud forming. Behind the smiling face, hearty handshake, or hug, your boss is worried. And sometimes you should be, too.

"I was so happy we were having a child," said Shelly, the lawyer. "And my firm was saying, 'We care about women, we're going to make it work for you.' I thought I could write my own ticket. But the guys who run big firms don't know what it takes to be an engaged parent when your spouse works. And I didn't know going into it either."

Most bosses—even the best ones—don't know what it's like. About

85 percent of leaders in most fields are men and three-quarters of those have an at-home wife, so they just haven't had the same experience of sharing roles at home.[1]

And some bosses feel they have been burned before. "I would always get 'the promise'—the speech from the woman that she was coming back and wanted her job. But only half returned," said Brian, the ex-CEO of a multibillion-dollar company. "I don't think a woman can make that promise because I don't think she can really know in advance."

There is no experience more intense than becoming a parent, with its surge of responsibility, logistics, anxiety, and joy. By sharing the highs and lows of our journeys and those of other moms, we hope to show you that there are many ways to navigate your own. What we find is that when women ask for (and get) the right support, they keep their promises—to both their bosses and themselves.

WHY EMPLOYERS THINK MOMS ARE TOO EXPENSIVE

While almost all the industrialized world requires paid leave for new moms (and in some cases for fathers), the United States does not. The Family and Medical Leave Act of 1993 gives you the right to six weeks off to recover (unpaid) and your job back—if your workplace has more than fifty employees. But because small businesses employ a lot of people, 40 percent of the U.S. workforce is not guaranteed any leave.[2] Often, you're on your own to cobble it together from vacation and sick days.

A female partner at a consulting firm told us how one of her male peers reacted when a new maternity leave policy was proposed: "It will just encourage women to have more babies," he said. What if male breadwinners were the ones having babies? Then leaves for childbearing would be treated like all other employee benefits. (Believe it or not, there are still companies that pay for Viagra but litigate to avoid covering birth control.)[3] Like health insurance and pensions, baby leaves would be a cost of attracting talent for big employers. For the rest of the workforce, childbearing would be supported through tax breaks, just as health savings accounts and Keogh plans are.

In 2004, California became the first state to get clued in: Women actually *are* breadwinners. So the state enacted a law ensuring women are paid up to 55 percent of their wages for six weeks (capped at a total payment of $5,502 and financed by a new payroll tax—as of this writing, only Washington and New Jersey have followed suit).[4] When we agree as a nation that female earners are as important to families as male earners, then maybe paid leave will become more common.

While we are staunch advocates for paid leave, we also know that these policies have many costs—ripple effects that can be very difficult to manage and to fund, even in the best-run companies. And the most resented of those costs is the one you create if you don't return to your job (remember that replacing you can cost 100 to 200 percent of your salary).

Stuart is a progressive man who runs a firm of fifteen people. "I was surprised how much maternity leaves interrupted life at the company," he told us. "Two women went out at once and I had given them each a three-month paid leave. I hired interim workers whom I had to train and pay. It was a stress on the firm," says Stuart, who has three kids and a working wife. "And then one of the women didn't come back. I was really angry." The next time a woman gets pregnant, Stuart says, "I'm unsure I'll be as generous. I think there should be a quid pro quo. If we keep their position open and we pay them, the employee has an obligation to come back—or return what we paid them on leave."

"Apart from managing the pregnant woman, managing her stand-in was just as hard," says Brian, the retired CEO. His company actually retained a number of "floaters" to fill in for women on leave, workers who often resented being pulled off the job when the new mother returned. If a transition was rocky or mishandled, business would suffer. Deals would fall apart, problems would go unresolved, money would be lost. In addition, he told us, "The review process and compensation is hard. There are so many frictional costs, so many unknowns, you have to overpay to keep everyone happy.

"I've racked my brain and I don't know what the answer is. Sometimes maybe half our staff was female. When they go out on leave you don't know if you are losing them for four months or forever."

Talk is cheap—save costs (and misunderstandings) by communicating more

It's much easier to reduce the burdens for both employers and the women themselves when pregnant women and bosses feel free to talk candidly.

"The reason there are so many issues when women go on maternity leave is that we treat it as a supervisor-to-employee problem," says Michael, a partner at a large law firm who ran a regional office. Danielle, a talented associate, approached Michael before she got pregnant. "She said, 'I really want to talk about what happens when I have a baby.' Danielle and I wanted to make it work."

Instead of approaching the issue as a one-on-one negotiation, Michael opened it up. "When Danielle got pregnant, I realized that if we didn't talk openly about her situation, other associates were prone to imagine Danielle was getting a special deal," he told us. "When Danielle was ready to talk about it, we had a meeting with the whole office. We went through her workload case by case and mapped out what we thought she could do. We broke out all the phases—producing documents, flying places, retaining experts, the trial. We mapped out her caseload through her pregnancy and her child's infancy. We asked what other associates could or would do.

"We made it explicit for both sides. Danielle understood that there were implications—she'd have to make up the work or have her partnership clock slowed. For the other associates, Danielle's child meant more hours and more responsibility. I said, 'Look, you'll be getting more work and visibility and you can look at that as an opportunity. And we'll do the same for you if you have to look after someone someday.' " Not only did Danielle return to work productively, but two non-parents (one male) took leaves to address other family issues. And they, too, returned to work productively, rather than quitting.

Bosses who are open, candid, and constructive can talk through the logistical issues, save themselves a lot of expense, and support working mothers at the same time. We need to train more managers to be like Michael.

"Having kids is such a flux. Before you know it you are in so deep you can't see your options clearly," says Elena, the surgeon, recalling the birth of her first child. "What would have helped is a person with perspective—someone who had gone through the same thing and could check in as the demands of parenthood grew. If someone had just talked to me when I was pregnant, or just had my first child, I would have said, 'Don't worry, I can handle it.'

"What you need is a real mentor to say, 'Great. We're going to meet every two months after you have your child and figure out the issues and what adjustments need to be made.' It sounds expensive to have such tailored mentoring but think about what happens now. After kids, many female faculty leave just when they're becoming profitable for their hospital. A new doctor takes three years to build a profitable practice and sometimes the hospital is so desperate to fill the slot they have to pay up just to recruit a replacement."

Your other new job: Maternal diplomat

Your colleagues may be genuinely happy for you, but if they end up with a lot more work (and no extra pay) they will resent you. Rather than direct their unhappiness at your boss, who may be mismanaging the situation, they will focus it on you, particularly when you return to work and are hoping for a smooth transition. Again, if you don't work for someone like Michael, who carefully talks through the details, then you need to step up and play that role yourself. Yes, in the midst of going to the bathroom (again) and all the other angst (and joy) that comes with pregnancy, you'll be wise to add another job to your list— chief diplomat.

"Why is this all on me?" you may ask (we certainly did). Until there are more people like Elena—women leaders who've lived through these things—both the social and legal environments make it tough for a lot of bosses to raise issues that need to be discussed.

If you have a male boss, even if he is a father himself, he may be uncomfortable talking about what you are going through. A pregnancy is public, but still very personal. Talented managers know they can discuss pregnancy in a way that's abstract and doesn't make anyone squeamish. Yet, they often get censored by something else: the law. Or the misinterpretation of the law.

As bosses of pregnant women, we've found that HR departments get worried at the hint of open discussion about maternity leaves. The standard HR response: "If you talk about pregnancy, you'll get us sued." Instead of training bosses to engage in legal conversations that will help women return productively to their jobs, many HR departments silence these discussions in favor of CYA (as in Cover Your Ass). With these fears afloat, many managers don't feel free to talk to you as they usually do ("We have this work to do. How is it going to get done?"). Instead, thanks to a baby in your belly, you'll have to articulate the questions your boss feels unable to ask—and answer them, too.

We'll give the last word to Brian, the ex-CEO who was honest about his concerns. "Women come off much better when they are candid. If they say, 'I realize you can't ask this question, that you may have questions about my career plans.' When you volunteer information, you help the employer get comfortable with the risk. If women gave more notice and were clearer about their plans, all of those things would help reduce the cost to the employer."

Breaking the news on your breaking news

When should you start talking? Getting this right is quite a challenge. Telling people early can leave you feeling awkward: "What if I have a miscarriage?" "What if I have to do IVF again?" Tell people too late, and colleagues often feel like you were holding out on them.

"The timing of when you tell people you are pregnant—it's always tricky," said one husband, of his wife's experience. "The other day, we were standing in our bedroom closet and my wife was saying, 'Well, if I wear this I could hide it. Should I do that? Or should I just be open because I don't want to be dishonest with them?'" As a working mom told us, "I try to be very sensitive to the concerns my clients may have. I want them to know their work is going to get done and get done well. At the firm, everybody knows that I'm a mom and I can do it. I've proven that. But clients who haven't worked with me a long time don't know that. I worry they'll take their business elsewhere if they know I'm pregnant."

Pregnant with her first child, Joanna had hoped to tell her colleagues after the first trimester. But two months into it, Joanna walked into an awkward situation. She arrived at a firm bonding event where she and her colleagues were to play fighter pilots aboard a flight simulator. Joanna, the only woman, blanched as she saw a sign saying "Dangerous for Pregnant Women." Pulling her boss aside, Joanna explained why she'd be sitting it out.

For our other pregnancies, when we knew they were viable in month four, we told our bosses. Maybe some colleagues thought we should have piped up sooner. But we did our best to strike a balance—when we knew we were really going to have a baby, we told the world. And we had five months to plan how we'd manage our jobs.

Women in career transition face a more difficult decision. Gina runs an analytical team and she was excited about a dynamic new hire. "But right after she accepted the job," said Gina, "she told me she was three months pregnant. We have a tiny team. I just hired someone who is going to be leaving us in six months, for an entire quarter of our fiscal year. That's a pretty big blow for us to absorb." Gina, herself a mother of three, fully understands her new hire was anxious. "I don't have a good answer here. Maybe there would have been less enthusiasm for hiring her if she had told us. But instead we feel a little deceived." Here is some tough advice (and yes, we'd have been scared, too): Tell it like it is. Long term, you need your boss's confidence. If you disclose your pregnancy *and* voice your commitment to work, your employer should respond well. And if they don't, better to know that and find another place to work.

"I'll be back"

When you break the news is a hard call, but if you plan to be someplace long term, we'd vote for more disclosure earlier. *How* you break the news is more straightforward: Leave no shadow of a doubt you're coming back—and offer evidence that you're for real to calm the skeptics. The words you choose are important.

Some women who fully intend to return make colleagues feel less than confident about their commitment when they don't think through this weighty announcement.

"It's going to be very upsetting to even the hippest, most flexible boss in the world," says *Business Week*'s workplace guru Liz Ryan, who suggests you "put yourself in your manager's shoes" when you disclose your pregnancy. You should strive to convey that "you are very committed to your job and that you want the period leading up to your leave as well as the time you are away to be as easy as possible for the company."[5]

"If a pregnant woman tells me she's not sure how she's going to *feel* about her work arrangements after pregnancy, I just want to run out of the room," a male employer told us. "I think, *I'm going to have to tiptoe, and be extra nice, and then she's going to cry a lot.* It may not be fair, but a lot of guys react that way when women start to talk about feelings in the context of kids."

The first words out of your mouth after you break the news and graciously accept the good wishes should be straightforward and reassuring, not peppered with doubt about the future. We think Arnold said it best in his classic line above (if "Terminator" and "pregnant lady" don't connect in your head, consider your body volume—use your big presence to be convincing).

You need a plan *before* you talk to your boss. Even at very well-run firms, managers may be clueless about leave policies (if they exist). Do the homework for your bosses—they'll appreciate that you saved them time and you'll set the right tone. If your firm doesn't have an employee handbook that covers maternity leave, it probably means you'll need to negotiate one. Regardless, go talk to working moms outside your workplace—you'll get some good perspective without the risk of a news leak. As you get closer to going public, talk to women you trust at your workplace and get their tactical advice.

"Control the spin," working moms told Sharon when she was preparing to announce her first pregnancy. "Tell all your managers directly—

don't let them hear secondhand. If they imply you might not come back, smile and say, 'You know, I'm the working sort.' Give them a written plan for your leave as soon as possible. You'll be more credible."

When you approach a boss, remember that your employer's outward reaction may be positive and full of warmth, but this person is thinking about how they'll manage without you—either for the short term or permanently. Ease their pain.

"When she told me, 'Hey, we need my income,' I heaved a sigh of relief," says Chip about his talk with a pregnant employee. As we've said throughout this book, whether your family "needs" your income is a matter of attitude and you can argue that *every* family is more secure with a mom's paycheck. So have no qualms about saying, "I'll be back. I need this job."

It's hard to foresee all the things that will happen while you're out, so just do your best. Make a spreadsheet showing who might cover each of your tasks while you're out. Write a memo detailing all your projects, what could go wrong, and how you can be contacted if they need you. "As a practical matter, who knows your job better than you?" said one mom. "If you come up with a plan yourself, you're more likely to design something successful. And by taking charge, you send an important message—that you care about your job and that you're coming back."

Entitlement vs. disability: Setting expectations—both yours and theirs

Your mother is calling with advice about varicose veins and stretch marks, you're gobbling calcium to feed that little person growing inside you, your immune system is down, and you get more colds—it's hard not to feel a little embattled between the rosy moments of baby showers and childbirth.

Bearing children is an incredible gift women give the world and they deserve a lot more credit than they get. Until more women run things, our workplaces generally won't reflect that view. So while we are learning to cope with false-alarm contractions and pregnancy fatigue, we need to remember that some colleagues won't be sympathetic. We don't do ourselves any favors if we let ourselves believe they are going to be.

One hardworking woman had to spend the last months of her first pregnancy on remote assignment—in sweltering heat. "I hope I'm getting extra credit for this," she told us. Probably not. Most men around you have the view that you chose to be pregnant and your job is to make it as small a deal as possible for everyone else.

Even other working moms may wish you had more perspective. Bettina, herself a mother, was a little surprised by an otherwise sensible colleague who regarded her pregnancy as a trump card to move to their bank's most desirable branch. The pregnant woman was still relatively junior but felt she should be able to leapfrog a lot of her colleagues who'd also petitioned to make that transfer. "That branch is ten minutes from my house and right now I have an hour commute. I'm pregnant. I should be the one to get it," she told Bettina.

It's a bad idea to go into pregnancy with a sense of entitlement, and it's the fastest way to reverse whatever good feelings your colleagues really do have for you. The same applies when you go out on leave.

"It was really frustrating. She had the baby and left town," says one working mom of her colleague on maternity leave. "For three months she never checked in, never responded to e-mails or voice mails from internal people. Maternity leave is not a vacation—we were paying her. She should have stayed in closer contact." We're going to guess that this situation is a fine example of what happens when neither pregnant women nor their bosses set expectations up front. Not only does the employer lose but the new mom earns herself a reputation as a flake.

BRINGING BABY BY

Let us start by confessing: When we were on leave, we do recall bringing our babies into the office at midday—mostly because it suited our schedules. But when we talked to Brian, the ex-CEO, we thought he had a point on this we should share.

"I called it 'The Baby Shower Syndrome,'" said Brian, whose staff was about half female. "The new mom comes in with her baby and the whole office comes over to say, 'What a beautiful child.' And then they have to go out for lunch. I think we lost a good half day of work every time someone came in to do the baby tour," said Brian. While workplaces need to get more sensitive about new mothers, new moms need to be sensitive, too—to their bosses' desire to keep the workplace productive.

So maybe save your baby's office debut for the end of the workday.

Although there are risks in letting yourself feel "entitled" by your pregnancy, there's a bigger risk if you fail to understand why time out for babies is sometimes called "disability leave."

If you've never given birth, it's easy to think "disability" is an overstatement. Before she had her first child, Joanna imagined that labor was where the tough work ended. Then a very organized (and clean) friend told her that she'd been so busy with her newborn she didn't even have time to take a shower. Joanna didn't understand how that could be.

While bringing children into the world is no longer the deathdefying feat it once was, it remains a pretty extreme sport. Newborns feed every two hours. If you nurse, you can easily spend eight hours a day just getting milk into the body of your beautiful new child—and while your body "rests," it's making more milk and burning almost five hundred extra calories a day.[6] Meanwhile, unless your spouse is right there with you, you have another six hours of burping, changing, baby laundry, and remembering to eat and (occasionally) sleep yourself. You've worked a fourteen-hour day and you're on "leave."

All this while you're recovering from the most intense act an otherwise healthy body ever performs, your biochemistry lurching in new directions as your cells try to readjust to being nonpregnant. Top that, Iron Man.

If you've successfully mapped out your leave, you've handed off your work and your boss knows how things will function without you, and when you will return. But there's still the question of how much contact to have while you are out. If there's a crisis, if only you can fix a problem, your office needs to be able to count on you (assuming you and your child are healthy).

Making yourself available will not harm your ability to bond with a new child. Successful working mothers know this. In our survey over 75 percent of the respondents stayed in touch with the office during their leaves. Does this mean you should volunteer to jump into things? While your intentions are good, colleagues can get confused and may think you're back at work and not doing as much as you used to.

"I was lucky to have a long leave but I worried I'd lose everything I'd worked for while I was out," said Kara. "I was in love with my baby but also felt obliged to make sure things didn't fall apart at the office. So, while she was napping, I'd go in to the office—I thought that was one way to show my commitment. But I wasn't really up to speed on what was going on and put my foot in my mouth without even realizing it. I had huge arguments with colleagues I respected—I was too exhausted, my body was out of whack, and I lacked perspective. In the end, I think it would have been better to stay home and just check e-mail."

If you're lucky, your boss will help you strike the right balance. "I'd call in on my leave because I was worried about getting out of the loop," says Ann, a management consultant on her first maternity leave. "My boss said, 'I hate to tell you but you are expendable and I mean that in the nicest way. And we will need you when you come back.'" The best advice we've gotten: Stay home, rest up, but don't disappear.

"MANNING" BABY LEAVES

Maternity leaves will get less difficult for women when paternity leaves get more common for men.

The 2008 National Study of Employers by the Families and Work Institute found that about 60 percent of employers offer twelve weeks of unpaid leave to *both* moms and dads. But while 22 percent of employers offered maternity leave longer than twelve weeks, only 13 percent offered these longer leaves for fathers. And as for pay, 52 percent of employers studied offered some sort of pay to mothers, but only 16 percent of dads got any kind of pay while on leave.[7]

But utilization of leaves is where the gap between men and women may be largest. While some large employers (like accounting firm Ernst & Young) have high male usage rates, most employers don't.[8] Many men (and some wives) worry that taking an extended paternity leave is "the kiss of career death," as one dad told us. Indeed, some of our favorite guy friends resolutely refused to take paternity leave despite strong advocacy from their wives.[9]

Among all the men we interviewed fewer than 5 percent took leaves. But those who did found it was great for their marriage, their babies, and themselves—and did not damage their careers at all.

Peter worked at Microsoft when his third child was born and he took a month's paternity leave. "When I said I was going to do this, people kept telling me I was such a rock star. Lots of our female friends would tell me, 'You're our hero,' and pointed to me when they asked their husbands, 'Why can't you do that?' It felt great. And at work, no one gave me the 'you are such a slacker' vibe."

Don is a partner at a national law firm and his wife works for the police department. Though there are skeptics, many successful men at Don's firm take paternity leave. Don himself took three weeks with his first child and a month with the second.

"The day after Jenna was born, one of my clients demanded a conference call," Don recalls, but a partner intervened and told him, "your daughter will be one day old exactly once in her life. You can talk to clients every day. I'll cover for you." The client was fine.

Jon, a doctor in his first job, negotiated two months off to care for his first child while his wife, Beth, was finishing her residency. "For that time, I was home with the baby eighty hours per week. I was the nap tsar—I got the baby on a schedule and Beth was really impressed. I learned Tara's personality. I'd talk to her and walk around parks. It is one of the best memories of my life. It gave Tara a great foundation having bonded with both of us."

In 1990, Henry (also a big-firm law partner) took paternity leave and decided to work part time. His example was so notable that he ended up on national TV. Opposite Henry on the show was a headhunter. When asked if working part time would hurt a man's career the headhunter responded, "absolutely." When the show cut to commercials, the cameraman told Henry, "Don't let him get away with that. We all need time with our families and what you are saying sounds right." Today, Henry runs a practice area and sits on his firm's management committee.

We're not saying it's easy for men to take paternity leaves—or that they'll enjoy every moment.

"I think for any person pulling themselves out of the workforce, it's a shock. At home with the baby, I couldn't put my finger on what I had done at the end of the day," says Peter, the software executive. "As wonderful as our baby is, there is no reprieve and very little chance to unwind. It was time consuming and difficult. If I had my choice, I'd do paternity leave when my kid was three."

And there are the standard annoyances of having someone stand in for you at work. It's hard to feel anyone does your job like you do (often they don't), and it's easy to feel your colleagues are grabbing territory (often they do). "Some things totally shut down. 'You never called that client the whole time I was gone?' I'd ask," says Peter. "There was some friction over getting my accounts back. I had to reassert my authority and let people know I was back, and up and running."

But, frictions aside, it may be easier for husbands to take leaves than it is for their wives because they won't face the maternal wall—bosses and colleagues will assume that, in the end, the man remains committed to his job, that the special time-out to focus on parenthood is finite.

Many men really can't get over the hurdle of taking paternity leave (our own husbands didn't manage to do it—and we still love them). But every time a man joins in and takes a leave, he helps pave the way for other men—and helps change the perception that baby leaves are "women's work." As one female executive said to us, "Real men take paternity leave."

Buying peace of mind: Shop for child care early (cute baby clothes come later)

Mapping out a leave you can return from has one final step: figuring out who is going to look after your child when you (and your husband) are fully back at work.

We find that an educated consumer is a happier consumer, particularly when it comes to child care. Don't wait until your leave is nearly up to check out your child-care options. Start when you're pregnant. Give less time to selecting the perfect crib and more time to teaching yourself about the many types of child care you can choose from. You'll enjoy greater peace of mind if you've done your homework—and your husband knows the subject as well as you do.

"A lot of women who stop working really stopped because they're not comfortable with their child care," says Rose, a media executive, who has two young children. "I can understand how when you're not comfortable you feel much more pulled between work and home, and you can feel so bad you want to quit."

A waitress told us, "My mom went back to work when I was a baby and put me in a home-based day care. She liked one caretaker but not the other woman who worked with her. My mom couldn't get over it and she didn't feel she could find something better. Even though we didn't have much money, my mom walked into her job and quit without notice. By the time she'd had her third child, my mom realized that she wanted to be working and found care arrangements she liked."

Dads need to be as comfortable with child care as you do. In Chapter 4 we reported on a study that said many men encourage their wives to quit. Many of these guys sincerely believe that no child care could compete with an at-home mom. Both for your husband's benefit and his support of your career, visit day cares for a lunch date and spend your Saturdays interviewing sitters. It will prompt all sorts of discussions that will make you a better parenting pair—before you're in the heat of battle.[10]

We were both so anxious about child care that we started looking at our options in our second trimester. Sharon took a working mom with five children to lunch to ask how she did it. Steve mass e-mailed friends and associates to get tips on finding good care. (Steve gets credit for hiring their caregivers of eight years—found through business contacts.) Together, Sharon and Steve discovered what many parents do—that they enjoyed learning about child care (and got more confident about it) because they could use each other as sounding boards.

You think the day care looks joyful and the children are free to express themselves. Your husband sees a hole in the fence and toddlers climbing through it. He loves the lady down the street who offers child care in her home: "She's so mellow and speaks in a soothing voice." You think the woman is depressed and needs more time with grown-ups. Either way, talk it through, and you're more likely to make a better decision than if you were doing this on your own.

Good child care comes in many shapes and sizes

As the NICHD study and many others show, child care can be a positive in your child's life. How do you find it? The good news is that child-care quality is not just about what you are able to pay. Harvard's Kathleen McCartney points out that often good-quality care is not necessarily the highest-priced care. While higher cost may imply better location and a lower ratio of kids to caregivers, that's not all that counts. What psychologists call "caregiver sensitivity" makes a big difference—how caregivers speak to children, how often they intervene to help a child cope with something. The problem is that looking for sensitive caregivers takes a lot of work—by you—whether it's time sitting in different child-care centers watching how the staff behaves or interviewing lots of sitters. (In Resources, you'll find a link to the NICHD's checklist of qualities to look for.)[11]

As one child therapist told us, "There is no perfect child care. But then parents aren't perfect either. Find people you trust and stay close to your child so you can make changes when you need to." And, as with all child-related issues, nothing fits forever. "You have to find people who are right for your kids as they grow," says Linda, the medical professor. "They need to want to interact with your kids, and as your kids grow up, they need to know when to step back—to stop hovering and let them have playtime alone with their friends." You may choose a relative, a child-care center, a small group of children in licensed home care, a shared sitter, a nanny—or a combination of the above, which will shift as children grow.

Shanti, a cardiologist, was born in India and brought up in a family where grandparents were deeply involved in raising children. Shanti and her husband, Raj, who live in the United States, asked their mothers to come from India to help them out with their first child, Loli. "We were very lucky that our family was in a position to help out. Our parents are in good health and our moms didn't have other obligations—and they really wanted to be with their grandchild. So when I asked for help, they were happy to do it." The grandmothers took turns visiting for Loli's first eighteen months. Was it always easy? "We think it was great for Loli but it's really different to live with your parents again after you've grown up." As another mom said, "It might be hard to have grandparents as full-time child care. But as part-time child care, grandparents can be great."

Matthew, who works at a large technology firm with his wife, seconds that. "My dad covers one day a week for us. He moved out here when our son was born and chose a job where he did not need to work on Wednesdays. He set his life up with the question 'How can I get to know my grandson?' He does totally different things with our son than we do: They go swimming, to the boardwalk, to Chuck E. Cheese. He totally spoils our son. When we get home on Wednesdays, we don't ask what he had to eat because we don't want to know," Matthew says with a smile.

Some parents prefer the environment of a day-care center. "My son had lots of friends there and I knew where he was all day," says Darcie. "It's different when you have a nanny. In a sense you have to let go of the control." Zelda, a mother of three, said, "I tried a nanny but after a few months I put my six-month-old into a local day-care center. My other two I put into day care at four months. I felt like they did much better in a social environment. I thought the kids really thrived in a place where they had peers to play with."

Good day-care centers hire trained staff—and research shows that training does, in fact, produce better results for kids. Research also says that caregiver training may rub off on *you* and help you be a more effective parent. As one mother told NICHD researchers, lauding her child's day care, "I've learned so much about mom stuff by watching the staff interact with the kids...this kind of place is priceless. I think I would choose to work just so my kids could go here! And *that* gives me a feeling of great joy."[12]

Like the researchers, parents also say they find that the high-cost option is not always the best one. "The benefits of a shared nanny are great," says Jody, a public defender who found a sitter with a friend. "Certainly there is a cost savings, but they also get socialization, learn to share, learn to get along. It would be much harder to achieve this with one child, one nanny. The sharing stuff is really important, I am really glad we have him with another child during the day." Randy, the consultant, has tried a variety of child-care arrangements for her three children. She recently found a student who relates well to her children. "I love my au pair. She lives in so if my meeting schedule changes, she can be flexible. My kids really like her—she connects really well with them. And she costs less than half as much as a full-time nanny."

When both parents work in less flexible jobs, a full-time nanny may be the best option since day-care pickup times and coordination with other families get difficult. But parents often worry they won't know how to choose the right person. Stuart, a business owner, told us, "We were so nervous about finding a good nanny that we started interviewing before we even had the baby. We immediately felt relieved that any one of the five candidates we interviewed on the first day knew more about babies than we did. I could see they would do more than a fine job—they could teach us what to do."

Working couples sometimes find they can reshape their work hours (at least temporarily) and cover a bigger portion of child care themselves. Joan and Paul, who have two kids, now share a sitter with a family across the street. But for the first three years of parenthood, they managed mostly on their own. Joan, a reporter, chose to work the night shift so she could be with their child while her husband worked during the day. Paul would take over at bedtime and stay up late to play with their daughter. That kept the baby on a schedule that allowed mother and child to sleep until midmorning (important since Joan returned from the night desk around 2 a.m.).

WANT AFFORDABLE CHILD CARE? GET OUT THE 50/50 VOTE

When you ask why the United States has such a hard time figuring out affordable care for children, you hear a variety of explanations.

"The American public sees education as a public issue and child care as a private one," a pollster said to a group of advocates for lower-income women. Really? Eighty-eight percent of voters under thirty think the government should subsidize child care, according to a 2008 poll by *Time* magazine and the Rockefeller Foundation.[13]

We hope this batch of thirty-year-olds holds on to that point of view—and votes that way. We Gen-X and boomer parents don't get high marks for making progress so far.

"Maybe the French can do it. But this is the U.S. and we don't know how to provide large-scale, quality child care at a reasonable cost," said another expert we talked to.

There are many examples of clever child care where the costs are well managed, but perhaps the best is the largest—run by Uncle Sam himself. The U.S. military provides care for over 200,000 children, recognizing that this benefit is an important retention tool for dual-income families. Round-the-clock care is available on 90 percent of U.S. bases. Fees vary from $43 to $126 per week based on need—you, the taxpayer, subsidize the rest. The real surprise: Military child care is lauded by the experts and scores far higher than the average child care available to U.S. civilians (they enforce standards and invest heavily in the training of child-care workers).[14]

But the military has some unique features (for example, people follow orders there), so government-run options still make a lot of people skeptical, even us. So what if we spent more effort helping more companies understand the economic case for on-site child care? According to surveys by Bright Horizons (a leading provider of employee-sponsored care), "Eighty-six percent of employees who do not plan to return to work after the birth or adoption of a child would return if work-site child care were available." Lower absenteeism and turnover, as well as higher productivity and job satisfaction (for both moms and dads), are among the rewards for employers—which more than offsets costs when we have the will to see child care as something good.[15]

"We'd bankrupt the country if we really subsidized child care," one man objected.

Right now, the only child-care bankruptcy risk sits squarely on the shoulders of working parents. The biggest subsidy today is the IRS Child and Dependent Care Credit. Its stingy scale ($6,000 per year maximum—regardless of how many kids and aging parents you care for) implies the feds think we can all rely on the old model, the one where moms and daughters care for everyone for "free."[16] If you pay for anyone else to do this work, the numbers are tough. Let's say you can limit your child-care needs to forty hours per week (you and your husband ingeniously figure out how to stagger your work hours to handle drop-off and pickup). Let's say that you are getting a good deal at $10 per hour. That $6,000 will last you about fifteen weeks of the year—for the rest, you're on your own.

One funding idea: When your boss takes you out for a fancy lunch (and clients out for even fancier dinners), how much do we taxpayers cover for *that* bill? Six billion dollars per year.[17] We have an obesity problem in this country so let's vote less money for foie gras and more to cover your child care. And 50/50 parents know where dinner is best—at home with the kids.

Ambivalence about working moms and misinformation about child care are the real reasons we've made so little progress toward affordability. Getting to 50/50 is good for everyone, so write to Congress or your state legislature, petition your employer. When the 50/50 vote starts speaking, we'll get better child-care options at better prices much faster.

Chapter Nine

The Post-Baby Uphill: Test-Driving 50/50 and Getting Back Up to Speed

Between us, we've had five babies and five leaves. Each experience was unique except for one lesson: No matter how princely the man you married, pregnancy, childbirth, and breast-feeding just aren't splittable. And it takes a lot of faith (and holding your tongue) to stay on the 50/50 course.

Having a baby inside you prompts you to think about the baby more than your husband does. Breast-feeding has the same effect. And if you take more time off than he does, you're accruing knowledge about your baby at home while he's at work. How can you keep your equal footing as partners if you are losing touch with your old life and he's losing touch with the new one? How do you avoid growing apart?

Your baby expertise is one example where knowledge is power, and new moms often get a little power crazy. "If I'd been a little more laid back it would have helped—I'm a very type A personality, this was our first child. I was getting excited and anxious about everything," says Shanti. "I would drive everybody nuts on everything from diaper rash to missing a feeding. Maybe it will be better with the next one."

Moms and dads do experience the early parts of parenthood differently. And moms often (rightly) feel they've got more data points on the baby business. But families we talk to say they're happier when Dad stays in the race. So remember that 50/50 is a marathon, not a sprint, and Dad will have plenty of time to catch up—if you'll let him.

The first test of 50/50: It's your belly, not his

Even before your baby is born, you may feel your spouse is lagging behind you, failing to match your zeal about the miracle of pregnancy. Why isn't he constantly amazed at how huge your blue-veined stomach is or how skilled your child is at doing cartwheels in utero? Who is this guy?

You may take copious notes visiting your OB and study fetal development online, but don't be surprised if poring over the latest baby research is not at the top of your husband's to-do list. Your spouse may be like Rose's husband, Mark, who never missed a prenatal visit, or he may be like Lydia's husband, Rick, who "has a thing about needles," nearly fainted during her amniocentesis, and found *What to Expect When You're Expecting* scarier than anything by Stephen King.

Just because your husband isn't intimately familiar with the three phases of labor doesn't mean he isn't on board as a 50/50 mate. If you're growing frustrated with what you perceive to be his lack of baby interest, back off and consider this an early sign that you need to let him do things his *own* way. He may not make time to learn about prenatal neurology because he's more concerned about lining up child care or adding the baby to your health insurance.

If you really think he is missing something, find a way to bring him in—gently. Rebecca, a therapist, found her collection of baby books enthralling but saw that her husband did not. So she wrote up her own *Cliff's Notes* for her spouse so they could parent with the same information.

The second test of 50/50: It *was* your belly, but now it's *his* child, too

We all nod our heads about letting Dad be Dad, but it's amazingly hard to do when you're in the throes of new-mom-ness. Dads deserve a role beyond dispensing ice chips in the delivery room. Cutting the umbilical cord seems to be a symbolic step for involving fathers from the first moments of life. It also seems to be the extent of many a new dad's contributions—especially when new mothers fall prey to the cult of maternal supremacy.

Now is *not* the time to act like a ferocious mother grizzly guarding her helpless cub (we had a hard time with this ourselves). Your husband can't read your mind and when you're in new-baby overload, your powers of communication are somewhat impaired. Sharon was such a pill in her first weeks of motherhood, she vowed to do better with child number two. She and Steve wrote up a game plan to tie down what they would each do—and all the things that would not get done—in the first month of their new daughter's life. They found that helped a lot.

"Letting a partner venture forth in his own or her own way is a quiet vote of confidence; the more we try to control, the more we tacitly undermine that vote," writes Daniel Goleman in *Social Intelligence: The New Science of Human Relationships.*[1] This advice could easily apply to how you allow your spouse to "venture forth" as he attempts feeding, burping, diapering, bathing, and clothing his newborn child. You may be tired of repeating things you've read (and he didn't) about infant care. You may feel frustrated that he doesn't comfort the baby using the same hold you do—it sure *seems* to take longer that way. You may think that if he wastes one more wipe you'll go stark raving mad. But we know, in our experience, a dad's motivation declines with each helpful piece of "advice" we utter. So try to get perspective and know that your husband will do just fine.

Like many new mothers, you may be worried that your husband won't be as sensitive as you are to the needs of your newborn. However, there are plenty of studies that say fathers are equally competent as caregivers.

In the late 1960s, psychology professor Ross Parke conducted a study of new parents immediately after the birth of the child to compare the parenting behavior of mothers and fathers. (They chose babies who were bottle fed so that nursing would not create a difference in how parents *could* interact.)

After carefully observing one-on-one behavior of babies with mothers only, then babies with fathers only, Parke and his researchers found only one difference: Mothers smile at their babies more than dads do. "Women smile more at everyone," Parke told us. In all other measures, fathers and mothers were the same. Men paid attention and responded to vocalizations and distress from their babies, just as their wives did. Addressing a classic source of early-parent conflict, the researchers found that neither gender had a real edge in feeding a baby. Whether a mom or dad held the bottle, the baby consumed about the same amount of milk. Fathers equaled mothers in figuring out what to do when their infants stopped feeding, cried, or needed to burp.[2]

Child psychologist and researcher Michael Lamb also conducted a series of experiments on mothers and fathers, focusing on their physiological reactions to a crying baby. He measured blood pressure, heart rate, and galvanic skin response and found the responses of fathers and mothers were "indistinguishable."[3] Like Parke's work, Lamb's research shows that men and women are born with the same basic instinct to care for kids.

Here's one of the hardest things that you may face when you're staring down at your sleeping newborn: It turns out that you don't know everything. You just might when it comes to your regular job, but this motherhood gig is full of mysteries and surprises, and as the research bears out, your partner may be just as good at it as you are, and downright better at some things.

Sharon's new baby was a great eater but he took forever to burp, and would cry in discomfort after a feeding. She would walk him around and pat his back the way she'd seen the nurses do it in the hospital, but it took almost till the next feeding before Max would burp. Steve couldn't stand it. On the next doctor's visit, Steve asked the pediatrician to demonstrate burping. The doctor put Max on his shoulder and delivered several firm blows to Max's back. Sharon was alarmed—how could you apply so much force to such a small baby?—but Max belched and smiled (in a two-week-old sort of way). Sharon and Steve decided burping would be Dad's job. So Sharon wouldn't wince, Steve invented a variety of bubble-extraction routines for Max—putting his abdomen over a pillow, massaging his belly. Burping Dad-style became a more efficient and happy experience for everyone.

Joanna learned what all moms do: that sometimes babies cry for a very long time no matter how many infant books you read and methods you try to soothe them. Across the experience of three babies, this frustrated Joanna. Jason, in contrast, was very Zen about the crying—with each of their children, Jason was the one who would pick the baby up, speak soothingly, and walk (and walk and walk) until the yowling child calmed and fell asleep on his shoulder. Just knowing she had a husband with this magical talent greatly helped Joanna's psyche and let her become a more relaxed mother.

"Isabelle had a very difficult delivery and was basically in bed for the first eight weeks," says Don, the large-firm law partner who took two paternity leaves. "Jenna needed more milk so we started supplementing with formula, which meant that I could do a lot. I spent a lot of time being the one to soothe the baby. I kind of felt I developed a real bond with Jenna. That was an experience I would not have been able to reproduce any other way. It made it really worthwhile to have taken the time off."

The third test of 50/50: Home alone

One day, your 50/50 spouse gets up in the morning, not to change a diaper but to put on a crisp, spit-up-free shirt. He's going back to work with a fairly predictable routine and characters. He's back in the real world. You are not.

"When your life gets too different from your spouse's it gets hard," points out Vera, the attorney. "When I was on maternity leave, I was feeling kind of bitter because my husband would go out and he would be doing all these interesting things. And two hours of my day would be consumed washing and sterilizing baby bottles. I'm like, 'this is just drudgery.'"

And then, like a cherry on top of that cocktail of sleep deprivation and postpartum hormones, comes a question that pops whatever cool you have retained. "So, what did you do all day?" your spouse asks when he comes home one night. Don't strangle him with a nursing bra. This scene has unfolded in the lives of many parents we know, even if they've been through the baby drill before.

"When Jason would ask me, 'What did you do today?' I wanted to burst," says Joanna, recalling her third maternity leave. "I'd been working so hard all day, but he had no sense of what I was actually doing. And while Jason loved the new baby, he also seemed to miss talking about work and the world with me. And I missed it, too! On top of everything else, this made me feel guilty—I was supposed to want to be at home with our baby, right?"

Joanna and Jason realized the tension wasn't going away unless they talked about it. "We agreed that I really needed to take my maternity leave—that I couldn't be on call with my office all the time. We also agreed that the house would be a bit dirtier and our older kids might not get baths and meals exactly on time. And that when Jason got home, he might have to figure out what to make for dinner or toss a load of laundry in."

Maternity leave is not a permanent state and remembering that may make it easier. Yes, be available if your office needs you, but don't overdo it. The same goes for home. Now is not the time to plan four-course dinners or get the gutters cleaned. You'll be plenty busy, even if it feels like you have nothing to show for your time. Just watch your baby's evolving smile and know that someone thinks you're useful.

Husbands often struggle to empathize if they don't get enough direct infant experience. There's an easy way around that. As soon as you can, give your husband time with your child—without you. Baby Boot Camp is a surefire way to boost your spouse's confidence in himself as a parent, show him that you trust his 50/50 instincts, and help him understand how you spend your time at home. Go visit your sister, go get a haircut, find a hotel with cable—just go. After his stint at "camp," it's unlikely that you'll ever be greeted with "So, what did you do all day?"

"I went out for dinner with my mom and left my husband, Will, in charge of feeding our son and putting him down," one mom told us. "When I got home he told me the baby was fussy and didn't want to eat. So the baby woke up all night—and we were miserable. I told Will I wasn't leaving feeding to him anymore. But then a friend told me, 'Hey, if Will's in charge of the p.m. routine, let him do the whole thing. Get some earplugs and sleep in the study. Will's a smart guy and he'll figure it out with the baby—but only if he does night duty without you.'"

Finally, cut yourself some slack. Remember that you really are recovering. Days after childbirth, your estrogen levels dive to menopausal levels and do not return to normal levels for three months.[4] It's hard to be your best self when your body is still adjusting. During maternity leave, your husband may be a better 50/50 partner than you, because you're constantly tempted to push him away if he doesn't do things your way. Our maternity leaves were not a highlight of 50/50 life. But we held on to the hope that things would settle down as our babies grew and we returned to work.

BABY BOOT CAMP

No long good-byes. No lists of "what to do." No checking in from your cell phone. Walk out the door cold turkey. You'll come back to a spouse who feels like he has mastered the secrets of the universe. "I got him to stop crying—in less than a minute!" "I think he smiled at me!" "Have you seen how far this fella can pee?"

We call it Baby Boot Camp—not Daddy Boot Camp—because it's just as much about training moms.

Here are the camp rules.

Leave your husband alone with the baby. You don't need to leave the country, you may not even need to leave the house. How about leaving the room? Leave them alone, and *leave him in charge*. No cheating: no grandmothers, baby nurses, sisters, doulas. (Absolutely no baby monitor.) But if you have triplets, there's an exception to the part about helpers. Interestingly, research shows that dads have an easier time getting in on the act when new moms know they have too much on their hands—like multiples or medical complications. It's easier to ask for help and it's more obvious that help is needed. He can do this—and so can you.

From personal experience, we know this can be tough to do in the first few weeks of motherhood. Your postpartum biochemistry is sending you a message that may feel something like this: "PREPARE TO THROW YOURSELF IN FRONT OF A TRAIN FOR THIS HELPLESS CHILD FOR THE NEXT EIGHTEEN YEARS." But know your mother-protector self needs time out so Dad can get time in. So leave.

Start small. You don't need to go on an eleven-day wilderness hike. Go walk around the block. If you're breast-feeding, it's hard to go out for more than a few hours at a time, but one or two hours is better than no hours. So get a manicure, enjoy dinner with friends, or breakfast by yourself, or catch a movie. If you're not breast-feeding (or left pumped milk in the fridge), settle in for a double feature.

Remember that it's never too late to go to camp. Even if your husband doesn't sign up for the early weeks, this is a camp with many openings and round-the-clock sessions (at least for much of the first year). Perhaps you need to confess that you aren't a superhero after all, and you really do need help. Perhaps he will feel less nervous and more confident when the fragile, mysterious newborn fills out into a sturdy eight-month-old who smiles back at him and communicates with zeal.

Sign up for more sessions. Baby Boot Camp is basic training for 50/50 life as a parent—and it's most rewarding as a repeat experience. This is where we women tone those muscles we need to hold in the mother-knows-best reflex. And dads gain the experience to manage their kids with aplomb.

When you need to travel for work or want to visit your best friend two time zones away, it will feel totally natural to leave your husband in charge—because it turns out he learned all this great stuff at camp. And you did, too.

The fourth test of 50/50: Going back to work

Anticipation. It may be the hardest thing to live with as your maternity leave winds down. You're feeding the baby in the dead of night or strolling through the park on a brilliant sun-filled day and you're suddenly gripped by that old worry: *I don't know how I can do it.*

What kind of mess am I walking back into at work? What if I don't like the babysitter—what if she quits? What if the baby gets sick while I'm at work? How am I going to perform without a decent night's sleep?

Here are two thoughts that may get you through this phase: 1) the anticipation is worse than the reality, and 2) you aren't doing it alone—you have a partner in all of this.

"I was dreading going back to work," says Rebecca, a therapist. "I cried every night just looking at my son and thinking about not seeing him all day. The first few days were hard. I thought about him all day long and couldn't wait to get back home. But after about a week I remembered that I really like doing therapy, I like my colleagues, and I had missed adult conversation. I also realized that my son was fine. It was harder for me than him."

"I desperately wanted to postpone going back," says Jody, the public defender. "But the anticipation was definitely worse than the reality. Once I was back everything was okay and I liked using my mind again."

If you're bracing to feel sad or worried, you may surprise yourself. Sharon's friend Gloria called her saying, "I went back to work today. My husband is taking time off. We have a great sitter. I'm not anxious at all. Why should I be? My son is happy and he's in great hands. But I feel like I can't say that out loud because people will think it's not okay for me to feel okay!"

Whether you go back to work excited or with a little apprehension, it helps if you are lucky enough to have a husband on the same wavelength. Laila, a psychologist, loved her leave because she got to interact with more female peers—moms of other babies. "I loved observing the kids, playing with them. I did not want to go back to work," she says. And her husband, a lawyer who took two weeks off, felt the same way. "My husband also wanted to stay home, he was heartbroken to go back to work. We really bonded over that."

For us, the best way to reduce the stress was to see our child care in action: lots of dry runs before we *really* had to be back. Take your new sitter to visit friends with toddlers—you'll get a window on how she'll do as your child grows and maybe get some insight from more experienced parents. Or ask the day-care center if you can be a parent volunteer or just observe (with your sleeping infant in the BabyBjörn)—you'll see more than you did on the tour.

REENTRY: HOW NOT TO SURRENDER IN YOUR FIRST MONTHS AS A WORKING MOTHER

"When my first child was four months old, I returned to work and was put on the highest-profile case my firm had. When my second child was born, I returned to working on another huge case a thousand miles away for two months," says Shelly, the lawyer. "It's really enticing to be part of exciting cases and saying no means you can be blackballed. You've worked for years to build your credibility and all someone has to say is, 'Well, my experience is she didn't rise to the occasion,' and your reputation is shot."

Shelly's superiors weren't trying to make her miserable. But when employers don't intervene in the hard-charging culture of our 24/7 world, new moms often drown in a riptide. Trying to prove they still have the right stuff, moms may fear asking for slack or even temporarily declining big assignments. No one at Shelly's firm (as at many others) was willing to talk about how to draw the line—how to find the boundary between doing enough important work to remain credible and working so hard you fall over the edge. So Shelly quit—and went to a firm doing the same high-profile work, for the same high-powered clients, but with a culture where family mattered.

Policy research says that employers improve their chance of retaining women when they offer maternity leaves. In fact, a 2006 University of Maryland study shows how employers have benefited from the passage of the 1993 Family and Medical Leave Act—which merely requires a six-week unpaid leave, as we discussed earlier. "Women who had a child post-FMLA returned to work more quickly and were more likely to return to the same job," according to the study. In fact, the proportion of women returning to the same job following leave rose to 82 percent from 76 percent.[5]

From our experience and that of the working moms we've talked to, we think there's a way to improve these numbers: Good leave policies are important but what's also needed is a little humanity when the new mom walks back into the office. A few acts of kindness are often all it takes to make reentry a positive experience. Employers who exercise more common sense and empathy have far better luck helping talented moms return to work productively.

"I was in real pain when it was time for me to go back to work," says Shanti, a cardiologist who was serving a one-year term as co–chief resident when she went out on maternity leave. "I was actually ready to quit," she recalls, remembering how she agonized over leaving her baby daughter, though she lived close to her workplace and was leaving Loli in the care of her own mother.

Shanti fretted over the fact that Loli was still breast-feeding and that she was still so young (Shanti's "maternity leave" consisted of four weeks of vacation, followed by two weeks of sick leave). "I had a very hard time trusting anyone else, even my mother—it just felt like very strong maternal instinct on my part."

Shanti shared her chief residency with another physician, Jack, but knew they had a two-person job and that the hospital couldn't replace her for the balance of her term. "I didn't want to leave Jack in a bad spot...I told my boss I'd resign and come in and help Jack without pay, that I couldn't stay in my job," said Shanti. "But my director was a mom with four kids herself. She said, 'Let's try to work around it. The first few months are the hardest.'"

BEYOND THE MILKY WAY: BREAST-FEEDING AT HOME AND AT WORK

The American Academy of Pediatrics recommends exclusive breast-feeding for the first six months of life. (Our request to the AAP: Raise your public awareness budget so that bosses—not just nursing moms—know this.)

Once your milk supply is well established, you can pump and freeze extra supplies of breast milk and empower others (e.g., your husband) to get in on the feeding action. When you pump, you can leave home for longer stretches of time, without the anxiety of having to rush back for feeds.

Like us, you'll probably go to great lengths to protect your milk supply and suffer a keen sense of devastation if one drop is wasted. Power blackouts were common the summer Sharon was nursing her first child. The prospect of spoiled milk made Sharon so anxious that she priced out (but didn't buy) a backup generator and asked a neighbor to check on the freezer when she was out of town one weekend.

Joanna was traveling alone on business but pumping and saving milk. "Regulations say that you can't board with breast milk unless there's a baby with you," said an airport security worker, pouring out two days' worth of carefully stored milk. Joanna wept on the airplane home. (Thankfully, the TSA is now more humane and you can now carry on precious bodily fluids without fear.)

Once you're back at work, the challenge of finding places to pump—if you don't have a private office with a door that locks—is surmountable when you are determined to breast-feed.

Pumping in a bathroom stall at her office after she returned from her leave, Christina grew discouraged at how little milk she was producing. In tears, she called a lactation specialist. "Why don't I have enough milk? Everything was fine until I started working again—do I need to quit so I can feed my baby?" "Relax," the specialist said. "Milk production often slows down when you go back to work." She also told Christina to find a more comfortable spot—which is how Christina wound up pumping in her car. She managed to keep breast-feeding for a whole year—without getting arrested for indecent exposure.

Though breast-feeding is not a 50/50 task, we did find one couple who managed to share a related task, which saved time and aggravation for one working mom. Gayle pumped at work but loathed the nightly ritual of washing and drying all the "moving parts" of the breast pump. Patrick, the designated dishwasher, took on the chore, cleaning the mysterious plastic and rubber pieces and carefully setting them on the counter, ready to go for the next morning.

"I try to focus on the first year," says Nicole, a smart boss who runs a group that oversees new acquisitions at her fast-growing firm. When women come back from maternity leave, "you need to help them set reasonable expectations for themselves. There are just a lot of unexpected things that come up when your child is young. I say, 'Hey, if you were coming back from a ski accident, you'd cut yourself some slack.' On the other hand, I try to help them with what I like to call 'recency bias'—the fact that no one remembers the great things you did *before* your leave. We try to find realistic ways for returning moms to put points on the board when they get back." Nicole also encourages working moms on her team to think through their contingency plans. "Don't wait until you need it to try out the backup child-care center here at the office. Go visit on a good day when you and your child are calm and happy."

Many of our survey respondents told us about small acts of kindness that made a world of difference when they returned to work. "I was a transport nurse, riding ambulances," one woman said. "My boss let me walk home and breast-feed whenever. Frequently, we would swing the ambulance by my home and my husband would run out and get a fresh supply if I was running numerous calls. I'm not sure I could have done this if I didn't have the flexibility of the transport team."

Another working mom said, "I was given flexibility by my bosses to start at just a few hours a day and ramp up to full time (6 a.m.–3 p.m.) over the course of the first month back. As far as HR and payroll knew, though, I had started full time at the beginning of the month—I was very thankful for my bosses' flexibility and financial help."

When bosses make an effort to help moms get back in gear at work, "they send the signal that they still believe in you, that they still see you as a valuable player," one mom said to us. Beth, the doctor, admits it's hard when full-time doctors step down their hours. But she herself worked part time for many years and believes that it's a great way to retain talented women. "Now that I'm a boss, I know that if you let people work part time, as their kids get older, they will likely gear back up," she says. "It's an investment from an organizational point of view."

If you work in a place where new moms aren't seen as good long-term investments, where acts of goodwill are in short supply, show yourself a little love. We wish we'd done this better ourselves. Expect flack and don't be surprised when it comes your way. And even if you've never been able to do this in your entire life, lower your expectations—of *yourself.* You have many great accomplishments ahead of you, but do yourself a favor and know they don't need to happen exactly now. And try to laugh. If you can't find enough funny friends (because they're all exhausted, too), put the kids to bed, grab your 50/50 spouse, and switch on the comedy channel. We're not joking.

EVERYTHING MUST GO!

"Wisdom is the art of knowing what not to do." Sharon read this Confucian saying nine months before giving birth.[6] It made her feel free (and wise) to think like a corporate cost cutter and wipe out large tracts of her to-do list. And when Sharon returned to work, she just kept cutting away at the list and hasn't stopped since.

Young women tell us, "It seems like you have to have some superhuman level of efficiency to be a working mom." Based on our lives and interviews for this book, we can tell you there are few supermoms (or dads). Happy working parents need to be exceptional in one way alone: They outsource—by that we mean they ship tasks out of their lives (with a certain level of glee). Tasks can be outsourced in many ways—to another person, to technology, to another time, or to the dustbin.

Start with your inner rebel, the voice that says, "I HATE this chore." Take heed—it's telling you what needs to go. Only your own list will work for you, but here's a diagnostic tool to get you going:

1. **Food.** Omelet and salad for dinner—how about French toast? Do what's easy. Make five quarts of chili you can freeze and eat over months? Sign up with the farm co-op that drops a random sample of veggies for $25 per week (you don't get to choose, but neither do your kids)? Order-in pizza and Chinese work well, too.

2. **Tidiness.** When you've got an infant, just forget it. Cleaning up after a baby is like shoveling in a blizzard. Try to take pleasure in the mashed peas ground into your carpet (it needed some green). Skip Martha Stewart and strive for Cherie Blair, the lawyer wife of former British prime minister Tony Blair, who was apparently undisturbed by the merry disorder of 10 Downing Street when the four Blair children lived there.

3. **Helping hands.** Give the errand backlog to the sixteen-year-old next door who likes to drive. If you live in a city, find the Laundromat that actually folds (how much is that extra $10 worth in time to finish all your other work?). And know that your baby will grow up to be a competent child who in less than seven years can give you a better deal (Sharon's son charges $5 for two loads). When your mom offers to shop for kids' shoes, say, "Yes, thank you."

4. **Deferral.** Outsource to a less busy time in your life—as in, another decade. Scrapbooks? Save the baby pictures until she is twelve and you can both use a glue stick (and marvel at how cute she was). Holiday cards? Not until the kids can address envelopes.

5. **Hair.** Unless you have a crew cut, it takes too much time. Get a simpler do. Sharon went for a wash-n-wear cut to save the two hours per week sucked up by blow-drying. Bob Marley has become a hair-care role model for Sharon's four-year-old daughter, who's very happy that Mom's okay with her tangled tresses.

"While you were out..."

Most women we talked to grappled with how to ensure their work got done while they were out—and how to reclaim the turf they had before having their babies. The natural ups and downs of the business cycle can feel more off-putting (and potentially personal) when you are a new mom and you're worried about how you're perceived. Vera was pregnant with her first child the year she was up for partner at her law firm. She thought she was having a great year, and got lots of kudos from her manager. Then this: "My bosses said this wasn't my year. The business environment was weaker and they were naming fewer partners. 'You're one of the top people this year and if you come back next year and try it again, you're in as good a position as anybody,' they told me. And I'm sitting there thinking, 'My feet are tied together. I'm seven months pregnant, I can't take on new projects when I'm about to go out on leave. So how am I going to prove myself again, am I really going to get the trophy next year?' It was pretty hard," Vera said. "I was a little nervous when I came back, but it all worked out and I became partner. My colleagues were supportive, but I think it was mostly my husband who helped me through it."

Sandy returned to her job as a sports agent after a three-month leave. Her boss had recruited Sandy to represent his firm in her part of the country and had treated her well before her baby. While he said nothing explicit about her motherhood, Sandy's boss starting calling her at the office early in the morning and late at night, checking her whereabouts. While the skepticism drove her nuts, Sandy rose above it. Now pregnant with her second child, Sandy told us, "As I lay awake in the middle of the night (again), I was musing over the fact that—in the sixteen months since giving birth to my first child—I've not only had the most successful (and lucrative) year of my life and career, but also have closed the biggest and most innovative deal in my firm's history. Between me and my husband (50/50 baby!), it's working out great."

Kara returned to work as her firm did a widespread restructuring. She ended up with a less exciting job, with more travel and more hours. "I was really discouraged," she says. "I'd walk through the slush to the subway in the dark after work and I'd think, 'How did I end up here? I'm a grunt again and I've worked a decade at this place.'" But after six months, things improved. Kara's daughter was a happy kid and while her husband didn't love her travel, he told her, "We'll do what it takes for you to get back where you were." Two years into being a working mom, Kara was again running a group she enjoyed and the head of her business pulled her aside and said, "You know, the buzz on you has never been better."

Baby up all night? Good guys to the rescue— how 50/50 men save the day

Your baby is sick. Your meeting runs late. Your sitter needs an emergency root canal. The day care closes for the Columbus Day holiday— but your office does not. Early parenthood can feel like a place where Murphy's Law is the only rule on the books.

And if the bombardment of new problems weren't enough, you're having to problem-solve with a deeply sleep-deprived mind (unless you lucked out with the rare infant who sleeps the full night). Kara remembers commuting on the freeway one morning after a rocky night with her six-month-old. " 'The cops should pull you over,' I told myself. I could barely keep my eyes open." "I think it takes six to nine months to rebalance, to recalibrate your life," says Carol, the accounting partner. "You have to know you're going to have rough nights when your kid comes in your bed and throws up on you."

In these stressful first months of parenthood, it's easy to feel like the damsel in distress. If your husband is not rushing to be your 50/50 knight in shining armor, you might share this with him. James Levine, director of the Fatherhood Project and author of *Working Fathers,* says that we need to help men stand up and ask for flexibility as often as women do. Levine says too many of us play a game of "Blame the Culture." "Working parents assume that employers won't allow men the same leeway as women. But they rarely ask. Men don't ask their bosses; women don't ask their husbands."[7] How to change this? After you stay home with your sick baby once, you say, "I covered this time. Next time, it's your turn to call in and say you have a sick child." Levine points out (and we agree) that if only moms ask for flexibility the workplace will never evolve (and recall from Chapter 2 that men are at least as anxious about work/life conflict as women). Working moms alone don't have enough power as a voting block at work. But when dads report for active duty, the culture starts to change.

With 50/50 comes practice providing mutual air cover—Dad for Mom and Mom for Dad. Sharon took a four-month maternity leave offered by her firm while her husband, Steve, went back to his job running his new company after a week. But Steve agreed that he'd play parental quarterback for Sharon's first four months back at work. When Max cried at night, Steve got him so Sharon could sleep. When Max had a doctor's appointment, Steve took him. Disruptions in child care? Steve had it covered.

"You figure out who has the least demands tomorrow and you deal with being exhausted," says Carol about how she and her husband (also an accounting partner) managed. "A key factor is sleep. If you need to sleep until noon or 2 p.m. on a weekend, you and your spouse have to let each other do that periodically."

Going to the office after being up all night with your child is just no fun, but working when you're tired won't last forever. Quitting *because* you're tired will probably keep you awake at night long after your child has fallen asleep.

| Chapter Ten | Getting to 50/50: At Home, at Work, for Life |

You're doing it.

You're back at work. Your child sleeps most nights, walks, talks, and eats vaguely normal food (when not dropping it on the floor).

But some days are hard. Maybe it's an aggravating boss or a change in management that spells trouble ahead. Maybe the day care you so carefully chose is closing down (or isn't working out). Or it's one too many late meetings, or business trips on Halloween.

"It's okay if you decide to stop," says your best friend, your colleague, maybe your boss or mentor, or even your spouse. They think they're tossing you a lifeline in the midst of a crisis. They see your struggle and something they believe will ease it. And it's tempting to see quitting as the cure-all for moms because so many people do. You start to think, "Maybe I *should* quit."

Regardless what income bracket a family is in, at least 30 percent of moms are unemployed when their kids are small. In every income quartile, moms struggle with this question of whether working is a good thing. As we pointed out in the introduction, whether you think you can "afford" to quit is more a matter of culture (whom you hang out with and what you believe you need) than pure economics.[1]

When we're thrust into difficult situations and feel caught between work and family, it's easy to wonder if we've made the right decision. "Would the kids be better off if I stayed home? Either I go to work or I stay home, because it seems impossible to do a good job on both fronts."

Why is this an either/or? Why can't we adopt the attitude of male breadwinners? They never think, "I think I'll quit my job and stay home with my family because I simply can't do both."

If you can see that the gains from working can outweigh what you lose from quitting—and know you'll survive the bumps in the road—you can embrace working as a given, not a "choice" that must be constantly second-guessed. You can enjoy your family and recalibrate your work commitments as you go along.

GUILT IS NOT A REQUIREMENT

When we speak to groups of young women, often in college or graduate school, we are struck by how frequently we hear the same concern from these accomplished students. "When I have kids, I know I'll feel guilty if I keep working. I'll have to stop, at least for a while."

These women don't even have kids yet, but they're already signing on for the guilt that they believe is a natural by-product of working motherhood (though never a part of working fatherhood). They're quick to focus on the "guilt requirement," but they aren't thinking of their partners as equal contributors to parenting.

"A funny thing seems to be happening among young women now," observes Linda, the medical professor with grown children. "When I was in medical school, it was a time full of promise. Everything was going to work out great," she says, remembering how hopeful, perhaps even naive, she and other female students were about their futures as working women who could have it all. "I wish someone would have told me about the turmoil, about the fact that you'd have bad days," she says, thinking of how she and other women made their way without role models or mentors who were working mothers.

Linda persevered and succeeded, raising a strong family and build-ing a career in a field she loved. Now women regularly fill the classes at the medical school where she teaches, as well as staffing the hospi-tals, which are not as male dominated as they once were. But despite these strides Linda has noticed a marked shift in attitude: "this back-to-the-earth idea of motherhood, that the 'best' choice is to be with your kids full time. And to see this in really promising women, it is very worrisome."

The message sent to women, starting at a very young age, seems to be this: *You are neglecting your kids if you work.* It is this presumption of neglect that spawns so much guilt. And guilt causes many young women to put their careers on hold or sacrifice them entirely, no mat-ter how hard they've worked to attain education, experience, and skills. What would our world look like—inside and outside of the home—if all working mothers allowed themselves freedom from guilt?

The first step: Don't call it "guilt"

Guilt is a powerful word. We're not talking about the twinge you feel when you eat a piece of your kids' Valentine's candy. We're talking about an onslaught of bad feeling that causes us to question how we are living our lives. Guilt is what you feel when you do something wrong, something that causes harm. So, if you're leaving your happy, healthy children in excellent care when you go to a job you enjoy that benefits your family, is "guilt" really the right label for the emotion you feel when you can't take your toddler to a Mommy-and-Me class?

Maybe you worry that you're not there to watch out for your kids, to make sure your son has got his blankie and your daughter finished her term paper. As a loving parent, you'll be concerned for your child's welfare for the rest of your life—whether you work or not.

In the beginning of this book, we provided hard evidence from leading experts, as well as kids and parents, that children tend to fare the same whether you stay home or not. But our feelings sometimes do quarrel with the facts. We can show you all the proof in the world that your kids will do fine if you work, but we can't argue with emotion, and we can't stop you from worrying. We can, however, show you how worry and guilt are easily confused, and why we increase our peace of mind when we keep these emotions separate.

One type of anxiety that working mothers experience, says Elizabeth Ozer, the psychologist at UC San Francisco who has studied the impact of combining work and family, is a fear of missing out. "What am I missing when I'm at work?" we worry. A first step or first words? Playdates? School-yard stories you'll only hear if you do pickup? We often feel pulled to be with our children, though they are thriving without our constant presence at home.

"It's okay to feel this pull," says Ozer, herself a mother. But this pull is different from guilt, which suggests that you're doing something wrong and harmful to your family by working. You can reframe your "guilt" and feel loads better about working if you acknowledge that you want to be with your kids, not for their sake, *but for your own*. You will also feel much better about going to work if you recognize that your children are doing fine even if you can't act on this impulse every time it hits you.

"I feel pulled to do things for our family that my husband does not feel pulled to do," Ozer says. Perhaps it's sticking around for T-ball practice (though your son may focus more on the coaching if you just drop him off). Or maybe it's attending all three performances of the fifth-grade play—what if he forgets his costume? Like Ozer, you may feel the pull, despite how difficult the timing may be. You have a big day, an important lunch meeting or conference call you can't miss, but your husband can get off early—turns out he can make it to the game, the spelling bee, the science fair setup. "If my husband goes," Ozer says, "if he does it, I'm okay."

Jane visited her daughter's kindergarten classroom, where the children had posted notes of thanks to their parents. "All but one said, 'Thank you to my mommy.' My daughter had written, 'Thank you to my dad and my nana, and thanks to my mommy, too.' At first I was sad I wasn't first," says Jane. "But then I realized how lucky my daughter is to have so many people involved in her life and loving her. I was proud of my husband for being the only dad up on the wall."

When you have a 50/50 relationship, with a spouse who can be there when the situation warrants the presence of a parent, the fear of missing out dissipates. You satisfy "the pull" to be with your children—because one of you *is* there. The emotion that we mistakenly think of as working mother guilt shrinks, and is replaced by "Oh, my children are in good hands."

When you feel the pull, push back

Early parenthood is exhausting, as you adjust to facing the twin demands of your growing baby and your office. But if your family is healthy (and your job is, too), you'll find a routine and start to think, "Okay, it feels like chaos but I'm nailing this working parent gig—I can do this! *We* can do this!"

But then a first, a fourth, a twelfth birthday goes by (perhaps your family unit grows by one or two or more), and after all this time, you wonder if you really do have it nailed. Here come demands for allergen-free birthday cupcakes for twenty two-year-olds, and requests for playdates with a kid you've never heard of. Kids get sick. They flunk out of math. They get made captain of the debate team and have to compete three towns away. Just when you think you have all their needs, quirks, talents, desires, hot-button issues, and favorite foods squared away, they change right before your eyes.

Life at work is changing, too. You've been promoted (that's good). You have more interesting work (that's good). You have a new boss who wants you to travel one week out of the month (not so good, even if it's to Paris). Or, maybe you want to change jobs.

We've discussed the importance of getting your spouse on board with 50/50 before you become parents, but even more important is *keeping* your spouse on board for the long climb ahead, after the pureed carrots and footie pajamas are long gone. The challenges of parenthood are unknowable, as are the challenges of sustaining a fulfilling career. Having a 50/50 partner whom you can turn to, no matter where you are in your journey, gives you the strength to keep pushing ahead, even when you may feel pulled in another direction.

How you can put "pull" in perspective

Joanna and Jason got that dreaded phone call from school: Your first-grade son is having trouble reading. They panicked and started making lots of phone calls and doing research. After a few days and nights of feeling stressed, Joanna called her mom to talk. Even in the midst of writing this book, Joanna got a tinge of maybe-I-should-quit-itis. "Mom, do you think I should stop working for a while? Can I do enough to help him while still working?" Her mother's question: "What are you going to do for him while he is at school all day? Think carefully about what he needs. Maybe you should take a *few days* off to focus. But it doesn't make any sense to stay home all day just to worry about him."

Sometimes we need to put our concerns in perspective. If your child is chronically ill, maybe one of you *will* need to stop working for a time to take care of him. If your teenager is getting into trouble after school, perhaps one of you *will* cut back your hours so a parent is home in the afternoons. Just don't reflexively blame your work for all the pitfalls of child rearing.

Your child cries when you leave for work

When Christina's daughter turned two, she cried—not soft whimpering but Oscar-worthy, heartrending sobs—every time her mother left her at nursery school. She hadn't done so as a baby, but now that she was a preschooler, the tears ran freely. *She's old enough to know where I'm going...she's doing this because I work,* Christina assumed, as many of us do. It was extremely painful to watch her daughter get so upset until Christina realized that her child wasn't the only one crying. "It's a phase," one of the teachers assured her. "Lots of kids do this—whether or not their mothers work." Christina noticed that many other children were, in fact, crying, whining, begging a parent to stay—no matter if that parent was leaving for an office or heading back home.

"It is quite typical for children, especially those under six, to experience anxiety before a parent leaves for the day or for a more extended trip," says Karen Friedland-Brown, a parent educator at Jewish Family and Children's Services. "It is important for children to be able to express their strong feelings and see that the parent has confidence in their ability to cope. Sometimes crying and other emotional outbursts come from the child's need to test whether they can control the situation. 'If I cry really hard or hang on to Mommy's legs, maybe she will stay with me.' A very consistent routine for good-byes which include rituals that the child can control (e.g., carrying the briefcase to the car or getting a special story) helps a child gain a sense of mastery and feel more secure."

"I used to hate telling my son I was going to have to travel," says Kara. "So I'd wait until the night before and then there would be lots of tears. But if I told him the week before, 'Mommy has to go to Chicago for three days,' it was different. My son would say, 'I don't want you to go,' and I'd explain why I needed to. He'd get interested in where Chicago was on the map, and how many times I would call when I was gone. We'd talk about the trip several times in advance. By the time I left, it was old news—no tears and occasional help with the packing."

It's normal to feel anxious when your child is crying, and you should allow her to express her feelings. But you are the parent so you set the tone. "If my daughter asks if I have to go to work, I say, 'Yes, just like you have to go to school. That's what we do,'" says Maya. "If kids see you hesitating, if they sense you don't have conviction, it makes things worse." Before you let yourself think that these long good-byes mean your child is being harmed, remember that you're only going to work, not joining the French Foreign Legion, and that children outgrow separation anxiety (though we parents may not!).

You worry about your child care

Unless you're a saint, perhaps you've gone through a phase at work where you blame a colleague or assistant for everything that goes wrong, even if logically that person is not directly responsible for the messes that you're trying to untangle. The blame game is easy to play when it comes to your kids, too—and often a caregiver may bear the brunt of your bad mood (of course, sometimes it's your spouse). Until the black cloud lifts, it's easy to find fault with something about a sitter, a day-care provider, or a teacher. We find it's worth thinking twice. You may just be feeling the normal anxiety of leaving your child someplace where you won't be.

"William goes to a small family day care, three providers, fourteen kids. Of course I had a lot of anxiety when he started, but he adjusted quickly. He talks about his friends all the time," says Celia, the teacher. "Twice last week he cried in the car going home because he didn't want to *leave*."

"Our nanny's not perfect, no one is, but she has great judgment and is really responsible," says Rose, who adds that having a reliable sitter contributes immensely to her sense of security at work.

You already know that child care you trust is a key to working without worry. If you're suddenly unhappy with your arrangements, don't keep it to yourself; share your concerns with a 50/50 partner and get to the bottom of it. Is it really because your job is in flux that you feel stressed out at the end of each day? Is it a personal issue that has nothing to do with your kids? Or is there something really wrong with your child care?

Sharon and Steve flubbed an early hire. Impressed by the credentials of one caregiver, they talked themselves out of their instincts that told them she wasn't a good fit. In the first month, they realized the personality issues were too big for them and made a change. Sharon was really rattled by this mistake. But Steve pointed out that they had seen many other good candidates. "Listen carefully and trust your gut," Sharon's father, the shrink, told her. Following that advice, they found two wonderful sisters who have worked with them now for eight years.

Some working mothers find another reason to worry about child care: Their children *don't* cry when they leave. "Why isn't my baby attached to me enough to cry when I walk out the door? Is it because I spend too much time at work?" When your child enjoys the time when you are at work, that means you've picked the right care. Go talk to people who grew up with working moms and listen to what they say. As the grown son of a working mother told us, "I always knew who my mother was. Children are never confused." You may feel an unpleasant twinge when your child calls out for a sitter—and not you—in a moment of distress. You may feel hurt, but be thankful that he or she has another "safe" person to rely on.

You made room for your spouse to be an equal parent. For the benefit of your child, make room for a caregiver to do the best possible job as well.

You hate telling your kids "I can't be there"

As kids get older, they don't cry when you leave but they do ask when you'll be back. You may want to answer "soon," as we often do, even if the "soon" we mean is many hours away. But happy working mothers learn that minimizing gets you in trouble and kids prefer straight talk they can depend on.

"When my daughter asks, 'Mom, can you come home early today?' if I say yes, I make sure I do it. But if I really can't, I tell her so and we make another plan," says Maya. "I set expectations that I will be working late. If I get home early, that's something to celebrate. I don't want my girls to be mad at my work or to resent it."

"I've always tried to be honest with my kids about what I can and can't do. And every year, there are probably one or two things you miss that you wish you hadn't," says Alexandra, the executive. "But I find it's not my kids that really miss it. It's the parents that miss it." Know that your children will be okay when you miss an event or two—especially if you've been up front about it and your 50/50 spouse is there without you. Realize the loss you feel is your own, something to be weighed against all the other things you get from work.

Your child's school doesn't have your job in mind

"Work is engineered for efficiency and things at your kids' school seem organized for participation," says Grace, about the challenge of contributing at your child's school when you're a working parent. "Who wants to bring the knives? Who wants to bring the forks, the napkins? I feel like saying, 'Aren't they all in the same grocery aisle? Can't one person just pick all of them up—and for all five class parties we have this year?' Because things are engineered this way it creates this myth that you can't be involved if you're working. My greatest value is time. So I say to my kids, 'Mommy isn't going to bring the napkins, but I'll be at the party with you.'"

While most parents today *do* work, schools remain designed for a different era, when nonworking mothers were the only parents who got involved. "It's like the at-home moms are saying, 'We're a club and you're not in it,'" says Rob, who has run his own company and tries to get involved at his child's school, adding that it's particularly frustrating for working fathers. "We feel shut out. It's just assumed you won't want to go because you're a man."

Until schools update their assumptions, you'll need to improvise to be involved. Bring "job sharing" to the classroom. Anita is splitting the duties of PTA secretary with another working parent. If there's a two-hour time slot for volunteering at the school book fair, do a half hour and recruit three other time-strapped parents. Or just go when you can. If you can't do the whole field trip from start to finish, meet the class at the planetarium and let your child show you his favorite exhibit.

If you are feeling vexed at all the things you can't do on the volunteer sign-up sheet, remember that parents are wanted at school for only a brief time in their child's lives. Like breast-feeding, it is fleeting. As your kids get older, the level of parental involvement in class declines. Your kids will continue to need you for other things, but at some point they get downright embarrassed if you set foot on school property.

Most of all, know that your 50/50 partner can do this as well as you can and that when he shows up in class he's got an edge on you—his scarcity value. Until more men get to school, your husband is a hero when he appears in the classroom.

"When Jamie would show up at school events our kids really loved it," says Sara, who traveled a lot and whose husband volunteered at school. "Everyone else had their moms but our kids got their dad. It made them feel special and proud." On his way in to help with a class project, Steve was approached by one of the few male teachers at his son's school. "It's really great you do this. It makes such a difference for kids to see a dad come to school."

You feel that you don't have enough time for your child

In *The Blessing of the Skinned Knee,* psychologist Wendy Mogel tells the story of a mother who saw her for counseling. The woman worried she wasn't connecting with her kids and that she should cut back her hours at work. The mom said she felt like an army commander issuing nonstop orders: "Stop watching television! Finish your homework! Eat supper! Clear the table! Take out the garbage! Get in the bath! Stop playing with the bubbles and wash your hair! Get out of the bath! Get in bed! Hurry up and start sleeping! Wake up! Find your backpack!" Mogel's advice? "Cutting down might be part of the solution, but your attitude and goals when you are at home are just as important as how much time you spend there. If you are ambitious at home in the same way you are at work, you won't succeed."

Mogel told the mother that while it might ease "your general sense of anxiety to load the dishwasher and return phone calls the instant you get home, control the urge. You do your job better if you let the dishes and phone calls wait while your daughter tells you . . . about how her teacher's son once got lost on a camping trip and they couldn't find him for four hours." Families connect better if time at home can be more relaxed and less focused on "cleanup detail and logistical planning," says Mogel, and so do the many working parents we interviewed.[2]

Rose had a morning drill many working parents will recognize — the rush to get dressed, eat breakfast, brush teeth, grab backpacks and briefcases, get to school, then race to work. "I felt like the enforcer — it was a struggle getting the kids to eat their organic oatmeal and fresh blueberries, it wasn't the relaxed time I really wanted with my kids." Then Rose had an aha moment. If she was willing to forfeit the organic breakfast, she could gain something she valued more: Time with her daughter.

"There's a vendor who sells bran muffins outside of our building," says Rose, who lives in New York, where the sidewalks are awash with muffin men most mornings. "My daughter thinks they are cupcakes." So Rose changed her idea of breakfast and decided to spring for muffins that her daughter would eat, rather than spend time policing the oatmeal bowl.

"I can leave the house an hour earlier, go to my daughter's school, play with the things she likes there, be with her in her school environment. It made me so happy I told my husband about it and he came today."

How much happiness can we gain, how much more time with our kids, if we are willing to question our "normal" routine? "My mom was a phone operator and worked the late shift," says Steve, "so during the summer, she'd come home and take us outside for a picnic dinner—at 10 p.m. It was a wonderful time for us to have with our mom."

"My kids' Halloween costumes will never win awards," says Alexandra. She notes that you can spend time trying to be a "perfect mother," doing things no one else remembers, "or you can take that time and give your kid an extra hug. You do remember that hug and so does your child. It gets easier to let go as you get more confident in yourself. My kids really helped me get over these things—they said, 'Mom, who really cares?'"

What kind of time could you gain with your child if you asked yourself that question about more things?

With an open mind, even time away from kids can be time to grow closer. "My rule when I was commuting was that when the kids called on my cell phone I always answered. Even in the middle of a meeting. I'd say, 'I'm sorry, I've got to take this,'" says Sara, who ran a company out of state for a few years.

"My daughter gave me the best Mother's Day present ever. My friends were all struggling with their teenage daughters. But Katy gave me an empty book and a beautiful note. It said, 'Dear Mom, I bought this book so we can share our thoughts. One week you can take it with you and write when you are on the plane. And the next week, I'll take it.'" Katy still calls her mom in the middle of meetings—even though she's now off at college.

You've got no time for yourself

You may feel frustrated that because you work, you have no time for yourself (or for your partner). "I wish I'd learned French or how to knit," says Rachel, who worked full time while raising three (now grown) children with her husband. "Pretty much all of my time has gone to three things: my work, my family, and my church." But, Rachel points out, her desire to have done "more" is largely tied to her personality. "I think I would have been too busy to do everything I wanted no matter what I did. I'm interested in lots of things." If you're happier when you're engaged in many spheres, and bored when you're not, you'll never be one to have extra time on your hands.

Most of us fantasize about how we'd spend our hours if we had more of them. Besides more time for family, there would be more time for exercise, sleep, sex, reading, vacations, giving back.

There is no easy answer for being a parent. As one mom quipped, "Working moms are stressed, stay-at-home moms are depressed." And all moms are pressed—for time. Whether or not you work, rarely in life will you think you have enough.

BRINGING YOUR CHILD INTO YOUR WORLD

Employers (like Brian) will rightly complain if you disrupt work with your kids, but many parents integrate children into work life in a way that's good for everyone. If you're skeptical you can do much with a child in tow, recall the only working mom to grace a U.S. coin: Sacagawea, the Native American who led Lewis and Clark through the wilderness. After giving birth at the start of their trek, Sacajawea traveled hundreds of miles through river rapids and mountain passes, bartering with hostile tribesmen along the way, all with a baby on her back. Today's working parents tell their own versions of this story. You can be both productive and close to your kids if you look for selective openings to bring them into your work.

Helen and her husband teach at an all-boys boarding school and live on campus with their family. "Kids like to be incorporated into grown-up life. Jobs need to work in the larger picture of family. I'd just asked myself, 'What part of this job can my kids do with me?'" she says. With no formal maternity leave, Helen found she was back teaching a few weeks after her first child was born. Helen and her husband scheduled their classes so they could alternate care of their son—literally handing off the baby in the hallways.

Helen coached the track team with her son in the baby jogger, and later with her daughter in tow. "When our kids got louder they couldn't come to faculty meetings anymore, and so my husband and I traded off going and we represented each other." Helen's circumstances are fairly unique. But lots of parents in lots of jobs find ways to spend time with their kids while getting their work done.

School-age children love spending the occasional day in a parent's workplace. Carmen, a doctor, has found a way to include her six-year-old. "She comes to my committee meetings at the hospital. I started doing home visits and took her to see a 102-year-old man. Everyone thinks it's great, especially my daughter."

"For (my daughter) it was all about getting the free sodas," says Carol. Beyond the fun, when kids see what you do, you're planting a seed for them to respect and value work as much as you do.

Jamie, the ex–NFL player, was in sales, so he traveled all the time. When he and his wife, Sara, had their first baby, they were in Texas, far from both their families on the East Coast. How's this for making adversity work for you? "When Katy was a baby, if Jamie had a meeting in the New York area, his mom would meet him at Newark, take Katy for the day, and bring her back to the airport for Jamie's flight back to Texas. He'd find ways to connect through different cities where we had family. Katy got to see family and be with her father in a pretty unique way. My mom thought this was so great she made Jamie a sort of manly suit protector—kind of like a BabyBjörn with an apron so Katy wouldn't mess up his business suits."

While male executives take their employees with them when they go to the airport or get a shoeshine, Alexandra gives her direct reports the option to meet her in a cab, en route to her son's basketball games, and invites them to stay and watch. "I negotiated my bonus with a woman just back from maternity leave," says Kara. "We were walking her baby around the park and it made me feel very grateful to her. She was showing me how to hold your head up high as a working mom—to be great at your job and great with your kids at the same time."

"More time with the kids" is often at the top of the working parents' wish list, but you needn't bring your child to work or on business trips to achieve that goal. You just may stumble onto some simple ways of being together, of showing your child the world you both live in, that involve no advance planning.

"Yesterday, my car broke down and my wife had a meeting," says Gus, the CEO, "so I took the bus home to pick up the two kids from their schools. I thought, *This is going to be interesting.*

"After I picked up my daughter, I realized I didn't have enough cash to get on the next bus and we didn't have time to find an ATM and get to my son's school on time. So we walked and had a great time. Walking together put us in touch with all these things we usually miss when we drive. It makes you remember there's a bright side to everything."

You wonder how your kids will turn out

"When your kids are really little it's easy to worry. Society tells you you'll mess up your kids if you don't devote 100 percent of your time to them," says Mary, whose sons are successfully making their way toward middle school. "That's just not true. That's easier to see as your kids get older—the proof is in the pudding." Working mothers find things get easier as their children grow and demonstrate in real time what the experts say—that a child with working parents can turn out very well.

In fact, psychologist Wendy Mogel says that in order to thrive, children *don't* need the best of everything. They need what's good enough. That might include "good enough (but dull) homework assignments, good enough (but a little crabby or uninspired) teachers, good enough (although insect-infected) summer camps." And good-enough parenting.

Mogel comments that some stay-at-home mothers figure they better do a great job to prove to themselves that they are "succeeding at the art, craft, and science" of child rearing. Some full-time working moms "want things to be very special for their children because they feel guilty for not being around as much as their own mothers were." And "the moms who work part time do a bit of both." But Mogel thinks we should all *chill out.* Have a little less ambition for yourself and your children. Strive to be a "good enough" parent, not a great one. "It can make everyone in the family relax and paradoxically make life richer."[3]

"If I could have peeked ahead, I might have felt some comfort that our kids would turn out to be brilliant successes by the yardsticks that matter to me. They are strong and loving. They have very good relationships and care for other people. They are finding meaningful work in the world. It's nice to have a happy ending—though some of it is just sheer luck," says Linda, the medical professor, looking back on her years of child rearing. "There were so many times that I doubted and worried. But my husband is so much more accessible to his kids than the dads I knew growing up. And even working full time, I'm more accessible to my kids than my mother was to me. We have relationships with our kids that are so much better than what we grew up with." All the many moments when we get anxious about our own kids, we try to remember what so many working parents have told us: Look into the eyes of your children and trust what you see.

Keeping a dual-career perspective— what to do when your job changes

In our experience, 50/50 life is much easier when careers are going according to plan, but that never lasts long. Couples we talked with say that what matters is how you process the disruptions and how you set things up to keep both careers afloat.

A wretched job situation, even if it's temporary, can sometimes be enough to make you want to throw in the towel. If you have a little savings, can afford some time off, and don't want to settle for less than you've had, the fantasy of saying "I quit!" can be very tempting. Maybe you're anxious because your job has grown bigger—or gotten smaller. Or, maybe it's your husband's job. Things are going gangbusters for him, he needs more time at the office (or needs your family to move).

You get a new boss, your job cools down
Your employer merges or your boss retires. What does it mean for you? Is your hard-won flexibility in danger? Did they take away

personal days as well as the free coffee? Does the writing on the wall say something like "Hey you, clean out your desk"?

When Lydia's boss was suddenly fired, she immediately worried about her own position, thinking of the toddler whom she left each day and what would happen if her family income was suddenly halved. Within a few hours of her boss's dismissal, she was summoned to the corner office to learn her own fate.

"Waiting for that meeting, I sat thinking, trying to envision staying at home with my child, but I didn't really want to get fired," she said. Then a young colleague, a single women with no kids, showed up in Lydia's doorway. "She'd been particularly close to our old boss and she said to me, 'You're going to quit, aren't you? Out of loyalty? I mean, you have a good reason to stay home.' Later, I thought about her comments and I understood they were coming from her heart. But if she'd been in my position she would have known that it's just not that easy. I kept my job—I even got promoted. It wasn't easy to transition to a new boss, but eventually we adjusted. Quitting in the heat of the moment would have been a huge mistake."

Erin worked at a highly respected nonprofit but felt her position there was eroding. "Every morning, I wondered how much worse my job would be by the end of the day. There were lots of layers of management, there was incessant fighting. I always seemed to be on the losing side." Miserable at work, Erin started interviewing elsewhere. Over a year, she met other people in her field and found some interesting jobs. "That process alone, just getting out there, helped." Finally the board of Erin's nonprofit intervened and installed a new leader. "Thank God I stayed. I have the best job I could imagine—work I enjoy, a well-functioning organization, a great boss who is a great mentor."

THE ROLLING STOP

Sometimes the scale of your unhappiness with work may make it hard to surmount. "I'm amazed at how skilled we are at torturing women out of this firm," an experienced working mom said to us before leaving her job of more than twenty years and starting her own company. There may be a moment where you just need time to clear your brain and re-boot.

In our experience, if you leave a job without a new one in hand, there are two major things to safeguard: your own confidence and the fairness in your marriage. It's also worth knowing that there is debate over how difficult it will be to return and how long you can afford to be out before your rolling stop becomes a standstill.

Research by Sylvia Ann Hewlett, president of the Center for Work-Life Policy in New York, presents a less-than-rosy picture. Her survey found that one-third of highly qualified working mothers "off-ramp" for some period of time, and of those nearly all (93 percent) want to return to work. But only 74 percent succeed in rejoining the workforce, and only 40 percent are able to return to full-time jobs.

Leslie Morgan Steiner, editor of *Mommy Wars,* says her research shows that women can go back: "Most college-educated women, aged thirty-five to fifty-five, at home with kids for three to ten years can usually reenter the workforce." There are some important caveats: Moms must be willing to accept full-time work and they must be deci-sive about returning. It helps to stay in the same field and geographic area and not to take more than ten years off. It can take up to a year to find work, says Steiner, but if moms can practice what they preach to their toddlers—patience—it will pay off.

You're asked to be the new boss, your job heats up

What if things get more intense, but in a good way? You're offered a big-ger job, a bigger raise, a bigger range of plum assignments—and with this promotion come longer hours and more travel. With a 50/50 spouse, you have the option to take the job and know that your kids will be fine. You also have the option to say, "Not now, how about a rain check?"

"I'm not sure that, without Frank behind me, I would have been so motivated," says Vera, the corporate securities lawyer who made part-ner at a large firm. "I had three IPOs going on at the same time for a few months, nights where I was at the office or at the printer's. When that's going on, I don't put my son to bed and I might have to leave before he wakes up." But when Vera's schedule keeps her away, father and son keep each other company—and content.

"My colleagues were supportive," says Vera, describing the push she made to become partner, "because there's been major attrition in women at the senior levels. Their encouragement was helpful, but it was mostly Frank who helped me through it."

Sometimes, opportunity comes knocking when you don't feel like answering the door. "I was offered a promotion after I'd just had my second child, and the next one came when I just had my third," says Trish, the executive who currently works a four-day week and manages a team of twenty-five employees.

"I've given up a little bit of speed," says Trish. "Maybe I'd be farther along if I had taken on the slightly bigger jobs when I was offered them, instead of staying in jobs that I could do well in with my four-day week. A couple of my peers are VPs at this point. But I was asked to take on bigger roles when I just wasn't ready."

Many moms we talked to diplomatically postponed taking bigger jobs, but they often expressed a mix of anxiety and hopefulness when they talked about it. "It's not easy not knowing where your career is going from year to year," says Susan, the software engineer, who has both accepted larger roles and deferred them. "There was one case recently where someone was promoted, and I was a little peeved, because I wasn't even considered for it—and I told my manager that, but I also realized I didn't want that job. I don't want to be in the hot seat right now. But I have a good job and a good paycheck. I've had good opportunities at work. I think I can sort of stay in the game in a significant way doing what I'm doing now. I'm not marginalizing myself and when I want to crank it up, I can crank it up."

We hope that more women will find people like Carla, the medical researcher, to give them faith that pacing yourself can pay off. "I worked part time when the kids were young," says Carla, who recently won a prize for her work at her institute and is recognized as a leading expert in her specialty. "Now, in my sixties, I get to lead large projects in my field and do work I find really rewarding."

HOW MUCH IS TOO MUCH?

When it comes to your job and how many hours you work, how big is too big, and how many collective hours can you and your spouse work before things start to go wrong? In our own experience, there is no magic number. But there is definitely a limit and you'll know it when you get close.

"In the years since my daughter was born, my husband and I have punched the family time clock in multiple ways—both of us working forty hours a week, him working sixty hours and me working twenty hours, him working eighty hours and me working zero...The conclusion is always the same—cross the line for any extended length of time and watch all hell break loose," says one mother on the Silicon Valley Moms Blog. "It isn't just the hours—you can use extended day care to cover that. It's the being present. It's having someone aware when a child is struggling with a math concept, or getting picked on at recess—when they can't even articulate what's bothering them. You just can't do that with two parents working to the point that they come home drained and exhausted."

In every family, in any given week, kids need some amount of time alone with their parents. If you cut things too close, and we've certainly done this ourselves, you'll pay the price in the form of whining, arguments, and short tempers all around. The trick is being willing and able to see the lights flashing when trouble is near, to take action today—not tomorrow when your deadline's passed.

"All our decision making is around 'If we do this, how will it affect our child?' " says Frank, the entrepreneur married to a law partner. "We don't go out as much as our friends do and skip a lot of things that could be professionally useful to us. We want one of us to be here enough so our son really gets time with us."

Chip's wife had to travel a lot when their son was young. "I felt it was taking a toll on our son but I also knew that, short-term, Vicki had no choice. So I made a vow to myself that I'd take a couple hours off every Wednesday morning to give him some extra time. We went to breakfast together. We'd go look at ships in the harbor or take the train into the city. It really seemed to make a difference for our son, and I felt better, too."

Your partner changes jobs—and your job changes, too

Terri agreed to make a big change for her husband's career, and disrupted her own in the process. When they'd graduated from law school together, Terri ranked number one in their class, while Sanjay was middle-of-the-pack. Four years out, Terri's legal career was evolving well and she'd given birth to their first child. But Sanjay said he wanted to make partner at his firm and, to do that, he needed to transfer to his firm's Tokyo office. Terri's firm had no Tokyo office, and Sanjay's had a no-spouse policy. Because they agreed that Sanjay stood to make more money over the long term, she agreed to the move. But once in Tokyo, Terri could not find work and Sanjay never did make partner. Now she's home with three kids, trying to get her derailed career back on track.

When you're married, it's virtually impossible not to feel some impact when your spouse's job goes south, heats up, or takes a sudden sharp turn. If a job is lost, you may find yourself working harder as the sole breadwinner, at least temporarily. But if a juicy new job is dangled before your partner and it involves a move across the country, you may find yourself with work where you have no seniority, in a strange new part-time situation, or with no job at all.

"My husband got an offer to go work for a great company in another state," says Laura, who was working in business development at the time. Not entirely satisfied in her job, she agreed to move so her husband could take a position he was excited about. "My kids were ten and seven so I thought, *Well, I'll work part time, I'll* . . . you know, blah-blah-blah," she recalls, not having high expectations for how that part-time "blah-blah-blah" would unfold. "But after we made the decision to move I did these big deals for my company and they asked me to do it from across the country, so that's what I did for two years. I worked from home in the suburbs."

THE HIS-AND-HER JOB SHARE

As young management consultants, Inez and Matthew watched a senior colleague learn she didn't even have time for a dog. "She couldn't leave a meeting at eight o'clock at night for twenty minutes to put her dog out," says Matthew. "Her boss said, 'No, dogs are resilient.' " This unfortunate woman had hoped pet ownership would be a successful pilot for having a child.

"We looked up at the partners and there were failing marriages and unhappy people not making it work—a lot of divorces and families falling apart," says Inez. Matthew watched his boss's marriage dissolve. "His wife was not working and he was never home," Matthew says. "When Inez and I started talking about marriage, we knew that we both wanted to raise children and we both wanted to be involved." They also both wanted to work. "We went to business school together and didn't see the need for one of us to work and the other one not to," says Matthew. "What happens when one of you wants to get back in and you've been out of the market a long time? You're way behind and don't have many choices."

So Matthew and Inez have engineered a life that is the most impressive form of 50/50 we've yet seen. Taking jobs at an industry-leading Fortune 500 firm, the couple focused first on building their credentials and looking around at options they might want when they became parents. "For the first two years we worked our butts off so we would be considered top performers," says Matthew. They also learned about several successful job-sharing teams at their firm and, when Inez got pregnant, they petitioned to join their ranks. The plan: that they would each work three days a week, overlapping on Wednesdays.

But they were the first married couple to suggest a job split, and "it was not smooth sailing," says Matthew. "You'll collude," said their boss. "One spouse can't have an influence on another spouse's review." Matthew and Inez pointed out that job sharing wouldn't let them raise each other's *pay*, but it might allow them to lift each other's *performance*. (Five reasons: 1) two people have twice the good ideas; 2) each person's bad ideas get screened out early; 3) you are always fresh; 4) two people have different strengths, so you likely get twice the number of strengths; 5) two people have twice the bandwidth of one person.)

The job share has paid off at home, too. "We can barter everything. We might say, 'Hey, I'll do this task at work if you'll change the next three dirty diapers.' That probably doesn't happen in every job share," says Matthew with a smile. "You can be fresh at home, too. At the end of my two days at home, I can say to Inez, 'Here's our son, I had a wonderful two days and now I'm ready to go back to work. We can go full force for the two days we are with him."

Matthew and Inez have built a life that serves their family and their firm. While they give up some income and pass on some promotions, "We've been getting enough experience so that both of us can have big jobs if and when we want them," says Inez. For seven years, the couple has performed so well that they continue to be offered new roles in their company. "When we think about our next position, we ask ourselves whether it meets three criteria: 1) is it good for our career? 2) is it interesting? and 3) will it let us be good parents?"

BOTH DREAMS COUNT: THE 50/50 PAYOFF

What do you hope to get from 50/50? The peace of mind that comes with knowing that another caring parent is with your child when you can't be? The sense of achievement you get from your job and the security you have from two incomes? The feeling of relief that you're not the only one in charge of doing the dishes, the carpooling, and reminding your children to floss? The connection that comes from loving a partner who gets it, who knows what you're going through every day and is living life the same way you are?

"You've got to value the dreams of your spouse, be respectful of what that person really wants—even if you don't agree. It's not about what you think. It's about honoring what your spouse cares about," says Laura, who has taken turns with her spouse for decades. Sometimes he had the bigger opportunity, sometimes she did. And sometimes they each just had a goal they felt compelled to pursue. "Whatever it is, your job is to appreciate and try to understand it. And say, 'Okay, well, let's think about what it would take for both of us to make that possible for you and see whether that trade-off is really the thing that makes sense in the context of our mutual life.'"

Taking turns can be hard, but it's easier if you have committed to the kind of fairness that 50/50 is all about. Christina had great success in her early thirties. "It was really exciting. I worked crazy hours but it was really satisfying." Through the birth of two kids, Christina had the support of her spouse who actively managed his own job so that he could do his part at home. For a while, it looked as if the arrangement was paying off more for Christina than for George. But then, things went south at Christina's firm. As she considered her next move, Christina realized that if she took a job as big and demanding as the one she'd left, it wouldn't be fair to George, who had been waiting to accelerate his career. "I felt boxed in. As much as I wanted to pay George back, it was really hard to limit the kind of jobs I looked at. There were days when it made me miserable," says Christina. "But I knew it was the right thing to do. I also know that George is a good guy and I'll have my turn again."

Isabelle was recruited for a big government job in the Midwest, but she and her husband, Don, lived in sunny California, where Don was a partner at a large law firm. Don recognized that it was Isabelle's moment. "This is a huge opportunity for Isabelle, albeit one that's enormously challenging," Don said in an e-mail he proudly sent out to friends announcing her new appointment and their relocation. "Like any dutiful spouse, I asked my law firm to let me move for a year or so, after which we'll reevaluate whether the arrangement is working out (I figure if I can survive the weather after thirteen years in Southern California, I'll be able to manage almost anything)."

Laura, who moved cross-country and worked out of her house for her old company, eventually got another turn herself. "My husband wasn't loving his new job. So I told him we should move back home." And they did. "My company was thrilled to have me back—I was in charge of business development and it was clearly better to have me back at headquarters." Laura's husband found a new job, while she continued to move up the ranks and get recruited for bigger jobs. She let him take the reins for that two-year stretch, but eventually she got another chance to shoot for the top (which landed her as the CEO of a growing company).

Carol and Eric both became partners the same year at a national accounting firm. While raising two kids, the two CPAs built their practices and each ran parts of their firm's business—but at different times. "I asked Eric, 'When I was managing partner, did you feel you had to sacrifice?'" says Carol. "Eric told me he'd realized that if we both went full bore at the same time, we'd never see our kids. So he decided he was not going to do that extra ten percent in his job that was required for further advancement. We try to have very supportive, honest give-and-take."

Even when your jobs look equal in scale, one may entail two qualities that interfere with family life—travel and unpredictability. But 50/50 couples find ways to divvy up those things, too, in a way that leaves neither spouse permanently out of the game.

"I chose not to travel much when the kids were little. That was okay, because I was at a big lab and just marching along," says Kathy, the physicist. "But then we had a big funding crisis and we needed to attract new projects so I travel as much as my husband, probably six to eight times a year. For part of my job, I work on a very specialized telescope out in Hawaii, so when it's my shift on the telescope I have to travel for that, too. When I'm gone, Jim really steps up to the plate."

There's another benefit to sharing the glory, which we touched on in the first part of this book. Two bets in the workforce are better than one, because there are very few jobs that are truly safe. Jobs are more uncertain than they've ever been. But the good news is that today women can be real economic partners. Families win financially if two parents work and keep their options open, even if one runs behind for a while until the other takes a breather, by necessity or by choice.

Embrace change, skip resentment

"Sometimes I get the 'I-can't-stand-it' feeling. That I'm starting to resent doing the dishes or dealing with a teacher I don't like, that's when I say to Chip, 'We need to swap, I need a change,'" says Vicki. "I saw how resentment built up between my parents because they felt they were 'supposed to' do X or Y. Like those were God-given tasks they each had to separately do forever. Our goal as a couple is to mix it up and avoid that."

Change can be as small as the way you look at something. "There's this assumption out there that moms are 'supposed' to be with their kids more. And Shelly liked to imagine this was true in our house, too. But I felt I was doing something pretty special as a dad and I wanted credit for it," says Derek, who got home to be with his sons earlier than his corporate lawyer wife, Shelly. "We'd have arguments about who watched the kids more, so I created 'The Waking Hours Spreadsheet.' For a week I logged the hours I watched the kids and the hours Shelly did. When Shelly saw the tally for the week, she didn't say much—but I 'won.' And it made us laugh."

Or change can be big—a deliberate overhaul of how you work so you can have more of what you want. "Over the years I started to feel more peripheral," says Jon, the doctor who had taken paternity leave when his first child was born. Seven years later, Jon wanted more time with his children than he was getting while working fifty-hour weeks plus being on call. "I knew I wanted something different. I wanted the kids to seek me out, to confide in me. I didn't want to be the distant speck on the horizon to my children. I wanted to be equal to Beth in intimacy and trust." Jon got that balance once Beth returned to full-time work.

Knowing that it's never too late to do more 50/50 also helps—it allows change to emerge over time. Even if a dad doesn't do half the diapers and listen to half of the crying (or get half of the cuddling and the toothless grins), there are countless opportunities beyond those first months (and years) of life for him to become an equal parent, especially if you make room for him.

Bob was "not a baby person," says his wife, Maya, "but he left his finance job and consulted from home for a while when our girls were in grade school. Bob really bonded with both of them. Before, the girls would always come to me if they fell down or got sick. But then one night, after Bob had been home for a while, my daughter woke up in the middle of the night and walked past me and around to Bob's side of the bed to say 'Daddy, I don't feel good.' I knew it was a great thing. Instead of being jealous, I said, '*Yes!*'" As an added bonus, "Bob now truly appreciates the work that's needed at home and is less likely to say 'Hey, I'm going away with the boys for the weekend, can you cover?'"

And while change is good, it can take a while to embrace it. Ben is now in college but when he was young, his mom ran a big company and his dad was a busy consultant. "My dad retired when I was twelve, and my mom continued to work. And it was only then that I started to know my father better. But it took a lot of effort for my dad to adjust to retirement. He felt guilty about not working even though my mom thought it was great that he was hanging out with his kids. So he took up a lot of hobbies. He saw me taking singing lessons so he signed up with my teacher, too. We had lessons back-to-back so we'd listen to each other."

It's never too late for a father to sing with his child, even if it's not a lullaby.

Keeping doors open so you and your spouse can share more of life's experiences—that's what 50/50 marriage is all about. More people need to know that. "Equal relationships are widely viewed as more stressful than the more traditional relationships. Yet, contrary to expectations, study findings showed exactly the opposite," writes psychologist Janice Steil about the advantages for two-career couples. "Those in equal relationships reported feeling stressed by their responsibilities arising from their marital relationships least often and traditionals reported feeling stressed most often. While equal relationships require more frequent negotiation and compromise, it may be precisely the need for continued interpersonal contact and involvement that contributes to high levels of satisfaction found among dual-career couples."[4] When neither career is assumed to be primary, couples learn to respectfully sort out the conflicts.

"After five or six years of exhaustion, we realized we were starting our weeks without having chatted, just the two of us," says Carol. So she and her husband began comparing calendars on Sunday night, open to the idea that no entry was indelible. "We'd each say, 'This is my greatest need this week. Here's what I *have* to do. Here's what I'd *like* to do.' We wouldn't just say, 'Hey, I'm not home on Tuesday night.'"

"It's about mutual respect. You have to agree on the goals and the expectations for yourselves—both as individuals and as a couple. Then you have a benchmark that makes decisions easier. You can say,

'We agreed these were the goals, we have this opportunity or this choice, how does it measure up?'" says Matthew about how to make dual-career life work smoothly. "If you are not super clear on those things, that's when people get in trouble."

In other words, working couples need to problem solve more than "traditional" couples with one breadwinner simply because daily planning tends to be more complex. But the ongoing negotiating and interacting is its own kind of intimacy—common ground, common interests, common life.

FINDING GOOD COMPANY

Getting to 50/50 is a lot more fun when you have like-minded friends to share the journey.

In his study of dual-career marriage, sociologist Scott Coltrane found that couples who successfully share roles shape their environment, "constantly making decisions about whom to spend time with, how to portray their family arrangements to others, and whose comments they should take seriously."[5] These couples saw value in building their "own networks rather than passively accepting one's local and kin ties." So think about the company you keep and whether it supports your commitment to working—and the 50/50 life.

In our lives, we've found this makes a big difference. The happiest working couples are those who build a community around themselves—one made up of friends, family, colleagues, and other working parents who support what they do. Let the naysayers do their naysaying. They won't get you down when you surround yourself with women and men who share your way of life.

When our sons were born, we didn't join traditional baby groups, the ones held during work hours. As we returned to our jobs, Joanna pulled together a different kind of moms' group, one scheduled for working stiffs like us. It was like an after-dark and sideways version of "mother's morning out," those a.m. gatherings at the Y with coffee and Danish. With us it was pizza and wine. We'd eat, drink, and yak, exchanging tips, like how to get our sons to stop eating toilet paper, or comparing notes on what was up (or down) at work. We laughed, we complained, we solved problems and thought of new ones. Most of all, we took immense comfort in each other's friendship and were reassured by one thought: We had company.

So do you. We all have peers—we may not have grown up with them, they may not live on our street, we may not even know them right now. But we can find them, those other women and men who share the love of family and the conviction that working parenthood is a great thing.

Our bunch of working moms not only makes our lives feasible, our gang makes life fun. We help each other start businesses, find jobs, doctors, clothes. We go on road trips together (kids in tow) or to the 8 p.m. movie (kids home with Dad).

As an added bonus, the husbands of the moms in our group like each other, too. They launched a Sunday soccer league for our children. They held dad–kid pool dates in manly fashion, complete with tug-of-war and knock-down, drag-out water-gun fights (without moms shouting "careful!" as kids ran on wet pavement). We got to see our husbands channeling their inner boy, with boundless enthusiasm for just going nuts with their children. Though their gatherings are sometimes free-for-alls, there's a more serious principle at work here: These 50/50 dads enjoy the freedom of parenting the guy way, they're spending invaluable time with their kids, and they're finding community with other like-minded fathers.

Whether you join an organized group that meets every other Tuesday for lunch, or one that meets kind-of-every-six-weeks after work like we did, there's nothing like good company to make your life, at work and at home, easier. If you share your 50/50 solutions with your new friends, they'll do the same. You'll learn a lot from each other and have fun at it. We certainly have.

Share the work, change the world

If you take only one thing away from *Getting to 50/50*, let it be this: You and your husband have an equal commitment to pay bills and to care for kids—and you each can develop skill in both these callings that is equal enough. You may need to get one salary up or your expenses down. You may need to let the parent with less babysitting background catch up. But with this mind-set, you'll have a real shot at the reward of a 50/50 life: sharing your family's laughter and the triumphs of two jobs standing together on common ground.

Men and women need each other in all spheres of life. In one generation, we've seen the vast improvements that come from men and women sharing the stage in the workplace. Companies large and small, universities, hospitals, arts, institutions, government—all perform better when more women are included in their ranks. At the same time, our children, our marriages, our family life all gain a lot when men are truly engaged at home. Allow men and women to contribute in both parts of life and everyone wins. How do we make that an option for more people?

"Every male CEO in the country should be required to have a working wife," says Abby Joseph Cohen, the world-famous investment strategist, whose pronouncements on the economy are better known than her views on working families. "Without working wives, senior men, including CEOs, don't understand their employees' balancing act—not just those faced by the women but also the stresses on the younger generation of men."[6]

As one of our survey respondents wrote, "Most of the men I work with—I mean like ninety-five percent—have wives that stay home, so the playing field is not level. They have support at home that I cannot imagine. We all need a wife." Actually, we're not sure everyone needs a "wife" in the traditional sense. What we all *do* need is a spouse who shares the load at home and a workplace filled with sensible working parents.

Dream for a moment. Imagine if *everyone* you worked with, from the top down, fully understood the demands of working parenthood.

No one would stay later than they need to. Workers would get more done in less time because they'd have incentive to do so, and 24/7 would be reserved for times it's really needed, for real surges in work and crises. Managers would know that sending workers home to their families is good business. Reliable child care might finally be available on a scale that makes it more affordable. Schools would create systems, schedules, and policies aligned with grown-up work hours. A request for flexibility would not be considered a sign of weakness, and dads would ask for it as routinely as moms do.

Women would be promoted right alongside men because they wouldn't be devalued after they embarked on motherhood. They would work until retirement, not drop out years before their time—free of guilt, full of satisfaction. Families would have the security of two breadwinners. Children would have the benefit of two involved parents. Married partners would really be equals in all things.

As long as mothers leave the workforce in higher numbers than dads do (and remain less visible when present), the problems faced by working parents will never be challenged and changed.

Getting to 50/50 is a journey that can give you the life you want. And the more of us take it, the smoother the path will be for ourselves and for those who follow, including our kids.

Remember that workplace mountain, the one that got so hard to face after motherhood? With the 50/50 mind-set, our spouses become true partners. And when there are enough of us, 50/50 women and men, we won't just scale that mountain—together, we'll move it.

RESOURCES

"Be the change you wish to see in the world," Gandhi said. Here is our short list of resources that's helped us see how we might do that in our own lives.

PARENTING AND FAMILY

Ask the Children: The Breakthrough Study That Reveals How to Succeed at Work and Parenting, Ellen Galinsky. New York: William Morrow, 1999.
Want to know what kids think about working parents? The Families and Work Institute surveyed more than 100 children from various kinds of families to reveal how the children feel their parents' work lives are affecting life at home, and what parents can do to be more successful in both arenas.

Blackwell Handbook of Early Childhood Development, Kathleen McCartney and Deborah Phillips, eds. Malden, MA: Blackwell Publishing, 2006.
This book gets you behind the headlines to learn what top child-development researchers are finding.

The Blessings of a Skinned Knee: Using Jewish Teachings to Raise Self-Reliant Children, Wendy Mogel. New York: Scribner, 2008.
Joanna's favorite parenting book; very practical advice for all parents.

"Childcare Research at the Dawn of a New Millennium: An Update," Sarah Friedman, Ted Melhuish, and Candace Hill. In: Gavin Bremner and Theodore Wachs, eds. *Wiley-Blackwell Handbook of Infant Development, Second Edition.* Oxford: Wiley-Blackwell, 2009.

A hot-off-the-press overview of current research findings on child care by former chief scientists for the NICHD study discussed in Chapter 1.

Einstein Never Used Flashcards: How Our Children Really Learn—and Why They Need to Play More and Memorize Less, Kathy Hirsh Pasek. Emmaus, PA: Rodale, 2004.

If you worry your child can't compete unless you pack his schedule with fancy extracurriculars, think again. Pasek, a psychology professor, explains why chores and free time will help your child more.

Halving It All: How Equally Shared Parenting Works, Francine M. Deutsch. Cambridge, MA: Harvard University Press, 2000.

A comprehensive study of equally shared parenting. Good research and lots of interviews with 50/50 parents. Strong discussion of the philosophical underpinnings of equal parental involvement.

What We Know About Childcare, Alison Clarke-Stewart and Virginia D. Allhusen. Cambridge, MA: Harvard University Press, 2005.

Very accessible research by NICHD investigators from the University of California, which puts forth new insights on the child-care system and offers guidance for making the difficult decision about alternative care for your child.

ACTIVE FATHERHOOD

Family Man: Fatherhood, Housework, and Gender Equity, Scott Coltrane. New York: Oxford University Press USA, 1997.

Sociologist Coltrane conducted many interviews with couples in the early 1990s and offers a broad array of ways men and women look at sharing the load as well as a look into the evolution of man's role in the family.

Father Courage: What Happens When Men Put Family First, Suzanne Braun Levine. Orlando, FL: Harcourt, 2000.

Inspirational stories of men who are really involved in the lives of their children.

Marathon Dad: Setting a Pace That Works for Working Fathers, John Evans. New York: Harper Perennial, 1999.

A good, practical discussion of fathers who get involved in their children's lives. Good suggestions for working dads.

Working Fathers: New Strategies for Balancing Work and Family, James A. Levine and Todd L. Pittinsky. San Diego: Harvest Books, 1998.

If you need any evidence that men want change as much as women do, read this compelling book. Based on talks with smart managers and successful dads, the authors show what has to change in companies and homes to let fathers get more time with their kids.

MARRIAGE

And Baby Makes Three: The Six-Step Plan for Preserving Marital Intimacy and Rekindling Romance After Baby Arrives, John M. Gottman and Julia Schwartz Gottman. New York: Three Rivers Press, 2008.

Suggestions from a preeminent marriage expert on how to get through the tough patches after your baby is born.

How Can I Get Through to You? Closing the Intimacy Gap Between Men and Women, Terrence Real. New York: Fireside, 2002.

How do you talk to the person you love about difficult things? Therapist Terrence Real gives you the words to try.

Kidding Ourselves: Breadwinning, Babies, and Bargaining Power, Rhona Mahony. New York: BasicBooks, 1995.

How did so many women end up in marriages less equal than they expected? Mahoney helps us see how easily this happens when women overlook their BATNA.

The Lazy Husband: How to Get Men to Do More Parenting and Housework, Joshua Coleman. New York: St. Martin's Griffin, 2006.

If courage and a peaceful approach is what you need to start the 50/50 conversation, this book is very helpful. Funny and practical, marriage therapist Coleman shares the steps that help his patients find more fairness.

Love Between Equals: How Peer Marriage Really Works, Pepper Schwartz. New York: The Free Press, 1995.

A discussion of the positives and negatives of a 50/50 marriage. Book compares "peer" marriages with "traditional" marriages and "near-peer" marriages, and strongly outlines the benefits of the equal "peer" marriages.

Marriage, A History: How Love Conquered Marriage, Stephanie Coontz. New York: Penguin, 2006.

A great read on the quirky and occasionally sordid history of marriage from prehistory to the present. Coontz helps us see that we live in a very new time where equality in marriage requires a set of skills that our grandparents weren't required to cultivate.

Parenting Partners: How to Encourage Dads to Participate in the Daily Lives of Children, Robert Frank and Kathryn E. Livingston. New York: St. Martin's Press, 2000.

Dr. Robert Frank, a family therapist and stay-at-home dad, provides specific tips for fathers, from sharing the "on call" duty in emergencies to negotiating downtime, to create a more balanced living situation at home.

Role-Sharing Marriage, Audrey D. Smith and William J. Reid. Irvington, NY: Columbia University Press, 1986.

Engaged in a role-sharing marriage themselves, the authors describe their conclusions from in-depth interviews with sixty-four couples who share earning power, household tasks, and child-care responsibilities. Good discussions on how domestic labor negotiations occur in each marriage.

When Partners Become Parents: The Big Life Change for Couples, Carolyn Pape Cowan and Phillip A. Cowan. Philadelphia, PA: Lawrence Erlbaum Associates, 2000.

Marriage guru John Gottman says this is "the most important book on the prevention of divorce that has ever been written," and we agree. The Cowans share how their group training for new-parent couples teaches men and women to speak openly about their frictions—and see that they are not alone.

WORKING MOTHERHOOD

42 Rules for Working Moms, Laura Lowell, ed. Super Star Press, 2008.

Super practical advice for working moms, with suggestions on how to avoid guilt and why it's okay to be selfish sometimes. Also has a great sense of humor.

The Comeback: Seven Stories of Women Who Went from Career to Family and Back Again, Emma Gilbey Keller. New York: Bloomsbury, 2008.

Offers good insights on what women experience when they try to return to the workforce, and how it can be done.

The Feminine Mistake: Are We Giving Up Too Much?, Leslie Bennetts. New York: Voice, 2008.

All the stories you'll need to see that everyone needs a paycheck, no matter whom they marry.

Flux: Women on Sex, Work, Love, Kids and Life in a Half-Changed World, Peggy Orenstein. New York: Anchor, 2001.

Orenstein gives an intimate and politically astute vision of how women in their twenties, thirties, and forties negotiate life in a world only half-changed by feminism. Discussion of how both the home life and workplace need to change for women to be successful in each arena.

Getting It Right: How Working Mothers Successfully Take Up the Challenge of Life, Family and Career, Laraine T. Zappert. New York: Touchstone, 2002.
A clinical psychologist and working mother, Zappert interviewed three hundred Stanford MBA students about work and family. Short on practical advice, but good inspirational stories.

Get to Work: . . . And Get a Life, Before It's Too Late, Linda R. Hirshman. New York: Penguin, 2007.
While we disagree with some of her solutions, such as having only one child, Hirshman gives a very intelligent argument that women are creating their own glass ceiling by staying home and harming all women in society. Definitely worth reading and discussing.

Mommy Wars: Stay-at-Home and Career Moms Face Off on Their Choices, Their Lives, Their Families, Leslie Morgan Steiner, ed. New York: Random House, 2007.
Intelligently written stories by moms who stay at home and moms who work. Shows the complexity involved in this decision for each individual and the soul-searching behind these choices.

Not Guilty! The Good News for Working Moms, Betty Holcomb. New York: Touchstone, 2000.
A well-written argument against working-mom guilt.

Not Your Mother's Life: Changing the Rules of Work, Love and Family, Joan K. Peters. Cambridge, MA: Da Capo Press, 2002.
Wise advice for women, arguing that we don't have to choose between becoming workaholics or stay-at-home moms. Good discussion of how to find balance.

Opting In: Having a Child Without Losing Yourself, Amy Richards. New York: Farrar, Straus and Giroux, 2008.
A refreshing book reminding us that there is no "appropriate" way to be a mother, urging us all to forge our own paths.

Perfect Madness: Motherhood in the Age of Anxiety, Judith Warner. New York: Riverhead, 2006.
Another of our favorite parenting books, Warner discusses hyper-parenting and the pressures on both parents and children today to be perfect.

This Is How We Do It: The Working Mothers' Manifesto, Carol Evans. New York: Hudson Street Press, 2006.
More great examples of how working moms do their thing—happily—by the editor of *Working Mother* magazine.

CAREER AND WORKPLACE

Coming Up for Air: How to Build a Balanced Life in a Workaholic World, Beth Sawi. New York: Hyperion, 2000.
Sharon read this eye-opening book on her first vacation as a pregnant woman—between faxes from the office. Sawi shares how great world leaders, from Churchill to Confucius, fought to conserve time so they could focus on what mattered.

Finding Time: How Corporations, Individuals, and Families Can Benefit from New Work Practices, Leslie A. Perlow. Ithaca, NY: Cornell University Press, 1997.
Harvard Business School's Perlow shows how, even in the most intense work cultures, there is plenty of wasted time that can be reengineered so that we can get home to our families—and why that's great for the bottom line.

Giving Notice: Why the Best and Brightest Are Leaving the Workplace and HOW YOU CAN HELP THEM STAY, Freada Kapor Klein. San Francisco: Jossey-Bass, 2008.
Klein, a pioneer of diversity efforts in some of the most respected U.S. companies, tells why all the diversity dollars aren't having their desired effect—and why we still have lots of work to do.

Naked in the Boardroom: A CEO Bares Her Secrets So You Can Transform Your Career, Robin Wolaner. New York: Fireside, 2005.
Fun, helpful advice from a female former Time Warner executive that focuses on building your career and how women can succeed at work in today's environment.

Tempered Radicals: How Everyday Leaders Inspire Change at Work, Debra E. Meyerson. Boston, MA: Harvard Business School Press, 2003.
Want the phrase to explain why you have to leave before six? Meyerson interviewed successful professionals to see how they advocated—gently—for change across lines of ethnicity, gender, and sexual orientation.

FOR KIDS

Mommy and Daddy Are Going on a Trip, Ricki Booker. www.changeisstrange.com. Change is Strange, 2004.
Highly recommended by Sharon's daughter. Part of a great series of books by a Nickelodeon vet and a team of child-development specialists.

ONLINE

Equally Shared Parenting, www.equallysharedparenting.com
Excellent website by the Vachons, a couple who strongly advocate equally shared parenting—what they call 50/50. Provides real-life testimonials, tools to achieve the balance between work and life, and breaks down the benefits and challenges of working toward equally shared parenting.

Mommy Track'd, www.mommytrackd.com
A lighthearted but informative resource that offers working moms a survival guide for both home and office, as well as articles on working mothers in current affairs, from pop culture to politics. The site offers helpful and practical tools for parents, such as organizational sheets and discounts from their sponsors.

MomsRising, www.momsrising.org
The website for MomsRising, a nonprofit organization that seeks to create a family-friendly America, in both public policy and within corporations. The organization is cause-oriented, and the site provides updates on its progress, from standardizing paid maternity and paternity leave to securing accessible and cost-effective day care and health care for children.

NICHD Study of Early Child Care and Youth Development, http://www .nichd.nih.gov/research/supported/seccyd.cfm
This is the research from the NICHD study on child care. You can also go to our website, www.Gettingto5050.com, for a three-page summary from NICHD's parent booklet that shows you what to look for when you go shopping for child care, including the child/caregiver ratio recommended by the American Association of Pediatrics and a checklist of qualities you should watch for in potential caregivers.

Parentopia, www.parentopia.net
A website by Aviva Pflock and Devra Renner, the authors of *Mommy Guilt: Learn to Worry Less, Focus on What Matters Most, and Raise Happier Kids,* who promote increasing pleasure in parenting by embracing unique and personal parenting style. Includes updates on parenting issues in the news and topical and thoughtful real-life stories from the authors.

STRIDE slides, http://sitemaker.umich.edu/advance/stride
This PowerPoint presentation was developed by the University of Michigan STRIDE program to help hiring committees in math, science, and medicine understand research on bias and learn to keep their own bias in check. Share it with your hiring managers—or, if you work at a big organization, with the leaders focused on diversity. Data often speak for themselves—and inspire fresh thinking.

ThirdPath Institute, www.thirdpath.org

ThirdPath Institute is a nationally based organization that provides educational materials as well as coaching and training sessions in "Shared Care," their version of 50/50. The goal: to help parents redesign work and family environments to create more time for life.

NOTES

Introduction: Imagine a Full Life—There's No Need to Choose

1. Lisa Belkin, "The Opt-Out Revolution," *New York Times,* October 26, 2003.

2. E. J. Graff, "The Opt-Out Myth," *Columbia Journalism Review,* March/April 2007.

3. Julia Lawlor, "Earning It; Goodbye to the Job. Hello to the Shock," *New York Times,* October 12, 1997.

4. Lynn Prince Cooke, "'Doing' Gender in Context: Household Bargaining and Risk of Divorce in Germany and the United States," *American Journal of Sociology* 112, no. 2 (September 2006): 442.

5. Alison L. Booth and Jan C. van Ours, 2007. "Job Satisfaction and Family Happiness: The Part-Time Work Puzzle," *The Economic Journal* 118, no. 526 (January 17, 2008): F77–F99.

6. Philip N. Cohen, University of North Carolina, based on March 2007 Current Population Surveys. E-mail to author, April 26, 2007.

7. James A. Levine and Todd L. Pittinsky, *Working Fathers: New Strategies for Balancing Work and Family,* 21; Daryl Haralson and Suzy Parker, "Dads Want More Time with Family," *USA Today,* June 15, 2005; Ellen Galinsky,

e-mail message to authors, August 6, 2008. "In 1977, 35% of employed fathers in dual-earner families felt some or a lot of conflict between their work and family responsibilities, compared with 43% of women. Now, the percentage of these fathers experiencing conflict has jumped to 53%, while women's level has stayed the same. Even more interesting is the fact that 52% of men in single-earner families experience conflict, too."

Chapter One: Mom *and* Dad: How Kids Can Get More from Two Working Parents

1. NICHD Early Child Care Research Network, "Child Care Effect Sizes for the NICHD Study of Early Child Care and Youth Development," *American Psychologist* 61, no. 2 (February–March 2006): 113.

2. NICHD Early Child Care Research Network, *Child Care and Child Development* (New York: Guilford Press, 2005), xv.

3. "Child care and other child development experts at NICHD and from universities across the US spent two years discussing how to best evaluate the relation between factors such as family and nonmaternal care on the one hand and children's social, cognitive, achievement, and health outcomes on the other hand," says Sarah Friedman, one of the study's architects and scientific coordinator until 2006 (e-mail to authors, November 4, 2008).

4. National Institute of Child Health and Human Development, *The NICHD Study of Early Child Care and Youth Development: Findings for Children up to 4½ Years* (Washington, DC: U.S. Department of Health and Human Services, 2006), 9, 36–37.

5. Clarke-Stewart, Alison and Virginia D. Allhusen, What We Know about Childcare, p. 92.

6. Friedman, Ted Melhuish (of the University of London), and Candace Hill (the Institute of Public Research at CNA) have recently summarized findings about the effects of child care and child development (to be published in 2009 in the *Wiley-Blackwell's Handbook of Infancy Research*). They concluded that both the positive and negative statistical associations between features of child care and different developmental outcomes are modest and typically are half as large as those found for family and home factors. Therefore, the scientific literature to date suggests that the serious concerns about possible negative links between child care and children's development were largely unwarranted.

For further reading on recent research findings see:

Sarah Friedman, Ted Melhuish, and Candace Hill. "Childcare Research at the Dawn of a New Millennium: An update," In Gavin Bremner and Theodore Wachs (eds. 2009) *Wiley-Blackwell Handbook of Infant Development,* second edition. Oxford: Wiley-Blackwell.

A compilation of recent scientific papers pertaining to NICHD findings through the time the children were in third grade was published in December 2007 by the *Journal of Applied Developmental Psychology.*

Kathleen McCartney and Deborah Phillips, eds., *Blackwell Handbook of Early Childhood Development* (Malden, MA: Blackwell Publishing, 2006).

Alison Clarke-Stewart and Virginia D. Allhusen, *What We Know About Childcare* (Cambridge, MA: Harvard University Press, 2005).

For helpful guidelines for parents looking at child care, go to www .Gettingto5050.com for a three-page summary we extracted from NICHD's parent booklet that shows you what to look for when you go shopping for child care—including the child/caregiver ratios recommended by the American Association of Pediatrics and a checklist of qualities you should watch for in potential caregivers.

7. Aletha C. Huston and Stacey Rosenkrantz Aronson, "Mother's Time with Infant and Time in Employment as Predictors of Mother-Child Relationships and Children's Early Development," *Child Development* 76, no. 2 (March–April 2005): 467–482.

8. Ellen Galinsky, *Ask the Children* (New York: William Morrow and Company, 1999), 69.

9. Kathleen McCartney and Deborah Phillips, eds., *Blackwell Handbook of Early Childhood Development* (Malden, MA: Blackwell Publishing, 2006), 477.

10. Robert Pear, "Married and Single Parents Spending More Time with Children, Study Finds," *New York Times,* October 17, 2006. Statistics on the percentage of mothers who worked in 1965 came from a Census Bureau survey of the child-care arrangements of mothers who had worked twenty-seven weeks or more during 1964 and had at least one child under fourteen years old living at home.

11. NICHD Early Child Care Research Network, "Father's and Mother's Parenting Behavior and Beliefs as Predictors of Children's Social Adjustment in the Transition to School," *Journal of Family Psychology* 18, no. 4 (December 2004): 628–638; Cox discussion with author, January 25, 2007; Cox e-mail to author, July 15, 2008.

12. Laura Berk, *Awakening Children's Minds: How Parents and Teachers Can Make a Difference* (London: Oxford University Press, 2001).

13. Kathy Hirsch-Pasek and Roberta Michnick Golinkoff, with Diane Eyer, *Einstein Never Used Flash Cards* (Emmaus, PA: Rodale, 2003), 245.

14. Elizabeth C. Cooksey and Michelle M. Fondell, "Spending Time with His Kids: Effects of Family Structure on Fathers' and Children's Lives," *Journal of Marriage and Family* 58 (August 1996): 693–707; Paul R. Amato and Fernando Rivera, "Paternal Involvement and Children's Behavior Problems," *Journal of Marriage and Family* 61 (May 1999): 375–384.

15. NICHD Early Child Care Research Network, "Father's and Mother's Parenting Behavior," 628–638.

16. Ross D. Parke, "Fathers and Families," in *Handbook of Parenting,* ed. Marc H. Borns (Mahwah, NJ: Lawrence Erlbaum Associates, 2002), 57.

17. Joseph H. Pleck and Brian P. Masciadrelli, "Paternal Involvement by U.S. Residential Fathers: Levels, Sources, and Consequences" in *The Role of the Father in Child Development,* ed. Michael E. Lamb (Hoboken, NJ: John Wiley & Sons, 2004), 253.

18. Christina Winquist Nord, DeeAnn Brimhall, and Jerry West, *Fathers' Involvement in Their Children's Schools, National Household Education Survey,* NCES 98-091 (Washington, DC: U.S. Department of Education, Office of Educational Research and Improvement, 1997), viii–ix, 20.

19. Parke, "Fathers and Families," 47.

20. Kyle D. Pruett, *Fatherneed: Why Father Care Is as Essential as Mother Care for Your Child* (New York: Free Press, 2000), 52.

21. R. Koestner, C. Franz, and J. Weinberger, "The Family Origins of Empathetic Concern: A 26-year Longitudinal Study," *Journal of Personality and Social Psychology* 58 (April 1990): 709–717.

22. Pleck and Masciadrelli, "Paternal Involvement," 253; Kathleen Mullan Harris, Frank F. Furstenberg, Jr., and Jeremy K. Marmer, "Paternal Involvement with Adolescents in Intact Families: The Influence of Fathers Over the Life Course," *Demography* 35, no. 2 (May 1998): 203, 210–212.

23. Joan K. Peters, *When Mothers Work* (Cambridge, MA: Perseus Publishing, 1997), 105.

24. Kathleen Gerson, "Work Without Worry," *New York Times,* May 11, 2003.

25. There are many good studies on the benefits to kids from regular family dinners, including one by the Council of Economic Advisers to the President, titled "Teens and Their Parents in the 21st Century: An Examination of Trends in Teen Behavior and the Role of Parental Involvement" (May 2000). (Analysis of the Adolescent Health Study, using a national probability sample of adolescents and parents.) The largest federally funded study of teens, it discovered a strong association between regular family meals (five or more dinners per week with a parent) and academic success, psychological adjustment, and lower rates of alcohol use, drug use, early sexual behavior, and suicidal risk. Results held for both one-parent and two-parent families and after controlling for social class factors.

Additionally, more mealtime at home was the single strongest predictor of better achievement scores and fewer behavioral problems in children. Mealtime was more powerful than time spent in school, studying, church, playing sports, or art activities, as shown in a national study by Sandra L. Hofferth, "Changes in American Children's Time, 1981–1997." University of Michigan's Institute for Social Research Center, Survey, January 1999.

Chapter Two: What Your Husband Wins from a Working Wife

1. Catalyst, *Two Careers, One Marriage: Making It Work in the Workplace* (New York: Catalyst, 1998), 28.

2. Joyce P. Jacobsen and Wendy L. Rayack, "Do Men Whose Wives Work Really Earn Less?" *American Economic Review* 86, no. 2 (May 1996): 268–273; Younghwan Song, "The Working Spouse Penalty/Premium and Married Women's Labor Supply," *Review of Economics of the Household* 5 (2007): 279–304.

3. U.S. Census Bureau, "Historical Income Tables—Families," http://www.census.gov/hhes/www/income/histinc/f22.html (accessed August 8, 2008). In 25.5 percent of married couples, wives earn more than husbands.

4. Neil Chethik, *VoiceMale* (New York: Simon & Schuster, 2006), 119, 173.

5. John Gottman, *Why Marriages Succeed or Fail* (New York: Simon & Schuster Paperbacks, 1994), 155.

6. Carolyn Pape Cowan and Philip A. Cowan, *When Partners Become Parents: The Big Life Change for Couples* (Mahwah, NJ: Lawrence Erlbaum Associates, 2000), 107.

7. NICHD Early Child Care Research Network, "Factors Associated with Fathers' Caregiving Activities and Sensitivity with Young Children," 22.

8. Stephanie Coontz, *Marriage, a History: From Obedience to Intimacy or How Love Conquered Marriage* (New York: Viking, 2005), 292.

9. Josh Coleman, interview with author, June 22, 2006.

10. Coontz, *Marriage, a History,* 300.

11. Lynn Prince Cooke, "'Doing' Gender in Context: Household Bargaining and Risk of Divorce in Germany and the United States," *American Journal of Sociology* 112, no. 2 (September 2006): 442; Cooke interview with author, September 15, 2008.

12. Scott Coltrane, *Family Man: Fatherhood, Housework, and Gender Equity* (New York: Oxford University Press, 1996), 78.

13. Rosalind Chait Barnett and Jane Shibley Hyde, "Women, Men, Work and Family: An Expansionist Theory," *American Psychologist* 56 (October 2001): 789.

14. John Boswell, *The Kindness of Strangers: The Abandonment of Children in Western Europe from Late Antiquity to the Renaissance* (Chicago: University of Chicago Press, 1988), 3.

15. Brian O'Reilly, "Why Grade 'A' Execs Get an 'F' as Parents," *Fortune,* January 1, 1990, 36.

16. James A. Levine and Todd L. Pittinsky, *Working Fathers: New Strategies for Balancing Work and Family* (San Diego: Harcourt Brace & Company, 1997), 19.

17. Barnett and Hyde, "Women, Men, Work and Family," 784.

18. Ross Parke, interview with authors, January 30, 2007.

19. Robert Drago, e-mail message to authors, April 3, 2007.

20. John Snarey, *How Fathers Care for the Next Generation: A Four-Decade Study* (Cambridge, MA: Harvard University Press, 1993).

21. Levine and Pittinsky, *Working Fathers,* 21.

22. Daryl Haralson and Suzy Parker, "Dads Want More Time with Family," *USA Today,* June 15, 2005.

23. Ellen Galinsky, e-mail message to authors, August 6, 2008. "In 1977, 35% of employed fathers in dual-earner families felt some or a lot of conflict between their work and family responsibilities, compared with

43% of women. Now, the percentage of these fathers experiencing conflict has jumped to 53%, while women's level has stayed the same. Even more interesting is the fact that 52% of men in single-earner families experience conflict, too."

24. P. Kuhn and F. Lozano, "The Expanding Workweek? Understanding Trends in Long Work Hours Among U.S. Men, 1979–2006," *Journal of Labor Economics* 26, no. 2 (April 2008), 311–343.

25. William Pollack and Mary Pipher, *Real Boys* (New York: Henry Holt and Company, 1999), 133.

Chapter Three: What Women Gain from Working Motherhood

1. Coontz, *Marriage, a History,* 285–286.

2. Peggy Orenstein, *Flux: Women on Sex, Work, Love, Kids, and Life in a Half-Changed World* (New York: Doubleday, 2000), 19; Anne Machung, "Talking Career, Thinking Job: Gender Differences in Career and Family Expectations of Berkeley Seniors," *Feminist Studies* 15, no. 1 (Spring 1989): 35–58.

3. David Zinczenko, "Are Women Too Aggressive?" *Men's Health,* March 8, 2007.

4. Janice M. Steil, "Marriage: Still 'His' and 'Hers'?" *Encyclopedia of Women and Gender* 2 (2001): 681.

5. Steil, "Marriage: Still 'His' and 'Hers'?" 685.

6. Andrea Sachs, "Women and Money," *Time,* February 6, 2006.

7. Alicia H. Munnell, *Why Are So Many Older Women Poor?* JTF series, no. 10 (Boston: Center for Retirement Research at Boston College, April 2004); T. Heinz, J. Lewis, and C. Hounsell, *Women and Pensions: An Overview,* Washington, DC: Women's Institute for a Secure Retirement, 2006.

8. Sachs, "Women and Money."

9. Joan Williams, *Unbending Gender: Why Family and Work Conflict and What to Do About It* (New York: Oxford University Press, 2000), 115.

10. Francine D. Blau, Marianne A. Ferber, and Anne E. Winkler, *The Economics of Women, Men, and Work,* 5th ed. (Upper Saddle River, NJ: Pearson/Prentice Hall, 2006). In 2001, only 59 percent of custodial parents were awarded child support; of those who were supposed to receive

payments the same year, fewer than half (45 percent) received the full amount they were awarded, 29 percent received partial payment, and the remaining 26 percent received no payment at all (321).

11. Terry Martin Hekker, "Paradise Lost (Domestic Division)," *New York Times,* January 1, 2006.

12. A. McMunn, M. Bartley, R. Hardy, and D. Kuh, "Life Course Social Roles and Women's Health in Midlife: Causation or Selection?" *Journal of Epidemiology and Community Health* 60 (2006): 484–489.

13. Barnett and Hyde, "Women, Men, Work and Family," 784.

14. Myra Marx Ferree, "Working-Class Jobs: Housework and Paid Work as Sources of Satisfaction," *Social Problems* 23, no. 4, Feminist Perspectives: the Sociological Challenge (April 1976): 431–441.

15. Julia Lawlor, "Earning It; Goodbye to the Job. Hello to the Shock," *New York Times,* October 12, 1997; Elaine Wethington and Ronald C. Kessler, "Employment, Parenting Responsibilities and Psychological Distress: A Longitudinal Study of Married Women," *Journal of Family Issues* 10, no. 4 (December 1989): 527–546.

16. Elizabeth Margot Ozer, "Managing Work and Family: The Effects of Childcare Responsibility on Perceived Self-efficacy and the Psychological Health of New Working Mothers" (PhD dissertation, School of Education and the Committee on Graduate Studies, Stanford University, July 1992), 25–26.

17. Ozer, "Managing Work and Family," 123–124; E. M. Ozer, "The impact of childcare responsibility and Self-efficacy on the Psychological Health of Working Mothers," *Psychology of Women Quarterly* 19 (1995) 315–335; E. M. Ozer, R. C. Barnett, R. T. Brennan, and J. Sperling. "Does Childcare Involvement Increase or Decrease Distress Among Dual-Earner Couples?" *Women's Health: Research on Gender, Behavior, and Policy* 4, 4 (1998): 285–311.

18. Vanessa L. McGann and Janice M. Steil, "The Sense of Entitlement: Implications for Gender Equality and Psychological Well-Being," in *Handbook of Girls' and Women's Psychological Health,* ed. J. Worrell and C. Goddard (New York: Oxford University Press, 2006), 179–180.

19. Daniel Kahneman et al., "A Survey Method for Characterizing Daily Life Experience: The Day Reconstruction Method," *Science,* December 3, 2004.

20. Louise Story, "Many Women at Elite Colleges Set Career Path to Motherhood," *New York Times,* September 20, 2005.

21. C. S. Mee, *Middle School Voices on Gender Identity.* Women's Education Equity Act Publishing Center Digest, ED388914 (Newton, MA: WEEA Publishing Center, March 1995). Office for Sex Equity in Education, *The Influence of Gender-Role Socialization on Student Perceptions: A Report Based on Data Collected from Michigan Public School Students* (Michigan Department of Education, 1990).

22. McGann and Steil, "Sense of Entitlement," 178.

23. Anna Fels, "Do Women Lack Ambition?" *Harvard Business Review,* April 2004.

24. Nilanjana Dasgupta and Shaki Asgari, "Seeing Is Believing: Exposure to Counterstereotypic Women Leaders and Its Effect on the Malleability of Automatic Gender Stereotyping," *Journal of Experimental Social Psychology* 40 (2004): 642–658; Brian A. Nosek et al. "Pervasiveness and Correlates of Implicit Attitudes and Stereotypes," *European Review of Social Psychology* 18, no. 1 (2007): 36–88.

25. Mahzarin Banaji, interview with author, August 5, 2008.

26. Katherine Ellison, *The Mommy Brain: How Motherhood Makes Us Smarter* (New York: Basic Books, 2005), 177.

27. Catalyst, *Cracking the Glass Ceiling: Catalyst's Research on Women in Corporate Management 1995–2000* (New York: Catalyst, 2000), 75–76.

28. Philip N. Cohen and Matt L. Huffman, "Working for the Woman? Female Managers and the Gender Wage Gap," *American Sociological Review,* 2007, Vol. 72 (October) 681–704.

29. There are many studies showing that women are more likely to be fairly evaluated when they are fifty percent of the group. Some studies show that improvement may come when women simply reach a critical mass. For example, in one study, women were significantly more likely to be recommended for hire if they were three-eighths percent or more of the applicant group than if they were 25 percent or less.

See P. R. Sackett, C. L. Z. DuBois, A. W. Noe, "Tokenism in Performance Evaluation: The Effects of Work Group Representation on Male-Female and White-Black Differences in Performance Ratings," *Journal of Applied Psychology,* 76 (1991) 263–267; Madeline E. Heilman, "The Impact of Situational Factors on Personnel Decisions Concerning Women: Varying the Sex Composition," *Organizational Behavior and Human Performance,* 26 (1980), 386–395.

30. Mary C. Murphy, Claude M. Steele, and James J. Gross, "Signaling Threat: How Situational Cues Affect Women in Math, Science and

Engineering Settings," *Psychological Science* 18, no. 10 (October 2007): 879–885. Notably, while men did not behave differently when outnumbered by women, they are vulnerable to other forms of stereotyped threat: "Research has demonstrated that when White men are vulnerable to a stereotype—such as when they are compared with Asian men in a math context or with Black men in an athletic context—they show stereotype-threat performance decrements similar to those of women who are compared with men in a math context" (884).

Chapter Four: Women Don't Quit Because They *Want* To

1. National Center for Education Statistics, "Digest of Education Statistics: 2007," Table 181, U.S. Department of Education, http://www .nces.ed.gov/programs/digest/d07/tables/dt07_181.asp?referrer=list (accessed August 5, 2008). Women outnumber men in enrollment in degree-granting institutions. For full-time enrollment, women make up 6 million of the roughly 11 million students, or about 56 percent.

2. In hearings held in 2003, the American Bar Association's Commission on Women in the Profession found that despite recent progress, women were still underrepresented in top positions all across the legal profession. While women account for almost 30 percent of lawyers, they account for only about 15 percent of general counsels of Fortune 500 companies, 17 percent of law firm partners, and 23 percent of federal district and circuit judges. At law schools, women account for roughly 19 percent of deans and 25 percent of tenured professors. ("Charting Our Progress, The Status of Women in the Profession Today," The American Bar Association Commission on Women in the Profession, 2006. Women in the Law: A Look at the Numbers, November 2003.)

In an analysis of leadership of each company in the Fortune 500 in April 2007, Catalyst found that women still hold only 15.4 percent of Fortune 500 corporate office jobs (vice president or higher positions that require board approval). This number was 15.6 percent in 2006. Women held 6.7 percent of top earner positions. This number was the same in 2006. The number of companies with no women corporate officers increased from 64 in 2006 to 74 in 2007. ("2007 Catalyst Census of Women Corporate Officers and Top Earners of the Fortune 500." December 2007, www.catalyst.org.)

Studies about the advancement of women in medicine tend to focus on the numbers of women in senior positions in academic medicine, where status is clearly defined.

In 2000, only 8 percent of medical school chairs were women, and just 8 of 125 U.S. medical school deans were female. (A. S. Ash, P. L. Carr, R. Goldstein, and R. H. Friedman, "Compensation and Advancement of Women in Academic Medicine: Is There Equity?" *Annals of Internal Medicine* 2004; 205–212).

The proportion of medical school graduates who are women has risen over the past two decades, from 23 percent in 1979 to more than 41 percent in 1997. The representation of women on medical school faculties has also increased steadily during this period. The faculties of medical schools, however, continue to have substantially fewer women than their student bodies, and studies of the distribution of faculty members among ranks suggest that women are primarily in the lower ranks, whereas men are more equally distributed among the lower and higher ranks. (Lynn Nonnemaker, "Women Physicians in Academic Medicine—New Insights from Cohort Studies." *New England Journal of Medicine,* 2000 342: 399–405.)

3. Pamela Stone and Meg Lovejoy, "Fast-Track Women and the 'Choice' to Stay Home," *Annals of the American Academy of Political and Social Science* 66 (November 2004): 75–76, 78–79; Pamela Stone, *Opting Out? Why Women Really Quit Careers and Head Home* (Berkeley, CA: University of California Press, 2007).

4. Joan C. Williams, Jessica Manvell, and Stephanie Bornstein, *"Opt Out" or Pushed Out? How the Press Covers Work/Family Conflict: The Untold Story of Why Women Leave the Workforce* (San Francisco: University of California, Hastings College of the Law, Center for WorkLife Law, 2006).

5. Amy J. C. Cuddy and Susan T. Fiske, "When Professionals Become Mothers, Warmth Doesn't Cut the Ice," *Journal of Social Issues* 60, no. 4 (2004): 708–709.

6. Interview with Joan Williams, June 26, 2007; Monica Biernat, Faye J. Crosby, and Joan C. Williams, eds. "The Maternal Wall: Research and Policy Perspectives on Discrimination Against Mothers," special issue, *Journal of Social Issues* 60, no. 4 (December 2004).

7. Nancy Rothbard, "Enriching or Depleting? The Dynamics of Engagement in Work and Family Roles," *Administrative Science Quarterly* 46, no. 4 (2001); Nancy Moffit, "Challenging the Dominant Paradigm: Professor Nancy Rothbard Takes on the Work/Family Debate, with Some Surprising Findings," *Wharton Alumni Magazine* (Winter 2003): 34; Rothbard e-mail to author, November 5, 2008.

8. Erin L. Kelly, Alexandra Kalev, and Frank Dobbin, "Are Family-Friendly Policies Woman-Friendly? The Effects of Corporate Work-Family Policies on Women's Representation in Management." Paper presented at the annual meeting of the American Sociological Association, August 2007, New York.

9. Kelly, Kalev, and Dobbin, "Family-Friendly Policies."

10. Jenet I. Jacob, Sarah Allen, E. Jeffrey Hill, Nicole L. Mead, and Maria Ferris, "Work Interference with Dinnertime as a Mediator and Moderator Between Work Hours and Work and Family Outcomes," *Family and Consumer Sciences Research Journal* 36 (2008): 310–327.

11. M. H. Strober and J. M. Jackman, "Some Effects of Occupational Segregation and the Glass Ceiling on Men and Women in Technical and Managerial Fields; Retention of Senior Women," in *Human Factors in Organizational Design and Management-IV,* ed. G. E. Bradley and H. W. Hendrick (Amsterdam: Elsevier Science, 1994), 594.

12. *What Women Want in Business: A Survey of Executives and Entrepreneurs* (Korn/Ferry International, 2001).

13. Strober and Jackman, "Effects of Occupational Segregation," 596.

14. Paul B. Brown, "Measuring the Gender Gap," *New York Times,* April 7, 2007.

15. Tom Peters, *Leadership* (New York: Dorling Kindersley, 2005), 98.

16. *Creating Pathways to Success: Advancing and Retaining Women in Today's Law Firms* (Washington, DC: Women's Bar Association of the District of Columbia, 2006).

17. Cynthia Calvert, e-mail message to authors, July 12, 2007.

18. M. Shih, T. L. Pittinsky, and N. Ambady, "Stereotype Susceptibility: Identity Salience and Shifts in Quantitative Performance," *Psychological Science* 10 (February 8, 2008): 81–84; A. Dijksterhuis, J. A. Bargh, and J. Miedema, "Of Men and Mackerels: Attention, Subjective Experience, and Automatic Social Behavior," in *The Message Within: The Role of Subject Experience in Social Cognition and Behaviour,* ed. H. Bless and J. P. Forgas (Philadelphia: Psychology Press), 37–51.

19. Debra E. Meyerson, *Tempered Radicals: How People Use Difference to Inspire Change at Work* (Boston: Harvard Business School Press, 2001), 40, 41, 59.

20. Meyerson, *Tempered Radicals,* 61, 62.

21. Meyerson, *Tempered Radicals,* 50–51, 54.

Chapter Five: Success Does Not Require 24/7

1. Jody Miller and Matt Miller, "Get a Life! Ditching the 24/7 Culture," *Fortune* (November 16, 2005).

2. Jack Welch and Suzy Welch, *Winning*. New York: Collins Business, 2005.

3. Leslie A. Perlow, "Finding Time: How Corporations, Individuals, and Families Can Benefit from New Work Practices" (Ithaca, NY: ILR Press, 1997), 38.

4. Miller and Miller, "Get a Life!"

5. Craig Lambert, "Deep into Sleep: While Researchers Probe Sleep's Functions, Sleep Itself Is Becoming a Lost Art," *Harvard Magazine*, July–August, 2005, 33.

6. Miller and Miller, "Get a Life!"

7. Perlow, "Finding Time," 90.

8. Perlow, "Finding Time," xvii.

9. Perlow, "Finding Time," 15–16, 122, 134–135, 143.

10. Leslie A. Perlow, "Time to Coordinate: Toward an Understanding of Work-Time Standards and Norms in a Multicountry Study of Software Engineers," *Work and Occupations* (February 2001): 91–111; Leslie A. Perlow, Judy Hoffer Gittell, and Nancy Katz, "Contextualizing Patterns of Work Group Interaction: Toward a Nested Theory of Structuration," *Organization Science* 15, no. 5 (September–October 2004): 520–536.

11. Jyoti Thottam, "Reworking Work," *Time*, July 24, 2005.

12. Margaret Steen, "Stop Out, Hunker Down, Move Up? Challenges Faced by Women MBAs and Their Employers," *Stanford Business Magazine*, February 2007.

13. "Division of Labor–Historical Trends," Marriage and Family Encyclopedia, http://family.jrank.org/pages/407/Division-Labor-Historical Trends.html (accessed October 1, 2008).

14. Miller and Miller, "Get a Life!"

15. "Survey Finds Workers Average Only Three Productive Days per Week," Microsoft, http://www.microsoft.com/presspass/press/2005/mar05/03-15threeproductivedayspr.mspx (accessed March 15, 2005).

16. Miller and Miller, "Get a Life!"

17. Sylvia Ann Hewlett and Carolyn Buck Luce, "Extreme Jobs: The Dangerous Allure of the 70-Hour Workweek," *Harvard Business Review,* December 2006.

18. Robert Drago et al., "Bias Against Caregiving," *Academe* 91, no. 5 (September–October 2005).

19. Peters, *When Mothers Work,* 200. Background on Tilghman's scientific research is from her biography on the Princeton University website, http://www.princeton.edu/pr/smt/bio.html (accessed October 1, 2008).

20. Malaika Costello-Dougherty, "We're Outta Here: Why Women Are Leaving Big Firms," *California Lawyer* (February 2007): 22.

21. William G. Bliss, "The Advisor: Cost of Employee Turnover," ISquare, http://www.isquare.com/turnover/cfm (accessed August 7, 2006).

22. Louise Marie Roth, *Selling Women Short: Gender and Money on Wall Street* (Princeton, NJ: Princeton University Press, 2006), 176.

23. Robin Wolaner, *Naked in the Boardroom* (New York: Simon & Schuster, 2005), 174.

24. Catalyst, *Cracking the Glass Ceiling,* 74.

25. Lotte Bailyn, *Breaking the Mold: Redesigning Work for Productive and Satisfying Lives,* 2nd ed. (Ithaca, NY: ILR Press, Cornell University Press, 2006), xi.

26. Ellen Galinsky et al., *Leaders in a Global Economy: A Study of Executive Women and Men* (New York: Families and Work Institute, 2003); discussion with author, July 2, 2007.

27. Miller and Miller, "Get a Life!"; NewsCorp press release, July 9, 2007.

28. Edward Wong, "A Stinging Office Memo Boomerangs; Chief Executive Is Criticized After Upbraiding Workers by E-mail." *New York Times,* April 5, 2001.

Chapter Six: It's Not a Fair Game — but You Can Improve Your Odds

1. David Neumark, Roy J. Bank, and Kyle D. Van Nort, "Sex Discrimination in Restaurant Hiring," *The Quarterly Journal of Economics* (August 1996), 915–941; Claudia Goldin and Cecilia Rouse, "Orchestrating Impartiality: The Impact of 'Blind' Auditions on Female Musicians," *American Economic Review* 90 (September 2000): 715–741.

2. Madeline E. Heilman, "The Impact of Situational Factors on Personnel Decisions Concerning Women: Varying the Sex Composition," *Organizational Behavior and Human Performance*, 26 (1980), 386–395.

3. M. S. Schmidt, "Tennis: Upon Further Review, Players Support Replay," *New York Times*, September 5, 2006.

4. Stine Bosse and Peninah Thomson, "Ask the Experts: Women in the Boardroom," *Financial Times*, October 13, 2005.

5. Wolaner, *Naked in the Boardroom*, 25–26.

6. Katherine Lanpher, "The Conversation: Climb the Ladder or Build Your Own," *MORE Magazine* (September 2007), 98–102.

7. Wolaner, *Naked in the Boardroom*, 155.

8. Ashish Nanda, Boris Groysberg, and Lauren Prusiner, Lehman Brothers (A), *Rise of the Equity Research Department* (Boston, MA: Harvard Business School, 2006); Ashish Nanda, Boris Groysberg, and Lauren Prusiner, Lehman Brothers (B), *Exit Jack Rivkin* (Boston, MA: Harvard Business School, 2006); Ashish Nanda and Boris Groysberg, Lehman Brothers (C), *Decline of the Equity Research Department* (Boston, MA: Harvard Business School, 2001); Boris Groysberg and Ashish Nanda, Lehman Brothers (D), *Reemergence of the Equity Research Department* (Boston, MA: Harvard Business School, 2006).

9. Catalyst, *Cracking the Glass Ceiling*, 75–76.

10. Francis J. Flynn, "Thanks for Nothing: The Effects of Sex and Agreeableness on the Evaluation of Helping Behavior in Organizations," working paper.

11. Laurie A. Rudman, "Prescriptive Gender Stereotypes and Backlash Toward Agentic Women," *Journal of Social Issues* 57, no. 4 (2001): 758–759.

12. Francis J. Flynn and Cameron Anderson, "Too Tough, Too Soon: Familiarity and the Backlash Effect," working paper.

13. *Woman's Earnings: Work Patterns Partially Explain Difference Between Men's and Women's Earnings*, U.S. General Accounting Office report, GAO-04-35 (Washington, DC: General Accounting Office, October 2003), 29; Judy Goldberg Day and Catherine Hill, *Beyond the Pay Gap* (Washington, DC: American Association of University Women Educational Foundation, 2007).

14. Testimony of Evelyn F. Murphy, president of the WAGE Project, Inc., "Closing the Gap: Equal Pay for Women Workers" hearing before the U.S. Senate Committee on Health, Education, Labor, and Pensions, April 12, 2007, 2.

15. Testimony of Jocelyn Samuels, vice president for education and employment, National Women's Law Center, "Closing the Gap: Equal Pay for Women Workers" hearing before the U.S. Senate Committee on Health, Education, Labor, and Pensions, April 12, 2007, 2; Samuels interview with author, August 30, 2007.

16. Stephanie Saul, "Novartis Faces Class Action Over Sex Bias," *New York Times,* August 2, 2007, C5.

17. Wendy Sigle-Rushton and Jane Waldfogel, "Family Gaps in Income: A Cross-National Comparison," working paper no. 382, Luxembourg Income Study Working Paper Series, June 2004; Median 2006 earnings for men and women fifteen and older working full time, year-round. Social and Economic Supplement, March 2007, Current Population Survey, U.S. Census.

18. "Board Cafe: How Much to Pay the Executive Director," CompassPoint Nonprofit Services, e-newsletter, www.compasspoint.org/boardcafe, June 1, 2005.

19. Neela Banerjee, "Clergywomen Find Hard Path to Bigger Pulpit," *New York Times,* August 26, 2006.

20. Linda Babcock and Sara Laschever, *Women Don't Ask: Negotiation and the Gender Divide* (Princeton, NJ: Princeton University Press, 2003), 1.

21. Hannah C. Riley and Linda Babcock, *Gender as a Situational Phenomenon Is Negotiated,* paper presented at the International Association of Conflict Management 15th Annual Conference, Salt Lake City, Utah, June 9–12, 2002 (Kennedy School of Government working paper No. RWP02-037, September 2002).

22. Linda Babcock, "Preoccupations: Women, Repeat This: Don't Ask, Don't Get." *New York Times,* April 6, 2008.

23. Laurie A. Rudman, "Prescriptive Gender Stereotypes and Backlash Toward Agentic Women," *Journal of Social Issues* 57, no. 4 (2001): 743–773; Neale e-mail to author, August 4, 2008.

24. Laura J. Kray, Adam D. Galinsky, and Leigh Thompson, "Reversing the Gender Gap in Negotiations: An Exploration of Stereotype Regeneration," *Organizational Behavior and Human Decision Processes* 87, no. 2 (March 2002): 386–409; Neale e-mail to author, August 4, 2008.

25. William M. Bulkeley, "A Data-Storage Titan Confronts Bias Claims, Some EMC Saleswomen Fault Office Culture; Visits to Strip Club," *New York Times,* September 12, 2007.

26. Catalyst, *Cracking the Glass Ceiling,* 75–76.

27. *Entourage,* HBO, Season 1, Episode 6, "Busey and the Beach."

28. Janet Shibley Hyde, "The Gender Similarities Hypothesis," *American Psychologist* 60 (September 2005): 581–592.

29. Janet Shibley Hyde et al., "Gender Difference in Mathematics Performance: A Meta-Analysis," *Psychological Bulletin* 107 (1990): 139–155; Elizabeth Spelke, "Sex Differences in Intrinsic Aptitude for Mathematics and Science?" *American Psychologist* 60 (December 2005): 950–958.

30. Matt Richtell, "In the Venture Capital World, a Helping Hand for Women and Minorities," *New York Times,* June 15, 2007.

31. The STRIDE slides are available online at http://sitemaker .umich.edu/advance/stride and would likely help any hiring committee. Here are some eye-poppers from the mountain of studies that impressed the scientists at the University of Michigan:

- With identical applications, "Brian" was two times more likely to be hired than "Karen" in a 1999 study of bias in evaluating academics. A broad survey finds female scientists have half the success rate getting postdoctoral fellowships compared to their male peers. [See Rhea E. Steinpreis, Dawn Ritzke, and Katie A. Anders. "The Impact of Gender on the Review of the Curricula Vitae of Job Applicants and Tenure Candidates: A National Empirical Study," *Sex Roles* 41, no. 7/8 (October 1999): 509–528.]

- A 2003 study looked back in the hiring files for doctors on staff at a large university, exploring whether recommendation letters differed for male and female applicants. They did: 25 percent of letters for female doctors contained "doubt-raising" comments, while this was true for only 12 percent of their male peers. Fifteen percent of the letters for female doctors (but only 6 percent of letters for men) contained what researchers called "minimal assurance" language, recommenders hedging themselves against a flop. Recommenders were four times more likely to discuss the doctor's CV and publications if the applicant was male versus female. But letters for women doctors discussed their personal lives five times as often as those for men. [Frances Trix and Carolyn Psenka, "Exploring the Color of Glass: Letters of Recommendation for Female and Male Medical Faculty," *Discourse & Society* 14 (2003): 191.]

Danielle LaVaque-Manty and Abagail J. Stewart, "A Very Scholarly Intervention: Recruiting Women Faculty in Science and Engineering," in *Gendered Innovations in Science and Engineering,* ed. Londa Schiebinger (Stanford University Press, 2008).

32. Kathy Phillips is a professor at the Kellogg School of Management and the co-chair of the Center on the Science of Diversity. In addition to showing the performance benefits groups can get from group diversity, her work has revealed some interesting nuances. Even when diverse groups perform better by objective measures, they may not be perceived as more successful (and may not perceive themselves as more successful.) Why? Because diverse groups frequently are less comfortable with one another and experience more conflict. Researchers are now starting to explore what kind of leadership is needed to help diverse groups understand how to see their differences as the source of high performance that it is.

As Phillips points out, this is not a new notion. She quotes John Stuart Mill as saying in 1848, "It is hardly possible to overrate the value . . . of placing human beings in contact with persons dissimilar to themselves, and with modes of thought and action unlike those with which they are familiar . . . Such communication has always been, and is peculiarly in the present age, one of the primary sources of progress."

See Katherine W. Phillips, Katie Liljenquist, and Margaret A. Neale, "Is the Pain Worth the Gain? The Advantages and Liabilities of Agreeing with Socially Distinct Newcomers" (Northwestern University and Stanford University Graduate School of Business); Phillips interview with author, November 5, 2003; Charlan Jeanne Nemeth and Julianne L. Kwan, "Minority Influence, Divergent Thinking and Detection of Correct Solutions," *Journal of Applied Social Psychology* 7, 9 (1987): 788–799.

Chapter Seven: The Great Alliance:
How Your Husband Solves the Work/Life Riddle

1. Michael Elliot, "Men Want Change Too," *Time,* March 14, 2004.

2. *Woman's Earnings,* 34, 62.

3. Sylvia Ann Hewlett and Carolyn Buck Luce, "Off-Ramps and On-Ramps: Keeping Talented Women on the Road to Success," *Harvard Business Review,* March 2005.

4. Williams, Manvell, and Bornstein, *"Opt Out" or Pushed Out?,* 31.

5. Leslie Morgan Steiner, "My Inner Mommy War, Part 1," *Today's Mama,* http://www.todaysmama.com/expandyourperspective (accessed September 2007).

6. Pamela Stone and Meg Lovejoy, "Fast-Track Women and the 'Choice' to Stay Home," *Annals of the American Academy of Political and Social Science* 66 (November 2004): 75–76, 78–79.

7. S. Rosenbluth, J. Steil, and J. Whitcomb, "Marital equality: What Does It Mean?" *Journal of Family Issues* 19, 3 (1998): 227–244; interview with Steil, December 11, 2007.

8. Coontz, *Marriage, a History,* 290.

9. Terrence Real, *How Can I Get Through to You? Closing the Intimacy Gap Between Men and Women* (New York: Simon & Schuster, 2002), 53.

10. Cowan and Cowan, *When Partners Become Parents,* 107.

11. John M. Gottman and Julia Schwartz Gottman, *And Baby Makes Three* (New York: Crown Publishers, 2007), 16, 18.

12. Ashley H. Beitel and Ross D. Parke, "Maternal and Paternal Attitudes as Determinants of Father Involvement," *Journal of Family Psychology* 12 (1998): 268–288.

13. Cowan and Cowan, *When Partners Become Parents,* 207–208.

14. Cowan and Cowan, *When Partners Become Parents,* 248–249.

15. Cowan and Cowan, *When Partners Become Parents,* 252.

16. Judith Warner, *Perfect Madness* (New York: Penguin, 2005).

17. Chethik, *VoiceMale,* 118–161, 125–126.

18. Joshua Coleman, *The Lazy Husband* (New York: St. Martin's/Griffin, 2005), 34, 69; discussion with author, June 22, 2006; e-mail to author, November 2, 2008.

19. Real, *How Do I Get Through?* 211.

20. Real, *How Do I Get Through?* 117.

21. Chethik, *VoiceMale,* 175.

22. Coleman, *Lazy Husband,* 81.

23. Robin J. Ely, Debra E. Meyerson, and Martin N. Davidson, "Rethinking Political Correctness," *Harvard Business Review,* September 2006, 4.

24. For great basic training in negotiation of all sorts see: Roger Fisher, William Ury, and Bruce Patton, eds. *Getting to Yes: Negotiating Agreement Without Giving In* (New York: Penguin Books, 1991); Douglas Stone, Bruce Patton, and Sheila Heen, *Difficult Conversations: How to Discuss What Matters Most* (New York: Penguin Books, 2000).

Chapter Eight: The Pre-Baby Road Trip: Mapping Out
a Leave You Can Return From

1. Galinsky et al., *Leaders in a Global Economy* 9; Anne Hendershott, "A Moving Story for Spouses and Other Wage-Earners," *Psychology Today* 28, no. 5 (1995): 28–31.

2. "Paid Leave for Maternity Is the Norm, Except in...," *New York Times,* op-ed, October 6, 2007.

3. "The Women's Contraceptive Equity Act" was signed in California in 1999. It was one of many efforts around the country to redress inequities in male and female health care coverage. As Speier said in her press release, "Despite the fact that the FDA approved oral contraceptives 39 years ago, many prescription benefit plans do not provide routine coverage for birth control. As a result, women pay 68% more in out-of-pocket medical costs than men. Most of these costs are attributable to reproductive health care expenses. In contrast, immediately following FDA approval of Viagra, insurers quickly moved to add this male impotency prescription to their formularies. For years these same insurers have argued that the cost of covering prescription birth control pills would be prohibitive. FACT: Viagra costs ($60 month—6 pills @ $10 per pill) while birth control pills cost $25–30 a month."

Jackie Speier, "Speier's Women's Contraceptive Equity Act Signed by Governor," California State Capitol Office, http://www.sen.ca.gov/ftp/sen/SENATOR/_ARCHIVE_2006/SPEIER/PRESS (accessed October 31, 2008).

4. See the California Employment Development Department website for an explanation of benefits available under the Paid Leave insurance program. www.edd.ca.gov (accessed October 2, 2008).

5. Liz Ryan, "Interactive Case Study," *Business Week,* September 13, 2007.

6. F. Matthew Kramer et al. "Breast-Feeding Reduces Maternal Lower-body Fat," *Journal of the American Dietetic Association* 93, no. 4 (April 1993): 429–433.

7. Ellen Galinsky, James T. Bond, and Kelly Sakai, *2008 National Study of Employers: When Work Works,* Families and Work Institute, http://familiesandwork.org/site/research/reports/2008nse.pdf.

8. Jeffrey E. Hill et al., "Studying 'Working Fathers': Comparing Fathers' and Mothers' Work-Family Conflict, Fit, and Adaptive Strategies in a Global High-Tech Company," *Fathering* 1 (October 2003):

239–261. The study found that 58 percent of working mothers used work–family programs compared to 34 percent of dads. (As cited in *Father Facts,* 5th Edition, 2007, by the National Fatherhood Initiative.)

9. Families and Work Institute, *The 2008 Guide to Bold New Ideas for Making Work Work,* http://familiesandwork.org/3w/boldideas.pdf, 38–39.

10. Stone and Lovejoy, "Fast-Track Women," 66, 75–76, 78–79.

11. Kathleen McCartney, Eric Dearing, Beck A. Taylor, and Kristen L. Bub, "Quality Child Care Supports the Achievement of Low-Income Children: Direct and Indirect Pathways Through Caregiving and the Home Environment," *Journal of Applied Developmental Psychology,* 28, no. 5–6 (September–December 2007): 411–426.

12. Alison Clarke-Stewart and Virginia D. Allhusen, *What We Know About Childcare* (Cambridge, MA: Harvard University Press, 2005), 163–164.

13. "Dents in the Dream," *Time,* July 28, 2008.

14. Kate Pomper, Helen Blank, Nancy Duff Campbell, and Karen Schulman, *Be All That We Can Be: Lessons from the Military for Improving Our Nation's Child Care System: 2004 Follow-up* (Washington, DC: National Women's Law Center, 2004), 2, 7.

15. Bright Horizons, "Benefits of Employer-Sponsored Care," http://www.brighthorizons.com/employer/benefits.aspx (accessed October 2, 2008); Patrick J. Kiger, "A Case for Childcare," *Workforce Management Magazine* (April 2004): 24–40.

16. "Claiming the Child and Dependent Care Credit," Internal Revenue Service, http://www.irs.gov/newsroom/article/0,,id=106189,00.html (accessed July 31, 2008).

17. In 2000, government subsidies for business meals/entertainment was $6.6 billion according to congressional testimony, http://www.ctj.org/html/corpwelf.htm (accessed October 2, 2008).

Chapter Nine: The Post-Baby Uphill: Test-Driving 50/50 and Getting Back Up to Speed

1. Daniel Goleman, *Social Intelligence: The New Science of Human Relationships* (New York: Bantam Dell, 2006), 212.

2. R. D. Parke, "Father-Infant Interaction," in *Maternal Attachment and Mothering Disorders,* eds. M. H. Klaus, T. Leger, and M. A. Trause

(Sausalito, CA: Johnson and Johnson, 1974); R. D. Parke and S. O'Leary, "Family Interaction in the Newborn Period: Some Findings, Some Observations, and Some Unresolved Issues," in *The Developing Individual in a Changing World (Vol. 2): Social and Environmental Issues,* eds. K. Riegel & J. Meacham (The Hague: Mouton, 1976); R. D. Parke and D. B. Sawin, "The Father's Role in Infancy: A Reevaluation," *The Family Coordinator* (1976), Invited article for special issue on Fatherhood, *25,* 365–371; Parke interview with author, January 30, 2007.

3. Levine and Pittinsky, *Working Fathers,* 20.

4. F. Gary Cunningham et al., *Williams Obstetrics, 20th ed.* (Appleton & Lange, 1993), 538.

5. Sandra L. Hofferth and Sally C. Curtin, "Parental Leave Statutes and Maternal Return to Work After Childbirth in the United States," *Work and Occupations* 33, no. 1 (February 2006): 73–105.

6. Beth Sawi, *Coming Up for Air: How to Build a Balanced Life in a Workaholic World* (New York: Hyperion, 2000).

7. James A. Levine, "The Other Working Parent," *New York Times,* March 4, 1999; and Levine and Pittinsky, *Working Fathers,* 87.

Chapter Ten: Getting to 50/50: At Home, at Work, for Life

1. Philip N. Cohen, University of North Carolina based on March 2007 Current Population Surveys. E-mail to author, April 26, 2007.

2. Wendy Mogel, *The Blessing of the Skinned Knee: Using Jewish Teachings to Raise Self-Reliant Children* (New York: Penguin, 2001), 118–119.

3. Mogel, *Blessing of the Skinned Knee,* 54–55.

4. Janice M. Steil, "Marriage: Still 'His' and 'Hers'?" *Encyclopedia of Women and Gender* 1, ed. Judith Worell (San Diego: Academic Press, 2002), 677–686.

5. Scott Coltrane, *Family Man: Fatherhood, Housework, and Gender Equity* (New York: Oxford University Press, 1996), 78.

6. Rahel Muslean, "Profile: Abby Joseph Cohen," *Hadassah Magazine* 86, no. 6 (February 2005).

ACKNOWLEDGMENTS

Writing this book has been a great experience for us thanks to the incredibly generous contributions of many people—from close friends and family to the many complete strangers who volunteered to share their stories and insights.

To all our survey participants and interviewees, whom we agreed not to mention by name, we'll simply say thank you for inspiring us with your wealth of wisdom and humor.

Thanks to our early supporters, all those who talked over our very rough ideas (and talked us out of bad ideas), read, wrote, edited, and provided valuable insights. With your kind response to our calls for advice, *Getting to 50/50* became a community effort: Naomi Andrews, Lisa Babel, Caroline Barlerin, Elizabeth Beier, Linda Bialecki, Talia Biladeau, Stacey Boyd, Betsy Cohen, Chris De Cunha, Dawn Davis, Cathy Dean, Catherine Crystal Foster, John Freund, Linda Grais, Ann Herbst, Michael Hirschorn, Christina Jones, Diana Kapp, Deborah Copagen Kogan, Claudia Kolker, Tali Levy, Patricia Nakache, Catherine Norman, Neill Norman, Anne Popkin, Amy Rabbino, Regan Ralph, Betsy Rappaport, Andrea Rice, Louisa Ritter, Sheryl Sandberg, Nadine Terman, Mary Jane Weaver, Doug Winthrop, and Susan Wojcicki.

As we got started, we had the special honor of talking with Gloria Steinem who encouraged us in one e-mail saying, "We've proved that women can do what men can do. Now we have to prove that men can do what women do." We thank her for giving so freely of her time and invaluable advice.

Special thanks to Robbie Baxter, Lisa Bernard, Holly Finn, Simon Firth, Lindsey Hogan, Kim Malone, Tanya Mellilo, Laura Missan, and Courtney Weaver (and our husbands) for rolling up their sleeves and digging into the manuscript to make it much better. And to Tom Kosnik, who engaged an incredible group of Stanford students and alums to review our work and help us see what we were missing.

We also want to acknowledge the important contributions of the many experts who, in addition to the numerous hours explaining and deconstructing their research, took time to give us guidance on the book as a whole, including: Josh Coleman, Scott Coltrane, Lynn Cooke, Frank Dobbin, Sarah Friedman, Ellen Galinsky, Deborah Gruenfeld, Andrea Davies Henderson, Rod Kramer, Kathleen McCartney, Maggie Neale, Leslie Perlow, Londa Schiebinger, and Joan Williams.

Great thanks to Debra Meyerson, whose early suggestions on where to focus our efforts shaped our initial message on "the man thing."

Myra Strober, Joanna's mother-in-law, and a professor of economics at Stanford University, was really the godmother of this project. Her invitation for us to speak in her Work and Family Class at Stanford's Graduate School of Business showed us the need for our book. Myra was instrumental in the design of our project. Her suggestions regarding research material, interview recommendations, and ongoing support during the project were essential. Without her this book would not exist.

We want to specially acknowledge Becky Cabaza. Your work as a writer-editor enabled us to find our voice and articulate ourselves better than we could have ever done on our own. Elyse Cheney was an amazing agent, willing to bet on us when we had nothing more than a basic proposal. We thank Toni Burbank for believing in this project, being a masterful editor and sharing our conviction that men and women belong on the same team. Thank you also to Allison Roche, Clare Swanson, and the rest of the editorial, publicity, and production staff at Bantam for their patience and care in bringing this book to print. And our sincerest appreciation also goes to our amazing research assistants Nicky Dyal, Tammy Gerber, and Amy Rosenthal.

These acknowledgments would not be complete without mentioning those who helped each of us throughout our work and parenting journeys.

From Sharon: Thank you to my mother and father who, in their different ways, in their eyes and laughter, conveyed a great joy in being parents; and thank you for giving me the faith that asking "why?" is always a good thing (even those inconvenient "whys" about baths and bedtimes). Thank you to my stepmother, Elizabeth, for being a wonderful working-mother role model and to my stepdad, Bill, for helping me to see how the Second Law of Thermodynamics (the one about entropy) underlies everything. Thank you to my siblings Kira and Erik (who contributed many ideas and hours of editing), Katie (for giving me the twentysomething scoop on our topic), Jim (who gives me insight into everything from stream ecology to football), and Kevin (for letting me observe how, from cradle-to-college, two working parents can produce a wonderful kid). I am grateful to the many people at Goldman Sachs who were wonderful mentors and gave me opportunities for which I'll always feel fortunate. Thank you also to our nannies Cecilia Inga, and Diana Inga-Ruiz—your incredible warmth, judgment, and partnership has made us better parents.

To my one and only love, Steve: I thank you infinitely for taking the leap—and helping me leap—into the adventure of building a life, calling the shots, taking risks, and smiling together. And special thanks for being my lead sponsor writing this book, the one who said "just do it" and invested so much in me to bring this project to fruition.

Thank you to Max and Samantha for the honor of being your mom, of looking into your wonderful eyes, of hearing the fascinating things you tell me, and for just being you. May the things we wish for in this book make your journeys smoother and more rewarding.

From Joanna: I would especially like to thank my parents for continuously believing in me and supporting my occasionally crazy goals, as well as their enthusiastic participation in raising their grandchildren and providing babysitting and dinner at a moment's notice. Thanks also for your extensive comments on various drafts of the book, especially your ability to tactfully disagree and add suggestions. Jason's parents, Myra Strober and Jay Jackman, and Sam and Linda Strober, are ideal in-laws for a working mom, providing only support, encouragement, and assistance without criticism. My sisters, Rebecca and Denise, have been great partners and helpmates. I would also like to thank two of my male bosses: David Cowan of Bessemer Venture Partners and Peter Stamos of Sterling Stamos. You made it easy to return from each maternity leave and provided invaluable mentoring and guidance. I am also grateful to Susan Carruthers. Your patience, compassion, and organizational skills are unsurpassed and I am forever thankful for the remarkable care you have provided our entire family.

Jason, you are truly my secret weapon. I love and admire you, and I look forward to many more years of sharing everything together. Finally, my love and adoration and appreciation for my children: Sarah, Jared, and Ari. Coming home to you is the highlight of my day! I hope the road to 50/50 will be easier when you grow up.

INDEX

ABOUT THE AUTHORS

SHARON MEERS was a managing director at Goldman, Sachs & Co. until April 2005, when she decided that it was time to write this book. In her sixteen-year career at Goldman, Sharon ran several businesses and served on the diversity committees of two of the firm's divisions. Sharon also serves on the board of the National Women's Law Center and on the advisory council of Stanford's Clayman Institute for Research on Gender.

Sharon lives in the Bay Area with her husband, Steve, a real-estate developer, and their son, age seven, and daughter, age four. A graduate of Harvard College, she holds an M.A. in Economics from New York University.

JOANNA STROBER has spent her career working as an attorney and as an investor in venture capital and private equity. She is currently Managing Director of a fund investing in private equity partnerships at Sterling Stamos Capital Management.

Joanna lives in the Bay Area with her husband, Jason, a software entrepreneur, and their daughter, age ten, and two sons, ages seven and two. She holds a B.A. in Political Science from the University of Pennsylvania and a J.D. from UCLA.

Visit www.Gettingto5050.com to do the 50/50 mind-set quiz, swap stories, share tips, and read Sharon and Joanna's blog.